arouNd the world

in eighty wayS

Robin Dunseath

Additional material from

Miles Hilton-Barber, Caroline Casey
Mike Mackenzie, Jon Cook, Aoife O'Connell

and

Mary Donaldson

SERENDIPITY

First Published in 2004 by
Serendipity
Suite 530
37 Store Street
Bloomsbury
London

British Library Cataloguing-in-Publication data
A catalogue record for this book is available from the British Library
ISBN 1-84394-119-8

Printed and bound by The Alden Press, Oxford

He felt the small hand slip into his.
He looked down at the child – her eyes smiling as shyly,
she placed the drawing into his hand.
'Thank you Mr Magic Hat' she said.

Ebenezer School and Home for
visually and mentally impaired children
Tuesday 5 November 2002 Hong Kong

All photographs taken by Jon Cook, Mary Donaldson, Aoife
O'Connell, Mike McNamara and Dr Chris Calton

I notice that the police escort is ready. I check the adventurers and they give me the all clear. 'Follow me' I cry, for the first of many times. The horses jerk into action, the crowd cheers and I am off!

I climb back on again. Having warned Miles about the jerk as the horses move off, I forget to hang on myself and disappear off the back of the carriage. Attempting to regain my dignity, I climb on board once more and resume my journey, top hat and pride somewhat dented. No horse will ever make an ass of me again, I vow.

We make a striking sight for the tourists as we gallop – well canter – no perhaps clip-clop – past St James Palace and approach our first destination, Buckingham Palace. I realise that we must look important – horse-drawn carriages, me in my top hat, Miles standing next to me looking very dignified and behind us there radiates a golden couple in Caroline, her blonde hair flowing out behind her and Mike sitting beside her. Clearly we are royalty of some sort on our way to the Palace. The tourists run towards us to get a better view. Cameras click and flash incessantly. We wave at the crowds and they cheer back. I give Miles a running commentary to help him enjoy the experience, but I can see he is drinking adrenalin and needs no help from me. Behind me, Caroline and Mike are also waving. The wind kisses my cheeks and a tear tries to slip out unnoticed. Months of worry, of bonding sessions with the team, of exasperation, fear and indecision, melt away to nothing as I realise that we are a team, we are as one and we are on our way. Thousands of miles, hundreds of meetings and as yet unknown challenges lie ahead of us.

I am on an adventure, I realise, with childish glee mixed with anxious anticipation.

I look back to the Reform Club where our dedicated Project Director Mary collects our bags to transfer them to our next destination. For all the hard work she has done, she should be up here with me enjoying the cheers. But no, only the team should be on the means of transport. Yet I sense that it is wrong. Throughout the two years of planning, plotting and training, Mary Donaldson has been a bulwark of sound advice, determined motivation and astute business acumen. It seems unfair not to let her share the glory of the horse ride to Buckingham Palace, but a Project Director simply does not fit into the Jules Verne story which we are trying to re-enact. No matter what happens, we must stick to the story of Phileas Fogg and three Passepartouts attempting to get around the world using eighty entirely different means of transport. That is the bet we have accepted, that is what we must achieve.

Jon, our team manager, runs alongside the horses, showing the fitness that will save us many times later in the adventure. Behind him, struggling with his television camera and trying to capture the action Carbonara (nick-named that by us, his real name is McNamara), tries to keep up without

Above: Mike, Robin, Caroline and Miles outside the Reform Club
Below: They make friends with their first means of transport

running into anything. I fear for his safety as he has his one good eye behind the camera lens. He is careering along at a right old gallop. Bizarre! We all have nicknames. Mike is James Half-a-Bond as he is so suave, even if he has no legs, Miles is Smiles the Philosopher, Caroline is Princess, after the girl in the book, Mary started as Sparkly Mary but that quickly became Mum as she lovingly bossed and bullied us all.

Soon we clatter into the mews of Buckingham Palace and have our first brush with authority. We arrive in a flurry of excitement and are surrounded by media keen to file their stories. Russian television approaches me. To my horror, they interview me about the qualities of Jules Verne as a writer, rather than on our story. I stumble my way through, but vow not to get caught again. Caroline, Miles and Mike are also surrounded by media. Then I notice a man bellowing at me from an arched doorway. He runs towards me, his face puce with anger. It seems we have only been allowed to use the mews on condition that no media can enter. I think of pointing out that the two statuesque guards we passed at the entrance should have stopped them, not me.

'Which of you is Nussey?' he demands in a voice that makes it clear that anyone who claims ownership of the name would be consigned at once to the Tower. Fortunately Stuart Nussey, our Route Director who played such a major role in the adventure and had been given the warning about the media, is elsewhere. Just as well, for now I remember Stuart did pass the message on to me, but in the excitement I have forgotten about it!

I decide to flee.

'Follow me' I cry for the second time and the adventurers, sensing from my tone that trouble is brewing, do so with enthusiasm. We leap into brand-new London taxis provided by London Taxi International, and roar off for Stapleford Airport. In the mirror of my taxi, I notice the angry Palace official still fuming against anyone who looks as though they are part of our crazy party.

Soon the taxis leave the hurly-burly of Buckingham Palace and with our starter 'means of transport' behind, we sit back and for the first time since breakfast, relax! It is easy to do so, for the taxis are brand new and wonderfully comfortable. We think of going around the world by taxi, if it were to be like this, but immediately eliminate the thought. Perhaps later ...

Clear skies greet us at Stapleford Airport. In front of the clubhouse, our third means of transport is lined up. Miles chooses to fly in the Chipmunk, piloted by owner Mary Munley, who is to play a massive part in the scuba diving adventure later on in our journey, whilst Mike, Caroline and I are to fly in a Piper Dakota, flown by Polly Vacher, who has recently flown it around the world.

Miles and Chipmunk

But first Mike asks me if I could take him to the Gents. There, with the nonchalance of someone who has seen and done it all before, he empties his colostomy bag and for the first time, I experience the extraordinary mechanical world of bags, filters and tubes that keep Mike alive, and some of the challenges he faces every day. I realise what a colossal inspiration he will be to the rest of the team. In the face of his challenges, ours are puny.

With some difficulty we load Mike into the seat next to the pilot. I think of Douglas Bader, who also had no legs, but then he was not paralysed from the chest down. Like Bader, Mike is a hero. I scramble in behind him.

Mike in Piper Dakota

The sky is perfect blue and we fly in formation. Caroline is in a hysteria of excitement as even with her rotten eyesight she is able to peer out of the cockpit and make out shapes and colours of land and cloud. Miles is in the Chipmunk, flown by Mary Munley, and is heard over the radio to be pleading with her to let him land the plane. Thankfully we are soon on our final turn to landing. I think of how difficult it will be to get Mike out if anything goes wrong. Escape hatches are not designed for double leg amputees suffering from paralysis from the chest down and attached to a catheter.

I remember the battle I had getting any kind of insurance for the team.

'I would like to buy some travel insurance please. The group includes myself, I take six pills a day to keep my heart beating properly, and there are two blind people and a third who is paralysed from the chest down. We have a manager who is partially deaf in one ear and a one-eyed cameraman. We are going around the world using eighty entirely different means of transport, which will include riding elephants, ostriches, camels, hot-air balloons, sailing down the River Liffey in a cardboard boat on Friday 13 September ... no don't hang up on me please ... hello? ... hello?'

Eventually a wonderful insurance company called Optima who specialise in adventure travel insurance backed us. They offered a policy at a manageable premium and are rewarded with the fact that we did not need to make any claim from them.

Now fully insured and into our adventure, we are landing at the airfield and the usual media scrum explodes onto the runway for their pictures and interviews, terrified that they will miss something. Soon they focus on Mike and swarm around him.

Mike had been six foot four, now he is four foot seven. A tall, fit, charismatic man, he decided in 1993 to go to Bosnia to help restore water supplies after the war. He became involved in an incident, his two companions were killed, and Mike suffered horrific injuries. At first, they treated him for a serious bash on the head that threatened permanent brain injury, major chest injuries, a broken hand and broken legs. They amputated one leg and they also took out his spleen. Then, two days later when the general inflammation had subsided and they had flown him home, they discovered that he had severed his spinal cord at level two which lies at the top of the chest. He would be paralysed for the rest of his life. The other leg was subsequently removed due to blood pressure problems.

Taking Mike with us had been a difficult decision. I had been warned that as he no longer has an immune system, even a mosquito bite could kill him, that it was almost certain that he could not last the pace, let alone meet the challenges of the means of transport – whoever heard of a legless man paralysed from the chest down and with limited lung capacity scuba diving? It was even pointed out to me that should Mike not survive the adventure, I would be the one responsible, having ignored the advice not to take him as it was too big a risk.

Mary and I talked to Mike at length, consulted his medical advisors, and in the end we decided there was no way we were going to back down on taking Mike. He is such a determined character and if he was prepared to take the risk, so were we. My confidence in the decision was severely tested when, some weeks before our departure, he was back in hospital and we were told, very close to death. When Mary and I visited him, we felt there was no way he could recover in time. But, showing the determination that stunned people around the world, he did recover.

I received the following letter from his consultant at the National Spinal Injuries Centre at Stoke Mandeville.

This letter is to certify that at the present time Mr Mackenzie is medically fit to undertake the journey that he has planned. If you require any further information regarding his general medical condition I am happy to provide that, but this should not detract from his ability to undertake the trip.

Signed   Dr A Graham
            Consultant in Spinal Injuries

Later, from his diary, I learned what had been going through Mike's mind. He writes:

As the day for departure came closer, I began to think about how I would cope with the implications. I started to think about accessible loos, the task of getting up and being ready for the start of each day, the problems of hotel bathrooms, showers, long haul flights, time changes affecting medication, checking my INR (blood clotting measurement for warfarin doses) diet changes and potential illness.

The warfarin measurement problem was solved by a brilliant machine, a Coaguchek from Roche, which enabled me to carry out the checks myself. But my biggest concern in the lead up to the start was some broken skin which steadfastly refused to heal and I became increasingly worried that it might prevent me from going. As always, Dr Allison Graham, my long suffering consultant, kept her usual sense of perspective and although she felt it would not heal whilst going around the world, I was able to go if care was taken. If I was concerned, I should email a photograph of my posterior for her advice. I was concerned that sending pictures of my backside could be misinterpreted by the vice squad!

Our team manager Jon had issued a very strict list of kit we were allowed to take, most of it provided by Rolls-Royce, I was allowed to take an extra bag of medical kit which included enough dressings for three

Sir Jimmy Savile and the gang

months as well as catheters and 4187 pills! Fortunately Coloplast were
willing to re-supply in Hong Kong thus making packing easier.

Now we are approaching Mike's second home, The National Spinal
Injuries Hospital at Stoke Mandeville. We arrive from the airport in an
ambulance – our fourth means of transport – and as Mike appears, an
enormous cheer comes from the gathered crowd of nurses, doctors and
patients. Mike comments on how funny this is, as he was with them all a
couple of days ago and they did not cheer then! No business like show
business, he reflects.

Sir Jimmy Savile, who has done so much over the years first to raise
money for, and then to work at, the hospital, leads the reception. The
adventure is toasted in fine champagne, provided by Gerald Simonds of
Aylesbury, a major supplier of wheelchairs.

Mary our Project Director is there too, having raced down with all our
baggage from the Reform Club. Sir Jimmy Savile greets us and then we are
challenged to race in cycles made especially for people in wheelchairs.
Mike, Miles, Caroline and I line up, the flag drops, which gives Mike and
I a good laugh and a sneaky advantage as both Miles and Caroline are
registered blind. The starter, realising his mistake, yells 'Go' and the
disadvantaged duo set off in furious pursuit with no need for afterburners.

Caroline, who is fanatically fit, young and can see a bit, roars past unfit and doddery old me and heads off by mistake on to a public road. We shout a warning, she does a stunning U-turn and hurtles back to us, hotly pursued by Miles, chasing the sound of her laughter and having instructions shouted at him by Jon. Caroline and Miles are so determined to win that I fear for the safety of everyone at the grand prix race planned between them in Malaysia. Caroline wins, Miles is second whilst Mike and I, despite our advantage at the start, come in a competent joint third.

Sir Jimmy Savile and I have been together on a number of adventures, and I am delighted to meet him again. He makes a speech in which he expresses his admiration for what we are trying to do, and for the team for following me.

Mel Keeler is also there. When I first approached Mike, his doctors told him that he would need to take a nurse along with him. Thus Mike had the happy task of selecting a suitable person to accompany him.

'Would you like to come around the world with me' was a great chat line, but the intent was serious. Mike would need daily care and attention of a very special kind and it made sense to take someone along who was practised in these needs.

He chose Mel Keeler, a nurse who at the time was at Stoke Mandeville. Young, highly qualified, good-looking, vivacious, she seemed to fit the bill admirably. Sir Jimmy Savile made her decision to join easy when he offered to pay her wages whilst she was with us.

She came to the second bonding weekend held at Tenby in Wales and proved to have an extroverted personality and was very excited about joining our adventure. Mary worried that she might focus totally on Mike, and not get stuck in with all the menial tasks that would come in keeping the group on the road, but I decided we could handle this and that she would be an excellent all-round addition to our support team.

The day before we set out on the adventure, we learned that one potential financial sponsor had decided it was all too risky and pulled out. Without them, we were chronically short of funds. The problem was acute and Mary and I scour through our budgets to see where we could cut down. At first I can find nothing.

Then a chat with Dr Allison Graham provides a possible answer. Mike has made a spectacular recovery from his most recent rebuild and is very much fitter than we had anticipated. Dr Graham tells us that they no longer feel that a trained nurse is essential, as long as once we leave the UK, we establish a chain of medical advisors with spinal injury experience in each country along the route should they be needed.

Mary speaks to Mike about this, and he is happy with the suggestion. Mel is no longer essential and by taking her out of the equation, around £20,000.00 will be saved.

Now she is facing me and I have to make a very hard call. Due to previous commitments and because we always felt that she would not be needed in the UK, we had planned for Mel to join us in Nice. I decide to hold back on the decision to drop her from the party to give the whole team time to think about it and come to a consensus. In particular I have to be sure Mike is fully prepared to go along with the proposed arrangement.

Meanwhile, Mel is with us at Stoke Mandeville, fully believing that she is part of the team and telling us how much she is looking forward to joining us in Nice. It is very difficult and I feel I have handled it all very badly.

Sir Jimmy Savile calls the crowd to order and wishes us bon voyage.

We thank him, wave our farewells and climb on board our Land-Rover to travel to St Bees in the Lake District and sleep.

It is the end of day one. We have used six means of transport – horses, taxis, piston engine planes, an ambulance, hand powered cycles and a Land-Rover and have travelled halfway up England. It is a good first day for an adventure that will take over ninety days.

I reflect on the team. Miles and Caroline are ablaze with excitement and are performing well with the media, Mike has proved his ability to tackle difficult situations and overcome them, whilst our team manager Jon has begun to show his ability to win the loyalty of the team. In stage-managing the Reform Club departure, and then getting across to stage-manage the arrival at Stoke Mandeville, whilst ensuring that the baggage arrived safely, Mary has confirmed how impossible the whole adventure would be without her administrative ability and dogged determination.

I retire well satisfied and eager to move on – but I am also very tired and wonder if I am up to the challenges that lie ahead. Miles, Mike and Caroline are three very strong-willed people and are completely different from each other. During the day they have shown that they will do things their way. Will they accept my leadership for the three very difficult months that lie ahead, particularly as I have no executive authority over them? Will Jon fill the role I require of him, which is to provide a halfway stage between me and the adventurers, or will he instead become one of them himself?

Will Mike not survive the adventure as I have been warned?

And how about Mary, who has put in such very hard work in planning the whole adventure whilst holding down a full-time and highly responsible job, yet is not actually experiencing the excitement of being on the journey – will that cause a problem further down the line as we go to the more exciting locations?

We all sleep soundly, unaware that we have embarked upon an adventure that would change all our lives.

Today marks Jon's first day in charge. Having arrived by Land-Rover from Stoke Mandeville the previous night the adventurers are woken up at 5 a.m. in Fairladies medieval farmhouse, St Bee's in the Lake District where they are hosted by Mike and Karen Greene ... Strange and challenging means of transport lie ahead.

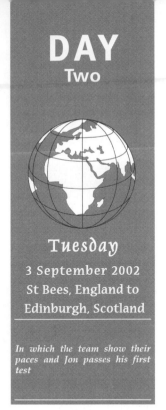

I have decided to see how Jon performs as a leader and how the team react to him, for in the months that lie ahead, there will be many times when I am going to be away from the team, preparing for their arrival and getting advance publicity, and it is important to me to know that Jon can take charge.

'They are all yours now, Jon. You are in charge, see you in Edinburgh.'

With that, having spent an exciting first day on the adventure, Phileas Fogg puts on his frock-coat, his top hat and departs for Edinburgh, leaving Jon to bring the team to Scotland's beautiful capital, using the various means of transport available to them.

'Don't worry Phileas, I'll get them there safe and sound, we will see you tonight.'

Difficult chap to read, Jon. Keeps his thoughts to himself. Not like Caroline who lets you know exactly what she is thinking and in somewhat blunt language. Her face gives her emotions away. Mike is up front with his views as well and lets you know very quickly when something is not to his liking. Miles is the philosopher, knowing that there is a reason for what is happening and that it will all work out fine in the end. But he too is well prepared to argue his point with some vehemence when roused. The potential for catastrophic argument is immense. Three powerful forces; get them working together and anything is possible, let them fall out and fireworks are guaranteed.

Apart from being Head of the Accident and Emergency Unit at nearby Whitehaven Hospital, Mike Green is deputy team leader of the Wasdale Mountain Rescue team and they meet up with Jon, Mike, Miles and Caroline at 6:30 a.m. At short notice Mike and Karen have arranged a whole day. Their first means of transport is to be carried on stretcher by the Rescue Team across rough terrain. For Caroline and Miles, it is a fairly straightforward situation but for Mike the challenge is different. Obviously he is the one to go in the stretcher and be carried by the others.

Miles and Caroline head up the stretcher party bearing Mike

The adventurers are shown a specially fitted harness that prevents back injury.

'Too late for me' jokes Mike, 'I already have a back injury.'

They are bounced to their next stop where Miles, Mike, and Caroline climb on board the Eskdale Narrow Gauge Railway and journey by steam through the Cumbrian countryside. Then they see it – a vintage tractor chugs its way towards them. It was originally used to pull Spitfires out of hangars in the Second World War. Caroline takes the wheel, but for safety reasons – for not only can Caroline see very little, she has never driven anything before – Jon decides that whilst she can have a go, the rest of the team must simply watch, or in Miles' case, listen.

Grinning mischievously, Caroline manoeuvres the gleaming vehicle around the car park, obeying the shouted instructions. Miles and Mike stand behind parked cars to ensure their safety. Route Director Stuart decides he cannot count that as a means of transport as they do not all

Robin gets to grips with a road roller

travel and Caroline goes around in circles, ending up where she began. Our first disqualification.

The next means of travel is courtesy of The Workington Life Boat Station. Miles, Mike, Jon, Aoife, our resident journalist and diarist and cameraman Mike McNamara tuck into steaming mugs of coffee and chomp down custard creams. Caroline takes a short nap on their lifeboat haulage truck. She gets up and her long blonde hair has turned black! What she thought was a shiny black plate on which to rest her head turns out to be a big pool of black grease. Fireman John whisks Caroline off and washes her hair in the toilet, using toilet cleaner as conditioner. I later give full marks for initiative.

There is no time for Caroline to ponder on the effect of toilet cleaner on the scalp as the team moves on to Whinlatter Forest where Jackie and Derrick Archibald have provided their next means of transport – huskies pulling wheeled rigs. The dogs cannot wait to begin the task, and bark excitedly, filling Mike in particular with dread. After all, he is looking at them eyeball to eyeball!

The team sets off. Mike has his own specially designed dog-pulled wheelchair imported from Sweden and he and his dog race past at a wild pace. Derrick shouts out a word of encouragement.

'Don't worry Mike, they have not killed anyone yet.'

Husky Denver tears through the forest pulling Mike who now has a massive grin on his face. When they complete their journey, both Denver and Mike are panting, one with exhaustion, the other with elation.

'Wow that was brilliant,' gasps Mike. 'The acceleration is staggering and would put most sports cars to shame. Thankfully I was only on one dog power as the GT version with two dogs would have been rather too exhilarating. I no longer need a Ferrari, I will just get a husky.'

After a picnic lunch, the team travel to Derwent Shore, paddling canoes across the Lake to Keswick. From there they make their way in rally cars to The Calvert Trust, an adventure centre with the Back-up Trust, a charity enabling spinal cord injured people to attempt

Mike, with Husky, on sled in Whinlatter forest

skiing, sailing, abseiling and other outdoor activities. The adventurers practice the skills learned that morning from the mountain rescue team. Then it is off towards Edinburgh in a specially converted mountain rescue vehicle.

It is evening and I am at the Apex International Hotel, in Edinburgh's famous grassmarket. It is a fantastic hotel – newly opened, and with special facilities for the disabled. I have spent the day checking out arrangements for the rest of the Scottish sector of our adventure. Now I am back with the Passepartout adventurers, and with Mary, Jon, Aoife and Carbonara.

We are all in one room, reviewing the day. Caroline is excited and is trying to get her hair back in order. Mike, a wine connoisseur, is sipping champagne with deep and appreciative satisfaction. Mary is watching over us all, just like mothers do. Jon is reflecting on his first day in charge, Carbonara is looking at the film he has taken during the day. Miles is lying on the bed, with his mouth wide open. Aoife is standing the other side of the room lobbing jelly babies into the air trying to get them into Miles' mouth. Miles catches several, and not for the first time, I have to remind myself that he is totally blind. He is amazing.

Aoife O'Connell was a late edition to the party. An Irish student of journalism she had met Caroline and suggested she should come along to be our diarist. She said she would cost nothing, as she would raise all her own funds to pay for herself. I met her in Dublin and she impressed me. I thought that having a diarist that would cost us nothing but could file back reports to the media would be a good addition. I also knew she would have an instinctive understanding of what we are trying to do, for Aoife has a significant facial birthmark that had caused intense problems as she grew up.

I spoke to Mary and we both agreed to bring her along. Mary was very keen to give her the wonderful training experience of going around the world on our adventure and recording it for the media. She wished someone had done something like that for her when she was a teenager, and hoped that Aoife would appreciate the chance that we had given her at the start of her career.

So Aoife joined us in time to attend the last bonding weekend at Hollins Hall, near Leeds. She blended well with the adventurers and both Mary and I felt that although she was young and lacking in experience, she was a good all-round addition to our project.

But now at the Apex Hotel, Edinburgh and in the second day of our adventure we have a problem. We have included Aoife in the group, but she has not yet managed to raise more than half the funds she needs, and even this sum is a loan which needs to be paid back. Mary is worried about what will happen if Aoife does not raise the full amount needed to pay her way. We are already chronically short of funds and can take no more costs on board.

But that decision is for a later time. Now it is the end of the second day and we are all together. There is warmth, a passion, an affectionate rapport between us, as the shared experience of our adventure begins to blend us into one highly dedicated team and former strangers become good and intimate friends.

I make three judgements. The first is that the three adventurers are up to the challenge. The second is that if Aoife cannot raise the rest of the funds needed, we will have to drop her out of the adventure once the heavy costs start. The third is that Jon has led the adventurers well and they have accepted his leadership.

Jon Cook had posed a problem in his selection. I had found it easy to take on board my Project Director, Mary Donaldson and my Route Director Stuart Nussey. The three adventurers, Miles Hilton-Barber, Caroline Casey and Mike Mackenzie had also been easy to select, though Mike's particular challenges had exercised the decision-making process. Aoife O'Connell and Mike McNamara had both selected themselves by saying that they would raise the money to come with us, Mike to make a television documentary and Aoife to do a daily diary and send feature material to the media.

It was Miles who suggested Jon as our team manager. He and Jon had undertaken many adventures together, and from Miles's description he seemed ideal. At first, I had not included a team manager, intending to do that job myself. However, at the first bonding weekend, it became clear that we needed someone who was fit, young and strong in this position, and with a bad heart, aged sixty-six and a life as a city-dweller, even I knew I did not qualify.

Jon worked for Rolls-Royce. I spoke to him by phone a number of times and then met him at Tenby in Wales, at the second bonding weekend. When I saw him, I immediately thought of Indiana Jones which was a good start. Tall, dark, wiry, with a black beard, he looked the part and over the weekend, he made a significant contribution on practical points. I was well pleased. I asked him if he would like to come with us as team manager, he said he would, but would first need approval from Rolls-Royce. I told him I would speak to them if that would help. He did not want me to do this and I let him have his way, a decision I was later to regret as it put me at a distance from one of our major sponsors. It was one of many mistakes I made.

Our next meeting was at our third bonding weekend – his second – which we held in a beautiful cottage in Shap, in the Lake District of England, found for us by Mary. Once again he impressed; this time I learned that he was a deep thinker, often questioning and probing to make sure he understood. If he did not agree, he let me know in no uncertain terms. But I felt uneasy that although he had come along to the bonding weekend, he still would not commit, as the time for departure was drawing close. He explained that it was difficult for him to negotiate his release from Rolls-Royce. I asked him if I could help but again he preferred for me to keep away; he believed it could best be done by himself when the time was right.

It was at our final bonding weekend, at Hollins Hall Hotel, that I first felt real concern about Jon. By this time, worried that I still did not have a firm decision, I told him I had found a replacement and if he did not give me a quick decision, I would have to appoint the other contender. However, this was not necessary. A meeting with Stan Todd of Rolls-Royce and his enthusiasm for the project had enabled them to release Jon.

At Hollins Hall we first experienced the extraordinary warmth that people extended towards us and our adventure. We spent our first night with friends of Mary's. Robin and Christine Scott lived in a nearby farmhouse and they invited the team, along with their many neighbours for a social evening. The highlight was pig racing, where bets were placed on mechanical pigs that waddled an erratic way along a table top track. The friends and neighbours did us proud and collected enough money amongst them to pay for most of our hotel bill, a spectacular effort. Later we were to learn that their son Roddy, a news photographer, had been killed in Chechnya and we grieved with them at their massive and tragic loss.

It was a great night, we ate and drank copiously and made good friends with Robin, Christine and their friends. We had some sore heads when we sat down to business the next morning.

As it was our last meeting together before the 'off', I had carefully prepared the agenda to take things in a logical order. However, before I could start, Jon, speaking on behalf of the team, said that instead of dealing with the items I wished to discuss, we needed to attend to a major problem that had arisen on the Irish programme. It was so serious that unless a call with satisfactory answers went to Ireland by 12 noon, the Irish organisers would pull out. I asked Jon when he had heard about the problem and he revealed that he had met with the team the afternoon before and learned about it then.

I was furious that, rather than alert me at the time he first learned about the problem, he had held back until there were only two hours to go before the deadline. I dropped my agenda items, turned to the problems with Ireland, which were swiftly resolved – though we later discovered that there were more problems.

It was Caroline who made the call to Ireland to let them know all was well and that they could continue to be a part of the adventure. The person who supposedly was waiting for our answers before deciding whether or not to pull out could not be found. I wondered how important it had really been.

I decided to call a break in the meeting and went to my room, angry, hurt and upset that I had let Jon persuade me to alter my agenda plans and livid with him for not telling me about the problem when he had first heard about it. Not for the first time, nor the last, Project Director Mary Donaldson saved the situation. She told me to calm down, which was wise advice. I reconvened the meeting and we concluded our business.

Then I spoke to Jon. 'Why did you not tell me about the problem when you first heard about it?'

'Because yesterday evening was a social event and I did not want to spoil it.'

I asked him where as team manager he felt his prime loyalty lay – to me as his leader or to the team whom he was managing. He replied, 'The team I have been chosen to lead must have my first loyalty.'

I understood what he was saying, but it rang an alarm bell. I then realised that our first major problem had arisen, for Miles, Caroline, Mike and Aoife had backed Jon, Stuart had taken the middle course, whilst Mary had backed me.

It warned me just how easily a split could occur, and how difficult a job I had given Jon in trying to ensure that it did not. He had to lead the adventurers but not become one of them, and also uphold my decisions and ensure that they were implemented at the coal face, whilst retaining his position of respect and authority within the adventure team.

It was because of this and the need to make an early judgement that I had decided to give Jon a day alone with the adventurers right at the start, and I reflect on this that second night of the adventure in Edinburgh. Jon had taken control of the team throughout the day. They had completed it elated, successfully, and clearly having developed confidence in Jon's leadership. I decide to put my doubts aside and welcome Jon in my mind as being fully capable of carrying out the tasks I need from him in the way I want.

But Mary is still wary. She believes that away from our influence, Jon may forget his role and get too close to the team, as we both felt he had done at Hollins Hall.

I tell her not to worry, I can handle it. But I am not as confident as I sound and she gives me a look that says she knows this.

It is only day two and already there are concerns as to whether we can hold the team together throughout the difficulties ahead of us.

We breakfast at the excellent Apex Hotel in Edinburgh and then attend our briefing. Today marks our first test with schoolchildren.

On which we travel by Roman Chariot, are blessed and meet Santa Claus

They arrive in buses – some two hundred of them – ages ranging from 5 to 13, and wait patiently though noisily in Cramond Kirk for us. The Kirk is beautiful. Standing in tree-filled grounds in the village of Cramond, once independent of Edinburgh but now an upmarket suburb, it has a warmth and charm about it. Now it is full of children who are waiting excitedly and expectantly to meet the adventurers who are going around the world.

I lead the team to the pulpit area, look at their bubbling and eager faces and immediately get stage fright. 'Suffer little children to come unto me' (Luke 18:16) says the bible, and I suspect St Luke had me speaking to them in mind when he wrote the words.

I flunk it and ask Mary to introduce the session.

'Good morning, my name is Mary' she says, and at once the children are at their ease. She introduces each of us in turn. I go first, but I know I am using the wrong language for them and quickly pass on to Caroline. She leaves the stage and moves amongst them, explaining that she cannot see them unless she is really close.

'I love elephants' she says. 'I love them so much that last year I rode one across India.' The children are incredulous. How could a blind person ride an elephant across India – yet here she is, in front of them and they can touch her.

'Have any of you got a pet like an elephant?' she asks.

There is silence, and then a small girl holds up her hand.

'Please Miss, I have got a hamster.'

Caroline, like Mary before her, wows the kids and I make note not to interfere when children are involved. I lack the magic that Mary and Caroline possess to communicate with kids.

Now it is Mike's turn. To my astonishment, Mike also communicates with children who ask about his injuries. Mike tells them he has no legs and shows the stumps. The children crowd around and fire queries that adults would never dare to ask.

'Mister, how do you pee?' is not a question you expect to hear in a kirk, but they ask it on that day.

Then Miles talks to them and he too shows that talking to children is no challenge. He is an amazing adventurer to them and they listen to his story in silence, which is hard for children. Then it is time for them to take part. We all come off the stage and are surrounded by eager children, questions coming like machinegun fire. Mary cops the best of all.

'Miss, I know a way your people should use.'

'What's that?'

'Swinging from tree to tree, like Tarzan.'

But for one school, there is disappointment. Their bus fails to arrive and they never make the meeting. Mary notes this and makes a point of e-mailing them later on in the adventure so that they can share something special with us.

We pull out and think about the morning. This is our first meeting with children and the depth of their questioning, their lack of any inhibition over disablement and the completely natural way in which they treat Mike, Miles and Caroline as ordinary people who simply have a different challenge is stunning to us. It is the message we wish to put out to the world, yet these children already understand it. What happens to change them as they grow up?

But there is no time for more talk, we have some travelling to do.

We have taken time out to talk to the children but we must get on with our adventure. We go back to our start point, the Apex Hotel and await our next means of transport, which is to take us to a service of blessing, again at Cramond Kirk. An ancient bus takes us to a wood near the village of Cramond. A Roman chariot arrives for us, pulled by 'Roman Slaves'. They are from Cramond Kirk and they are dressed in togas. They have made the chariot especially for us and we ask why.

We are told that a Roman fort was once located in Cramond. The congregation of the church thought it would be good to remind people of their Roman background through Around the World in 80 Ways.

We board the chariot and they pull us to the pier. There we see a man in a wheelchair.

Cameron Sharpe was one of Scotland's best athletes, competing successfully with Alan Wells who later went on to win the 100 metre sprint in the Olympic Games. They were on a par with each other, some thinking that Cameron was the faster of the two, others choosing Alan. Alas, it was an issue never to be resolved because Cameron was involved in a tragic car accident. Some say it was the accident that caused the damage, others allege it was the treatment he received for his injuries, but whatever the reason, with both massive brain and physical injuries, he was written off as a vegetable and whilst he battled for some recovery, Alan Wells went on to become the fastest man on earth over 100 metres.

Over the years, Cameron, urged on by his wife, battled against his gross disabilities. Slowly he learned to make noises and then to attempt speech. He worked on his useless muscles and gradually some movement was restored. Now he is in his wheelchair sitting before us.

We stand in front of him. He pulls himself up from the chair and walks towards us. He makes a short speech, wishing us luck.

We later learn from the Rev'd Dr Russell Barr of Cramond Kirk how, when Cameron heard what we were doing, he decided to come and wish us well. Cameron, you do not know how much that inspired us as we undertook our adventure, and how much we drew on that inspiration when times got difficult. You are a real battler, you have our admiration and we wish you well.

We bid our farewells to a very brave man and go back to our chariot. It is only big enough to take two at a time, so two trips from the Cramond foreshore to the Cramond Kirk are made. Caroline and Mike board the chariot first and are pulled by the Elders of Cramond Kirk. Led by a pipe band, the strange group processes to the Kirk.

I follow in the second trip, with Miles by my side. By now, there is quite a large crowd. The pipe band leads the way, then come the slaves in togas pulling the chariot, and the supporting crowds follow. The sun dissolves slowly behind us, scattering sparkles of crimson jewels to dance on the waters of the Firth of Forth, with the massive Forth Bridge standing out dramatically behind us. A lump comes to my throat as a photographer captures the scene and produces one of the best photographs of the entire adventure.

We enter Cramond Kirk where former television presenter Jimmy Spankie interviews us and the choir entertain the audience. Dr Russell Barr gives us all a blessing. The Kirk's highly talented organist, Ian Macpherson, plays a selection of tunes from around the world including a wonderful version of Mad Dogs and Irishmen specially written by him for the occasion and then the choir sing the beautiful and haunting Irish Blessing:

Roman Chariot and slaves

May the road rise to meet you
May the wind be always at your back
The sun shine warm upon your face
The rain fall soft upon your fields
And until we meet again,
May God hold you in the hollow of his hand

We have been blessed for the safety of our adventure. Dr Barr gives us the words of the Irish blessing as a keepsake and it is time for us to go.

We leave the Kirk and the congregation are lined up outside. By now we are used to the unusual but even we have to stop and stare. The South Queensferry Rotary Club has produced, in September, a remarkable Santa sleigh, complete with Santa Claus. Surrounded by the members of the congregation, we push through them, returning their hugs and their love, and climb on board. The sleigh pulls out, the crowd cheer, we all cry and Santa chuckles Ho Ho Ho into the dark Edinburgh night. We travel along Queensferry Road, greeting the people walking by, who simply smile and wave back. A car creeps up to us. It has Mary and Aoife in it. Abruptly it pulls into the side. Mary is laughing too much to drive and they need time to recover.

Another car comes alongside. Jon sticks out his head, he is furiously taking video film, as is Carbonara. Our Police motorcycle escort takes us into Princess Street and then up Lothian Road.

Our third day ends. What have I learned? That Mary and Caroline are our best communicators with children, that Mike is also brilliant head to head with kids, that Miles is inspirational in his public speaking. I have learned that Aoife can really write and that a close bond, perhaps friendship is developing between her and Caroline. I have learned that Jon has persistence and a devotion to the success of the adventurers.

I have learned that Cameron Sharpe is inspirational in the way he has fought back from cruel injury, not knowing that he is the first of many such people we are to meet in our remarkable adventure. His short speech has made a thunderous impact on us.

We have not travelled very far for we are still in Edinburgh – indeed today our travels have only taken us from one side of the city to the other, but we have used a Roman chariot and a Santa sleigh to do so. We are confident that Stuart will add them to our different means of transport, so are well satisfied.

It has been a good day and I sleep well.

It is day four of our adventure, we have completed one twenty-fifth of the trip and all is well.

We have been told to keep Mike off his bottom as much as possible to avoid sores developing, which, being paralysed, he cannot feel. Indeed, once away from the UK are under instructions that if we are in doubt, we must send a digital photograph of this part of his anatomy to the hospital at Stoke Mandeville for inspection. So far, his bottom is in fine fettle and Jon, ready to take the pictures, is learning of a new niche market in photography.

The idea is that by noon on Friday we have to arrive in Glasgow, having crossed from Edinburgh by the Forth and Clyde canal. This part of the adventure is organised by British Waterways. Our first contact had been with Gail Macauley from the Waterways Trust and she had thrown herself into the project with fierce and competent enthusiasm. Just as we were getting used to her, however, she left to

Jon discovers a niche market for his photographic skills and like ducks to water the adventurers sail the canals where Caroline falls in love with a horse

take up a job with the Scottish Arts Council and was replaced by Rita Crowe who attacked the project with the same enthusiasm and drive.

Now it is 9:30 a.m. on day four and Miles, Caroline, Mike and I are ensconced in Canadian canoes at the Edinburgh end of the Forth and Clyde Canal. Mike has a problem as he needs both his hands to steady himself in the canoe and thus has no means of paddling! He later told me how inadequate he felt when he could not play a full part, believing that the crowds would just think he was being lazy.

The rest of us will paddle – except that in my fine Phileas Fogg outfit I am more concerned about keeping dry than paddling whilst Miles has no idea in which direction he is pointing. So what, steering is for others. His job is to provide the horsepower and being very fit and very strong, this is no problem for him. We are provided with some additional horsepower in the shape of a fitness guru from the local canoe club. I think that this is a fine preparation for Ireland where we are to paddle down the River Liffey in a boat made from cardboard. We are joined by Laura Bowden who is Development Officer for the Forth and Clyde Canal Community Association; she is also in a wheelchair. Once again, our friends the media stand poised, no doubt hoping that one of us will fall in. But they have no such luck. We are skilled on the water, thanks to Caroline and our first bonding weekend at her family holiday bungalow in Cross on the West Coast of Ireland.

I thought back to the first time we met there as a team.

The bungalow was situated by a lake in the West of Ireland and soon we had tried out canoes and found we could manage. Indeed, the canoeing had given us one of our funniest moments. Caroline and Miles had set off alone to cross the lake, being guided by Caroline's husband Fergal. Eventually they disappeared around a bend.

Back at base, Stuart and I were startled to hear shrill and desperate screams from Caroline and shouts from Miles. Immediately, determined like the American Cavalry to come to the rescue, I set off at maximum revs along the bank only to get stickily stuck in the marshes. Meanwhile Stuart, remembering in a very Stuart-like way to put on his life-jacket first, dropped into a spare canoe, and looking totally immaculate as if he were out on a Sunday morning paddle, he set off calmly in the direction of the screams, leaving his leader floundering and unable to help.

As Stuart stroked powerfully and rythmically towards the crisis, he was suprised to meet Caroline paddling towards him with Miles and Fergal following in their canoes. Crisis? What crisis? They had gone for a swim and the water was ice cold – thus the screams. And so Stuart, Caroline, Miles and Fergal returned to base to rescue their trapped and embarrassed leader, now up to his backside in mud. Leading from the rear became a standard joke throughout the rest of the adventure.

The weekend at Cross was the first of a series of bonding weekends that had been planned to help to knit us into a team. The location was ideal – a beautiful modern bungalow by a small lake, deep in the heart of the West of Ireland and not far from Donegal. Owned as a holiday home by Caroline's dad, he had generously agreed to let us stay there for a weekend.

Mary and I arrived first in mid afternoon. Finding genuine Irish peat turf in a basket, we lit the fire so that when the others arrived, they would simply smell Ireland. Then we made an Irish stew, with carrots, onions and finest mutton, strong enough to fill the home with a wonderful aroma.

Miles, Stuart and Caroline arrived, complete with Caroline's husband Fergal. Without sight, Miles absorbed the atmosphere through his sense of smell – a warm welcoming peat fire, the magic of stew cooked to perfection.

'This is just wonderful' he said, sitting down in a long sofa in front of the fire, sipping his glass of Paddy's Whiskey and settling into the night.

Sadly Mike could not be with us for he was paying yet another visit to hospital to get parts of him serviced and rebuilt. We made sure we phoned him at regular intervals, so that as far as possible he would feel included.

The next two days were a wonderful kaleidoscope of fun, seriousness, business, pleasure and wonder at the task we had set ourselves. We planned a route, set out conditions that would have to be fulfilled on each sector, tried to think of eighty different means of transport, worked out budgets, clothing needed, means of coping with our special requirements. And we set a date to set out on the adventure – 2 September from the Reform Club, Pall Mall London. We also decided that it was not practical to try to do it in eighty days, but we felt that it should last no longer than one hundred days. Then on the phone Mike pointed out that 3 December was the United Nations Day for Disabled Persons, a piece of information that settled our return date.

As a means of getting to know each other, our first bonding weekend at Cross was a huge success and we left exhilarated and confident that we could pull it off.

But it is time to start our fourth day so I stop reflection and turn my attention to the present challenge of crossing Scotland on the Forth and Clyde Canal.

We are in a high state of tension, waiting for the 'off'. The flag drops, we pull on the paddles and our canoes lurch forward. Caroline and Miles keep themselves very fit and at once they are paddling furiously, each determined to outclass the other in reaching the next staging post. They trade insults about each other's efforts. Being Phileas Fogg, dressed in frock-coat but now helmeted instead of wearing my trusty topper, I decide to work at a more dignified pace, and use a steady Fogglike methodical rhythm. Mike, his hands holding him upright in the canoe, experiences the sensation of letting someone else do all the work. He does not like it, he wants to do it himself and is frustrated that he cannot paddle the canoe. I

Cruising on a horse-drawn barge

make a mental note to watch out for this in the future and to make sure that as far as practical, in all our means of transport, Mike has a role to play and is never again left as a spectator, relying on someone else.

By 11:30 a.m. and after a lot of splashing of misplaced paddles, we reach our next means of transport. Clydesdale Mac is a celebrity, having appeared with Ewan McGregor in a film. He is also a horse, and is massive – one of the few surviving members of a diminishing number of these magnificent beasts. Normally he pulls a beer dray, but this morning he has been recruited to pull a barge, with an even more precious cargo – us – along the canal. I am not sure what he thinks of us but we think he is just smashing.

We climb on board the barge and with the gentlest of tugs, quite unlike the jerk of the horses outside the Reform Club, this massive and dignified animal plods off on his journey.

It is a wonderful world of total tranquillity. I am aware that only a few metres away, the hectic Edinburgh to Glasgow motorway is packed with cars scurrying between the cities in 45 minutes. We plan to take two days. Clydesdale Mac takes his own time clip-clopping along the tow path, trees line the canal, the sun beats down on the water and life is good.

Mike is placed at the rear of the barge, by the tiller, and tries his hand at steering. Miles stands at the front, doing a passable impression of Admiral Nelson. Caroline falls in love with Clydesdale Mac whilst I wonder what Phileas Fogg would have thought of it all. I wonder if Jules Verne is looking down and laughing.

But soon it ends, for we are bound for the Falkirk Wheel, a short diversion to an amazing contraption. Caroline has difficulty in leaving Clydesdale Mac, for her love of animals is legendary. She is reminded of Bhadra, the elephant on which she crossed India. Parting from her was also difficult.

Caroline was a late arrival to the team. With Miles and Mike already chosen, I had decided it was time to read the book. To my concern, I learned that early in his travel, Phileas Fogg's companion Passepartout had rescued an Indian Princess from being sacrificed on a funeral pyre and that she had then accompanied the dynamic duo on their voyage around the world.

At once I decided to find an Indian Princess. The girl I found was Irish.

Miles told me about Caroline, a registered blind Irish girl who had made her name crossing India on an elephant. He had her mobile phone number so I asked him to contact her and see if she would like to join us. He got her first time, she told him to call back when she was at home. She was still on her elephant in India! Such are the now accepted wonders of mobile phones.

I met Caroline at the headquarters of the RNIB in London. She told me that she had been born with a sight defect and could see little in front of her.

'I am extremely short-sighted' she explained. 'I've got astigmatism and I have got ocular albinism which causes problems with the pigmentation in my eyes. I do have some vision but unless you are standing no more than one foot away from me, you are a blur.'

With enormous foresight, her parents had brought her up refusing to accept her condition and treating her like any normal child. As result, Caroline grew up unaware of the extent of her disability and only learned this when she applied for a driving licence! She went on to university, then worked in the high-powered world of management consultancy.

But she found this a dull world and so threw up the job to ride an elephant across India, a challenge that she completed with aplomb. This adventure was featured in Marie Claire magazine and shown globally in a television documentary.

I decided she was just the kind of person we needed and invited her to join us. Thus I got my Indian Princess. Enter the scene, Caroline Casey aged thirty-one.

Now a fully-fledged adventurer, she and the rest have reached the Falkirk Wheel, the only one of its design in the world. It is an astonishing construction, built as part of the Millennium Celebrations, and we are told it is Scotland's third most visited tourist destination. I presume that Edinburgh Castle is the first and mull over what the second might be. I think of the Loch Ness Monster and then rapidly put the thought out of my mind as I am on water at the time. I have enough to worry about as it is.

The Falkirk Wheel is as it says – a giant wheel rather like a mill-wheel. We sail our boat into the specially designed car, and are moored. Then the wheel begins to turn and we travel on it down to the lower level of the canal. It certainly beats the conventional lock. We are told that a few days before it opened, vandals managed to smash the water gates at the top and millions of pounds of damage was done. Today the only damage is to our nerves.

The Provost of Falkirk has turned out in his regalia. I stand with him resplendent in my Phileas Fogg outfit, and the media go to work. I check my team. Caroline is still on about Clydesdale Mac and is wondering if she can see him again. Miles talks about the colours of the surrounding area, and once more I forget that he is blind, as does the media interviewer, who simply lets the remark pass her by. Mike is exhilarated by his big wheel ride. A new life is opening for him. Mary is attending to the management of the occasion. We are fit to continue.

Scotland is famous for shortbread and we enjoy our first sample on board the Seagull Trust boat which takes us from the Falkirk Wheel back along the Forth and Clyde canal. The Trust operates day cruises for people with disability and we are glad to help them. Apart from providing us with a boat, they have also provided the sandwiches for our luncheon with the dignitaries of Falkirk and we try not to eat them all and let the other guests have their turn. It is on this occasion that we first hear Jon sing his Fish Song. It is an extraordinary production and Aoife asks him if he made it up.

'Made it up! You would not ask Wordsworth if he made up his poems. I wrote this piece of work, I penned it myself, yes!' As Aoife says, 'Indeed the tortured artist.'

The Fish Song

We have no fish today
Didn't have any yesterday
Won't have any tomorrow either
Have you tried the fish shop?
This is the library

(All rights reserved, says Jon)

Quite!

But it is time to stop and attend to our programme of speaking.

The evening is spent with the South Queensferry Rotary Club, who provided us with the Santa sleigh and who played a large part in our adventure. They have also presented us with the Around the World baton, specially commissioned as a cylinder of wood holding a parchment certificate. They charge us to get the signatures of Rotarians we meet along the route and to present it back to them on our return.

It has been quite a day. We have made our way from the Reform Club, Pall Mall London to halfway across the Forth and Clyde Canal in Scotland. We are all well and in excellent spirits.

What have we learned? That in Jon's fish song we have found something truly original – what to do with it remains a mystery.

I think back on the evening spent with the South Queensferry Rotary Club. Right from the start, they have been strong supporters in our adventure. Apart from providing the Santa sleigh at Cramond, they had contacted other Rotary Clubs around the world seeking help for us. And of course, we now have their wonderful Around the World baton to take with us.

I knew that Mary was a Rotarian, but was surprised to learn that Miles was as well.

I had first met Miles at a private luncheon being hosted by the Duke of Westminster at his offices in London. The Duke was Patron of the RNIB. He had invited me to be his guest as I had just introduced them to spectacle king David Moulsdale from Scotland, founder of Optical Express and who had just agreed to become active for the RNIB in Scotland.

Miles was sitting on my left. The first thing I noticed was that he was a meticulous eater, cutting all his food into small squares, and placing all his drinking glasses in a straight line in front of him and to a set order. After dinner he spoke about his adventures, and it was only then that I realised he was blind!

Miles Hilton-Barber is a remarkable man. He had been blind for twenty years when I met him. Whilst blind, he had completed the Marathon Des Sables, the toughest foot race in the world, a 250 kilometre Ultra Marathon through the 120 degree heat of the Sahara Desert. He had also climbed to 17,500 ft in the Himalayas and conquered Kilimanjaro and Mont Blanc. He set a world record as the first blind person to man haul a sledge over 400km across Antarctica; frostbite prevented him becoming the first blind person to reach the South Pole. He had also competed in The Silken Footsteps, a 200km marathon across China, including sections of the Gobi Desert. With Zambezi white-water rafting, abseiling, ice climbing, hot-air ballooning, scuba diving and sky-diving also in his experience bank, it is hard to remember that he is totally blind.

I outlined the Around the World project to him and he asked for more information.

We arranged to meet for luncheon and we talked at length about Around the World in 80 Ways. His enthusiasm was unbounded and his vision of the impact it could make was inspirational. I realised I was in the company of a very remarkable man and by the end of the meal, I knew he would be a superb addition to our adventure. I also liked him enormously but did not tell him that.

I arranged for him to visit Mike at the National Spinal Injuries Centre at Stoke Mandeville and they hit it off at once. So I welcomed Miles on board as one of the adventurers.

But first, he had to get permission from the Royal National Institute of the Blind to undertake the adventure. It would mean he would be away from his job as their project manager for at least three months. After a number of discussions with them, they very generously agreed to let Miles take the time to complete the venture on full pay. In addition, they became fundamentally helpful in the organisation of the adventure, allowing their communications manager Ciara Smith to help in our publicity campaign and their fund raising manager Gareth Edwards to assist in raising funds. Their understanding and support throughout was outstanding.

And so Miles became part of the team attempting to relive Jules Verne's remarkable book. But we are falling behind, for by the end of the fourth day, Jules Verne was well across Europe, we are still in Scotland. Who cares, we tell ourselves, he did not exist, we are living out a real adventure and if we want to go to Scotland and take our time, that is what we will do. As the day ends, we marvel at the Falkirk Wheel and the ingenuity that went into designing and building it.

We arrive in Glasgow, have our first accident, enjoy our first celebrity dinner and complete week one

Back on board the Seagull Trust boat, we sail from Lock 20 on the canal where we had left off the previous evening and head towards Glasgow.

There we arrive in considerable style in a - magnificent miniature steam puffer called *The Wee Spark*. The Captain and proud owner is Jimmy McFarland, and he presents us with Scottish Ale and a slab of shortbread, they are delicious. We alight on shore at the Applecross Basin, where the headquarters of Waterways Trust Scotland is located, and are greeted by the ebullient and very popular Lord Provost of Glasgow, Alex Morrison and by Roger Hanbury, Chief Executive of The Waterways Trust in the UK, who had flown up from London to be with us. We join them for a delicious buffet where hungry as ever we demolish sandwiches, snacks and tea. I notice a buzz of serious but controlled activity in the corner and go to investigate. It is Route Director Stuart who is ill and has the Glasgow medic team treating him.

Stuart Nussey is an immaculate man who seems to know something about everything, is totally unflappable and who pays meticulous attention to detail. After leaving the RAF, he got the job of organising the annual Scottish Business Achiever Awards Luncheon, which is one of the UK's largest annual fund-raising events. I was working for the sponsor of one, Sir Tom Farmer, founder of Kwik-Fit and needing someone to help, I recruited Stuart. He did such a good job that he was retained by future sponsors. Now, in addition to being Chief Executive of SBAAT, he is Route Director, in charge of ensuring that we complete at least eighty entirely different means of transport on our adventure, and that each means of transport is safe for us to attempt.

During the bonding weekends, Stuart had proved himself to be one of the most popular members of our party. He was always immaculate – I remember going into his bedroom first thing one morning at the Tenby bonding weekend and finding him waiting for the shower to be free. Even at that early hour his hair was impeccably parted, his pyjamas uncreased, his brain functioning properly, logically and efficiently. He gave a good impression of Verne's Phileas Fogg, who too was always impeccably dressed and totally unflappable.

But Stuart's major attraction as a member of the team was that he seemed to know something about everything. He knew that in Thame, where Mike lived at the time, there was a wonderful bakery and he knew who to ring up to get a taxi in Hong Kong. He knew how things worked, what you needed to do to fix things. I noticed that the curtain rail in the shower in Tenby, the location of one of our bonding weekends, had come down. After Stuart had completed his shower, yes, the rail was back up. Why was I not surprised?

At the Cross bonding weekend in Ireland, Stuart disappeared into the kitchen and produced the most marvellous breakfast for us all. He knew the rightness of the food we should eat, and the right amount of drink we could take without damage. He spent the whole of one evening in a pub in Ireland discussing serious politics with Caroline's highly intelligent husband Fergal, and held his own ground easily. We all found him totally lovable and utterly irreplaceable.

But right now, at the Appledore Docks in Glagow, four days into the adventure, Stuart is the one who is hurt and we have had our first accident. In lifting Mike out of *The Wee Spark*, Stuart had suffered a back spasm. However that is not what is causing most alarm. Stuart has never had a day's illness or injury in his life. Having the spasm has sent him into shock. Jon notices that he has gone pale and started to talk rubbish – something totally unheard of about Stuart – and sends for the medics. Under their care, the patient makes a speedy recovery and sets off for home, driven by a friend. But we are shaken. The incident shows us how close we are at any moment to disaster. It is a warning for the future.

I am upset at the incident but am comforted by the highly efficient and calm way that Jon handles it. Hardly anyone else in the tent knows that anything is wrong!

It is evening. We are in the Moat House Hotel, Glasgow, preparing for dinner. The team have shed their uniforms of T-shirts and combats and actually look clean for the first time in nearly a week. Dressed in monkey suits, Scottish tartan and with the girls in slinky dresses, we are almost unrecognisable to our hosts, the Waterways Trust staff. I knew we would all scrub up well when needed.

We prepare to enter the room, but Caroline is missing. Later I learn what happened.

As she put it in her diary,

After a week living dressed like an elephant in oversized clothes, boots and rain ponchos, it was like I had forgotten how to walk in a pair of heels. As we had little turn about time between getting to the hotel and getting dressed, I was running late. Pacing it to the lift I jumped in and immediately found myself attacked by Murphy and his atrocious law. The

Jon, Mary, Robin, Caroline, Miles and Mike polished up and ready for the first dinner

lift got jammed between the second and third floor. I know how to ride an elephant but stuck lifts are beyond me, so I waited for rescue. Eventually having listened to my pleas, the lift decided to resume normal service and arrived at the ground floor.

I leapt out with as much grace as a hippopotamus and set off for the function room. But there was a problem. My body was moving forward, my feet were not following. In all my haste, I had forgotten I was wearing 3-inch heels, and the left one was now firmly jammed between the lift and the landing. As I contemplated my latest predicament, the lift doors started opening and shutting on me, squashing me every few seconds.

The concierge seized up the situation, recognised a damsel in distress, and rescued me. Thus embarrassed, half squished and utterly dishevelled, I arrived at our first black tie function twenty minutes late.

We make our entrance and dine sumptuously. Then it is time for the speeches. Caroline and Miles are barnstormers when it comes to uplifting an audience. They have different approaches. Caroline talks about the challenges she has overcome, waving her arms around like a robot on speed and delivering her words like a demented machinegun whereas Miles tends to talk meticulously, with moderated tones and impeccable voice production as he outlines the rules for achieving full potential. Both are excellent and receive spontaneous and enthusiastic applause. Mike uses a much softer approach, but is nonetheless an attention grabber. He talks about his accident, and the moment he heard that, in addition to his horrific injuries to his brain, his hands, his leg and the loss of his spleen, he had also severed his spinal cord and would be paralysed for life.

'My brain told me that this is bad news, but I am going to make the most of it.'

Spoken in a soft voice and in total silence from those listening, it is a moment of high emotion. The audience ponder the fact that this man, paralysed from the chest down, no legs, and with little lung capacity, is trying to get around the entire world using eighty different means of transport to do so. The wonder of it all sinks in and they applaud loudly and enthusiastically.

We retire but Mary discovers there is a very 'girly' problem to be solved. We had now attended our first glittering evening, in Glasgow. Because of the need to keep our kit down to a minimum, only one formal dress is allowed and now Caroline and Aoife realised that at each function, they will be wearing the same dress, time and time again! They will have the same kit on at formal dinners in Glasgow, next week in Belfast and again the week after, in Dublin and so on.

They realise that there is no way around the problem, so Mary decides that when she is with the team and a formal event has to be attended, then she too will wear the same dress all the time.

So the girls agree to have only one formal dress, wear it at all formal events and then have a ceremonial bonfire at the end of the adventure.

The first week is over. We have used over 20 means of transport, but do not yet know if Stuart will allow them all. We are as fit as we can be, bearing in mind we carry heart failure, blindness and paralysis in our luggage, and we are all in good humour. We are still good friends and have not yet had an argument. We are not getting on each other's nerves. Most of all, we now have confidence to tackle the rest of the adventure.

Which is just as well, for ahead of us lie some gigantic challenges that will tax our courage, resources, initiative, determination, doggedness, loyalty to each other and organisation to the full.

We sleep soundly, innocent of the dangers that lie around the corner. Sleeping dogs are waking up, they are growling and getting ready to bite.

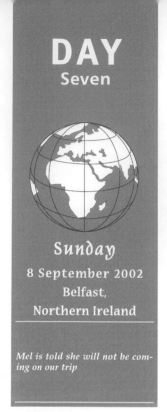

DAY
Seven

Sunday

8 September 2002
Belfast,
Northern Ireland

Mel is told she will not be coming on our trip

Over the weekend, Miles, Mike and Caroline fulfil a long standing engagement for the RNIB in England. On Saturday, day six of our adventure, Mary and I went ahead of them to Belfast to handle the Mel situation and to undertake some publicity calls.

It is Sunday morning, day seven in Belfast and we have finally found a café that is open. We order two hot chocolates with all the trimmings and decide that Mary should be the one to tell Mel. We feel the bad news will come more sympathetically from another female. As leader, I know it is really my job to tell her, but I know Mary has an instinctive understanding of other people's feelings and I know she will do it better. Mel will probably cry and men are not good when women cry.

Mary does it gently but firmly, explaining in significant detail the costs problem and how we have to find a way of reducing them. She talks of our discussions with the specialists at the National Spinal Injuries Hospital, and of the alternative that has made us come to the decision to drop her from the team.

Mel does cry and I can see that Mary is also crying quietly but her voice is firm, friendly and sympathetic.

Our admiration for Mel is total. Despite the massive disappointment, she accepts the decision. She shows enormous maturity and dignity, wishes us well and says she will follow us with enthusiasm on our web site.

It is a sad day for us and we cannot get Mel out of our minds. She had attended two of the bonding weekends, been involved in our regular team bulletins which we called 'Something for the Weekend' and had been fully kitted out with the team uniforms, bags and travel documentation. To have to make the decision so late was cruel and she took it wonderfully well.

We check into our hotel and wait for the arrival of the rest of the team from their engagement in England.

Airports are supposed to have staff trained in people handling so that folk like Mike can have assistance to board airplanes. It seems that no one has told Luton Airport. When the Irish talk of hurling they normally mean a sport played with a stick and ball. From Mike's experience, later repeated at the same airport, we formed the opinion it is disabled people the allegedly trained Luton Airport employees hurl.

As always, we ask for the airport people handling team to help load Mike into the plane. They treat him like a sack of potatoes. In full view of the other passengers, they heave and haul him, push and pull him and eventually throw him into his seat. Being paralysed, Mike does not feel the pain but when we get him to his hotel in Belfast, we discover he is sitting in a pool of blood in the taxi. The handlers have mishandled him so badly some skin has been torn. To make matters worse, his catheter is leaking.

It is a frightening and worrying experience and from then on, we decide that whenever possible, Mike will only be lifted by Jon and Caroline, both of whom are trained in the right way to lift him. We try to placate the taxi driver who has been wonderful to us, but there is not much we can do.

Now with Mike patched up, it is time for us to get on the road.

Later, Mike was invited back to Luton Airport to advise on people handling and on a recent trip to Edinburgh, was treated immaculately.

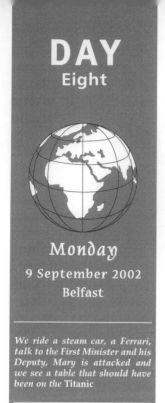
We ride a steam car, a Ferrari, talk to the First Minister and his Deputy, Mary is attacked and we see a table that should have been on the Titanic

Darlene McCormick is our project manager in Northern Ireland. She is Managing Director of Life Communications, one of the top public relations consultancies.

When I first outlined my project to her she brought me into contact with Safeway Stores, who were running a fund-raising campaign for Phab (Physically handicapped able-bodied). She introduced us to Phab Director Rainer Pagel and to Heather Lyons, Operations Support Manager of Safeway Stores. We agreed that the adventurers would visit each Safeway store in Northern Ireland using a different means of transport to every location and the stores would build a fund-raising programme for Phab around this.

I was excited about the Northern Ireland sector. Darlene had held a news reception some weeks before to announce our project and this resulted in major media coverage. For the reception she had brought together a group of people all of whom owned exotic means of transport and I was delighted to meet Gilbert Paton, who I had known at school and who was now an expert steam train model builder. Sadly his wonderfully built model replica of a steam train was too small to ride and we could not include it as one of our means of transport. But we marvelled at his skill.

Darlene suggested a picture of me dressed as Phileas Fogg, riding pillion on a Harley Davidson motorcycle and it looked so good that I decided I would travel around the world dressed as Phileas Fogg.

Finding a flowing black frock-coat presented no problem but the top hat was different. A visit to a hatter provided the information that a good topper would cost over £1,000.00, clearly out of the question. Indeed the most luxurious one I found cost £58,000.00! I would love a head that merits such an expensive hat.

However a visit to the costume department of the Royal Lyceum Theatre in Edinburgh provided me with a full Phileas Fogg outfit which they kindly donated. The frock-coat had last been used in a production of Hobson's Choice and had a deliciously fragrant aroma of make up and perspiration which I found very heady, whilst the topper was clearly one of supreme quality, for inside I found the words:

Manufactured Expressly for Extra Quality by J E Connelly, Glovery, High Street, Ayr.

Clearly from the markings inside the lining, it has been made individually for some top aristocrat, and it still looked magnificent.

The topper was called *The Arteleton* and the words *'with spring brim'* were proudly added. Whatever its previous life, how wonderful it should now be chosen to accompany us around the world.

Now on the seventh day of our adventure, I wear it proudly as we set out in a massive Safeway transporter to undertake our tour.

We are delivered to a car park where with a hiss of steam we head off for Belfast. Eric (we never did manage to get his second name) has built a beautiful but tiny steam engined truck. We all squeeze on board, Eric stokes up the boiler and off we go! It is an amazing experience. Despite the vehicle's smallness, we hurtle at 30 miles per hour along the main arterial road into Belfast, puffing out great belches of white steam as we go. Eric is up front, Miles and I sit immediately behind him, Mike and Caroline hang on at the rear clinging to a wooden bench. I think they are saying their prayers. We feel the blast of articulated trucks as they pass us, horns

Eric gets steam up, ready for the road to Belfast

Mike encounters a Ferrari. He bought one after the adventure!

blaring, drivers waving. Eric, oblivious to the consternation raging amongst his passengers and road users around us, hoots his way with glee. Every so often, his chariot runs out of steam and we have to stop at the side of the road until our driver has shovelled enough coal into the boiler to get under way. He is a wonderful, steam-crazed character and we want to pack him into our kitbags and take him along with us. He would have given Bogey of *African Queen* fame a close run. His is a wonderful contribution to our adventure and we thank him with enormous warmth, affection and gratitude.

But if Eric's vehicle seemed fast, on reaching Belfast our next form of transport is a lot faster. Canary yellow, costing £120,000, and so low to the ground that it hardly reaches up to my shoulder, it is the fantastic Ferrari Moderna provided for us by the motor firm of Charles Hurst. Thanks to them, we travel in some style to Stormont, the seat of Government in Northern Ireland.

Stormont is a truly magnificent building that stands high on a hill, dominating the countryside and looking every bit like a parliament building, its original purpose.

We meet First Minister David Trimble and his Deputy Brian Durkin. We talk about the need for a more positive attitude towards disability, and I am struck with a remark made by Caroline.

'We should all focus on the ability of the individual and not on what the label says.'

For me, the Stormont visit has an extra dimension. Born in Northern Ireland and old enough to have experienced the worst of the troubles there, it is wonderful to find a kind of peace had settled on the place, even if it is still a bit 'iffy'.

We stand for the obligatory photographs, with Darlene making sure that our Safeway T-shirts are well to the fore, rather than our Around the World uniforms. We feel it is a touch commercial, but are happy to comply to help Phab. Then it is back to our hotel to smarten up for the celebrity-packed fund-raising dinner to be held in the magnificent Harbour Commission building.

Preparing for the event, we have our second accident, for Mary is attacked by a shower – not of people, but the kind of shower you stand under and sing. Excess pressure has gathered in the shower rose, so when Mary turns it on, it shoots out of its socket like a cork from a champagne bottle before smashing down on Mary's nose, splitting it across the bridge. Blood pours everywhere. Summoned to the rescue I find her in tears, not of pain, but of the humiliation imagining her arrival at the ball – sweeping down the staircase, begowned in a glittering dress, with a bloody nose and a black eye.

But Mary is made of stern stuff. During a drama-filled life she has learned to make the best of whatever is happening. Wiping away the tears, she takes a deep breath, plasters on masses of make up and mascara, and makes a stunningly defiant appearance at the ball. I do not believe that anyone notices traces of the bloody battle she has just fought.

Mary Donaldson is a glass ceiling breaker. As Health and Safety Manager of a major firm of house builders, she is often to be found on top of scaffolding, dressed in hard hat, safety spectacles, overcoat, dungarees, woolly socks and thick safety boots.

'Don't talk to me about fashion in the work place' is one of her lines.

It is fun to see the reaction when someone who has met her at a building site sees her at a ball, for Mary is beautiful, but it is hard to appreciate that when she is dressed for a site visit.

Mary and I had first met in Northern Ireland when she worked as a consultant in a public relations firm where I also worked. I had lost touch with her, but met her again when we both came to Scotland. We lost touch again, but then, on 18 October 1999, standing in Leeds Bradford Airport, I felt a touch on my shoulder and a voice whispered in my ear, 'Hello Robin.' It was Mary. A graduate from the university of Life, she was now Group Health and Safety manager for a well-known development company spending most of her time travelling around the UK.

Mike grows accustomed to being centre of attention

She asked what I was doing and I told her about Around the World in 80 Ways. Immediately she said she would like to help and devote her spare time to the project.

Over the next two years, Mary proved herself to be irreplaceable. She set up a network of volunteer managers around the world, established procedures to be followed by them, supervised the building of their programmes, ordered them to find sponsored accommodation, routes and means of travel, organise publicity and find charities to help. On top of this, she 'mothered' the team. She also became second-in-command.

We had agreed that in her job as Project Director, it would not be appropriate for her to be with the team throughout the whole journey, but we selected a number of points on the route where her presence would be essential for the success of some of the major functions, of which the Belfast evening was one.

Now, with Mary's bloodied nose hidden by layers of make up, we wander around the magnificent Harbour Commissioners Building and find a table that should have been on the *Titanic*, but was delivered too late to make the disastrous maiden voyage. Thus it was saved to serve the Harbour Commission instead which it still does. The dinner has been organised by

Lady Stella Empey, wife of Sir Reginald Empey, former Lord Mayor of Belfast and leading politician. Everything glitters, including the guests who all sparkle with distinction.

I find Miles and take him to the *Titanic* table. He runs his fingers over the highly polished surface, seeking out shape and texture. He sniffs the wood and his enjoyment of that fine piece of historic furniture is as total as that of any sighted person.

The dinner is superb. Rainer Pagel has asked that Miles should be the speaker on behalf of the team and he rewards him by making a speech that stuns us all with inspiration, passion and power. He is on top form. Despite Rainer's request that we only put up one speaker, he invites Jon up on stage, praises the role of the enabler and invites him to say a few words. Jon quickly returns to his seat, but I am uneasy. Is this the first sign that Jon will find his role of manager becoming confused with that of an adventurer? Is he becoming a part of the story and not one of the enabling team? I let the thought pass. For now.

After the meal, I get an opportunity to meet some of the guests. Anne Hailes is there. I knew her as one of Ulster Television's top presenters. Anne and I used to work together for the Belfast-based public relations firm IPR, owned and run with enormous enthusiasm by Gordon Duffield. It is wonderful to meet her again and catch up with her life. I also meet the grandly named journalist Ian Jay McCartan Hill again for the first time in many years. He used to work for the Northern Ireland Tourist Board but is now a very prominent freelance columnist, critic and travel writer. I renew my acquaintance with Walter Love. In my time in Northern Ireland, he was a broadcaster, now he is one of the top radio doyens in the business. It makes me think back to my days in public relations in Northern Ireland, where there was a wonderful gang of media personalities. Two of the gang missing tonight are Gloria Hunniford, who of course became a massive star, and Henry Kelly, who found fame through national television and as the first presenter of classical music on Classic FM as well as being host of the television game show *Going for Gold*. We were a fine vintage and Anne, Ian, Walter and I reminisce about a time twenty-five years in the past when, even with the troubles at their height, we managed to have a wonderful life as young people starting out on our careers.

The Belfast Harbour Commission evening is a major success, thanks largely to the wonderful work done by Lady Stella Empey who undertook the responsibility of organising it and we return to our hotel knowing we have lived up to the very high expectations that had been placed on us.

We have been charmed by the warmth of the welcome from Phab, the people in general, and the Safeway team who did nothing for our waistlines by piling us up with tea and buns as we visited every one of their stores in Northern Ireland. They had been fundraising for Phab throughout the year and we were glad to have been able to reward this by giving them branding in the major media coverage that followed our adventure.

Our first day in Northern Ireland is now complete. We have travelled in a specially converted bus, a steam car and a £120,000 Ferrari. We have visited every Safeway store, the parliament building at Stormont, shaken countless hands, smiled for the cameras, told our story to the media, made speeches, raised funds for Phab at that glittering dinner and we are still all fit. Mary has a bruised nose but there is no further damage whilst the blood from the wound in Mike's backside has stopped, too. Jon does not have to take a photograph and send it to Stoke Mandeville!

All is well.

Elated by the success of the previous evening and the dinner which we have all enjoyed, we prepare to travel south into the Republic of Ireland.

DAY
Nine

Tuesday
10 September 2002
Belfast, N. Ireland to
Roscommon, Eire

We cross the border, take a ride in a tipper truck and sample Guinness in the land of its birth

But first we have to sort out a problem. Rather than wear the standard Around the World kit, Mike, Miles and Caroline have worn Safeway T-shirts during their time in Northern Ireland and have been photographed in them both by the national Northern Ireland media and by the media local to each Safeway store visited. It is very commercial but all have agreed to do this in return for the in-store fund raising. But we have all noticed that whilst there is plenty of media coverage, there is no in-store fund raising. As we still have a number of visits lined up, it is important to sort out why the promised fund raising is not taking place.

A check call soon reveals that there have been crossed wires. Safeway Stores had adopted Phab as their charity for the year, and whilst the original plan was to run special fund-raising schemes during our visit, it was subsequently decided that this would clash with the on-going programme and that our visit should be built in to the activity already on stream. No one had told us of the change but the explanation made us all happy and so we set out on the second day in Northern Ireland with equal enthusiasm. However, from now on Mary and Stuart decide to do a double-check just as the team is about to enter a new country, to make sure there are no changes of which we are unaware.

After a wonderful breakfast consisting of a massive Ulster Fry of fried eggs, soda bread, potato bread, rashers, sausages and black - pudding we set out from Belfast. We are joined by Tim Haddock, a wheelchair athlete and musician, who, like Cameron Sharpe at Cramond, inspires us. He challenges Mike to a wheelchair race along the pier at Kilkeel, snorts off in a spectacular wheelie and leaves Mike and a trail of dust behind him. We all think he is terrific, with a wonderful sense of fun and Mary promises him he will be there at the end when the team return from the adventure.

We get back on our bus which has been designed for transporting disabled people and we drive to the foothills of the Mourne Mountains for a very special meeting. It is held at an isolated cottage which serves as a conference and meeting place for Phab and as we arrive, we see that there are two buses full of children.

They are special. Severe disabilities, both mental and physical, mean they cannot live normal lives. Most of them cannot communicate. Remembering Cramond, I ask Mary and Caroline, both of whom have a magic with children, to board the buses and almost immediately love and excitement are everywhere. Mary, knowing that I am not at ease with children, leaves her bus and invites me to return to it with her. I am dressed in my top hat, frock-coat, tails, cravat, black shoes and as I enter, I am infected by the wave of excitement, the desire to touch, the attempts to smile. I am totally over-whelmed as Mary and Caroline somehow explain who I am to the children. And I remember what Around the World is all about – disabled people are not outcasts from the human race, but are people who have to live a different way. I realise that within these broken and twisted bodies and minds, real children with real feeling and real love spend their captive lives, and their needs for hugs, love and affection are those of any child. So I hug them, tenderly at first and then, realising they do not break, and that they respond in an unmistakable wave of emotion, I hug them with all the love and passion that I can, fighting the tears that try to escape.

Leaders don't cry I tell myself – at least, not in front of those they are trying to lead.

Oh yes they do.

The buses leave and we share lunch with the remaining children and their carers, parents and family. It is a wonderfully warm occasion, we feel we do not deserve our hero status but they accord it to us anyway.

Soon I am aware of a buzzing overhead. It is another means of transport, the helicopter which is to take us across into the Irish Republic and to Dundalk, our next stopping place. Caroline had told Joe Morgan of Mercury Engineering about her around the world adventure and to our total delight, he most generously offered his top of the range helicopter to take us into the Republic. But now there is a problem. The pilot cannot see us, despite our frantic waving, and circles around some distance away. We rip sheets off the beds in the conference room and lay them out on the grass, but still no luck. Then Caroline gets out her mobile phone, and finds the pilot's mobile number from Mercury Engineering. She rings it and to our delight, there is an answer. Caroline talks the pilot down and she, Miles, Mike, Aoife and I board, leaving Jon and Mary to travel by car to our destination.

We land for lunch at Dundalk. Caroline takes part in a video conference on disability which is being held in Dublin and as the link is set up and the picture comes through to us, the presenter at the conference asks her, 'Can you see us all right?'

'Not really' replies Caroline, raising a massive laugh from those at the conference and causing the presenter some intense embarrassment. Don't worry, I think to myself, for often I too forget that Caroline is registered blind.

We arrived in Dundalk in the Mercury Engineering luxury executive helicopter but we leave for the 200 mile drive to Roscommon in Mattie Early's giant tipper truck! It is so big, the cockpit so high off the ground that we struggle to get Mike on board. Eventually a genius borrows a scissor bed from the local hospital, Mike is placed on this, the bed is elevated and a triumphant Mike is downloaded to the cabin bunk where he takes the strain off his backside and lies down.

Miles clambers up next to Mattie and displays a comprehensive knowledge of engines as he quizzes him about his vehicle. Mike and Caroline fight for space in the rear of the cabin. There is no room for me so I take the car, along with Mary and Jon, who have successfully made it on the baggage train, from the Mourne Mountains, and Aoife.

At a rest stop in Paddy and Bridget Moran's pub, the Clohan Inn, Mullingar, I learn that I have been fortunate. Irish country roads (and the road from Dundalk to Roscommon certainly qualifies as a country road) are not known for their smoothness, and whilst Mike is OK lying down, Miles and Caroline find themselves being bounced and ping-pong balled all over the cabin. Supplies of reviving Guinness are called for, a pint is sent out to Mike, who has remained in his cabin, whilst the rest sup the white-capped black brew with relish in the darkness of the pub. There are nine other drinkers and when they learn who we are and what we are doing, the hat is passed around and a highly generous 130 Euro is collected from them. Mike and Miles are astonished at the kindness and genuine hospitality shown to them, Aoife and Caroline are proud to be Irish.

The rest of the journey is uneventful and we arrive at our destination in Roscommon, very tired, very late, and ready for some serious sleeping. Checks reveal that everyone is still well and able to continue. I notice that a degree of elation and possibly self-satisfaction at our success is creeping in. I am struck with the thought that all around the world, people are preparing for our arrival. How tragic if some simple mistake at this early stage means we let them down. What if Mike spends too long on his backside, Miles gets hit by a car, Caroline takes ill. Suddenly I feel the responsibility wearing me down and I decide to point out to the team that they have a duty to the rest of the volunteers working for Around the World to arrive in their countries fresh, fit, and able to sparkle. We have only done one week and it is far too early to think we have achieved anything. We have just made a promising start. We must not get over-confident, we must not take any chances.

I snooze off with that thought playing through my head, preventing the sound sleep that I crave. It is the end of day two of the second week and some problems are beginning to whisper to me, softly but persistently.

Go away, I want to sleep.

DAY
Ten

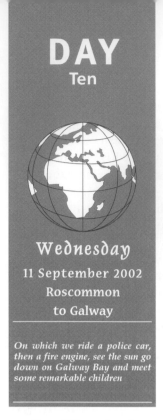

Wednesday
11 September 2002
Roscommon
to Galway

On which we ride a police car, then a fire engine, see the sun go down on Galway Bay and meet some remarkable children

There is nothing like an Irish hospitality, especially where breakfast is involved. Thanks to the incredibly hospitable Maggie Campbell, we are treated to a first-class Irish breakfast. Following hard on our Ulster Fry the previous morning, we all decide we will get fat if we keep on like this – but we ignore common sense and tuck in with rampant relish.

It is hard to leave the warmth of their home where we have stayed the night. We have reached Roscommon, it is time to move on. I check the party and they are all well. Mike used to take ages to assemble himself and get under way, but since his operation he has been able to get up with the same speed as the rest of us and he appears for breakfast, suave, eager and ready for action. Caroline, as ever, is bustling with energy, Miles, who enjoys his food enormously and who takes a terrific interest in everything that is happening, wolfs down his bacon and eggs and asks if the police car we are about to ride will have its siren on. We remember that without sight, noise is vital to his appreciation of any scene. As well known journalist and broadcaster Peter White writes, 'action is essential for blind people to experience beauty. If things are static and silent, they might well not exist for us.'

The police, or Gardai, are after us. Yes, our first means of transport is by Garda – or police-Jeep! It is there we meet Coman Kenny's mum and dad, who have turned out to help us.

Coman works for Caroline Casey's Aisling Foundation. When we first met him, he was a freelance public relations consultant but soon he joined the full-time staff of the Trust and became fundamentally involved in the public relations programme for Around the World. At the bonding weekend at Hollins Hall, it was suggested that he should take over the whole public relations operation, but fearing he would be unable to avoid subconsciously favouring his boss Caroline, I turned down the offer, and instead used Beattie Media, a top UK public relations consultancy based in Scotland but with a London office, who volunteered their services. Indeed, their Managing Director Gordon Beattie had been one of the original businessmen to make the bet with us for the challenge.

Coman applied himself to the project with enormous vigour and application. A man of strong views and one with a natural bias for the Irish dimension of the adventure, we often clashed, and it was difficult at times to reconcile the views of four public relations professionals in myself, Mary, Coman and the Beattie Media team, but somehow we managed to get through.

Coman and Mary became a strong and close-knit working team and many problems were solved by putting their heads together. We owed much to Coman, the enthusiasm he displayed and the time he devoted to Around the World in 80 Ways – and in particular the way in which he helped to mastermind the very difficult return to London at the end of the adventure.

We enjoy talking to his parents very much, they are delightful people and it is good to feel their friendship. But we have work to do and we climb on board the garda Jeep.

To Miles's delight, our driver Ollie Dempsey hits the siren as we drive through Roscommon town so that Miles can record it on his audio cassette. How can you refuse the charming request of a man who says he takes his photographs with his ears!

Next we transfer to the snorkel and fire engine at the town of Clare. We do this because it is 11 September and we want to pay tribute to the fire services who performed so heroically and who suffered tragedy at the World Trade Centres in New York. For many people today will be a sad one of remembrance, but one year on, it is timely to remember that life does go on and we want people, able and disabled alike to live life to the full.

We make our next stop – Galway – at noon and once again, sit down to a large meal. Caroline remarks on how much food we are consuming on an hourly basis. Miles does not mind, for no matter how much he eats, he still looks slim and debonair. I have been told that Mike has special food requirements, but I do not notice these as he gets stuck into a hearty lunch. I come to the conclusion that the special requirement is for there to be lots of it and ideally washed down with a fine wine, for that was his profession before his 'bump' as he calls it. Mary, as always, keeps a watchful eye out for potential problems or difficulties. Jon decides not to sing his fish song.

In Ireland we have chosen to help raise awareness and funds for the Jack and Jill Foundation. Originated by Jonathan Irwin, a highly successful Dublin businessman, the charity exists to provide trained helpers for those who have very young and mostly terminally ill children in their families. Jonathan started the charity when his own son Jack was born with such a condition and he discovered that there was no state help when, with no hope of survival, Jack was sent to their home to live out his short life. The Jack and Jill helpers take on some of the workload and help to reduce the stress on the fathers, mothers, sisters and brothers.

Rightly Jonathan has decreed that if we were to help his charity, then we must know more about it, so for our first afternoon in Galway, he has arranged a reception for some parents and their children.

We meet them in the office of the local Chamber of Commerce. Mary, Caroline, Miles, Mike, Aoife, Jon, Carbonara and I walk into a room, crowded with parents and children. The emotion is overpowering. The children are ill – desperately ill – and most of them will not live for much longer. Yet they are laughing, some only with their eyes. They are excited. Carbonara shows his television camera to one young boy, who has to haul a mechanical box around with him — without it he would die. The boy sees his image in the camera and squeals with delight. Carbonara gets down on his knees and shows him how to work it. Mary takes a grotesquely malformed child into her arms and hugs love by the bucketful into her. Caroline crawls around the floor and happy shrieks follow her. Mike again shows his wonderful communication skills with children whilst Miles chats to the parents. I stand aside, wanting so much to join in, but not knowing what to do. Again I find out that leaders can cry.

Miles speaks. He cannot see but senses that there is something special about the occasion. He talks of the role of children and the part they must play in bringing happiness to parents. I realise that he has not fully appreciated that the children in the room will almost certainly all be dead in the not-too-distant future, because he cannot see them and no one has fully briefed him. But it is a moving speech anyway. Caroline and Mary also talk to the parents, sharing their joy in their children, experiencing their love and warmth and happiness in tragedy.

And I appreciate and admire the wonderful vision of Jonathan Irwin and his wife Mary Ann, for seeing the need and doing something about it. We all resolve to do what we can to help the Jack and Jill Foundation.

Later in her diary Caroline writes:

In the afternoon, we met some representatives of the Jack and Jill Children's Foundation from the Galway area. Each of the Jack and Jill babies melted our hearts. Meeting these children you are reminded how valuable each of their lives are, but how much they have to offer and how much they can give regardless of their disability! You are also reminded though, how much the Irish State lets both the children and the families of the children down by having no care for the child and family before the age of four. What struck me most that afternoon was the positive energy and strength that the parents demonstrate. I just wish that our State would recognise how difficult it is for these families to survive and live normal lives. What changes when they become four years old, that then entitles them to help? Why not before they reach that age? That is if the baby lives to be four at all. It is a disgrace that considering that on average there is about only 250 of these babies a year, that nothing is being done to acknowledge the incomprehensible difficulties faced by these families.

But what is inspirational is that the human spirit refuses to rely on the State but finds enough spirit to succeed.

All of the team are inspired by meeting the Jack and Jill parents and children. We know we have tough days ahead in our challenge – I still fear the trip on the cardboard boat and wonder if disaster looms – but today belongs to the Jack and Jill children, to their parents and carers, and to the man who has done so much to promote the cause, Jonathan Irwin.

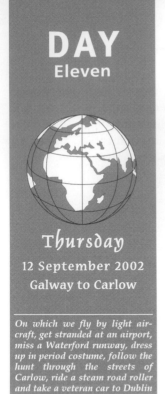

DAY
Eleven

Thursday

12 September 2002
Galway to Carlow

On which we fly by light aircraft, get stranded at an airport, miss a Waterford runway, dress up in period costume, follow the hunt through the streets of Carlow, ride a steam road roller and take a veteran car to Dublin

It is early morning which is not the right time to see the sun going down on Galway Bay, as the song recommends. Can't help that. Should have done it last night, but some enthusiastic vocalisation in a Galway pub got in the way. One of us even managed to sing Danny Boy to the tune of the Mountains of Mourne. We always said our adventure was about doing the impossible!

This day looks dodgy. We have arrived at Galway Airport where we are to fly by private plane to Waterford, but there is no one here – no one in the control tower, no one serving in the coffee shop. We learn that they only open when scheduled airlines are landing, so we have to wait until one does. We are told there might be one in an hour, but on the other hand . . .

There is a man in the coffee shop.

'Can we have a cup of coffee?' asks Jon.

'No I am closed.'

'But you are standing there, there are no barriers or anything up, your machines are turned on, it is 10 a.m. – please, can we not have a cup of coffee?'

'No, I am shut, completely shut and will not open until a scheduled plane comes in or sets out. You are not a scheduled plane. When no planes are scheduled I have to clean up the bar and café and I cannot do this if I am open,' he said as he downed his own cup of coffee newly poured from the machine.

We cannot beat his logic so Mary decides to try charm, aided by Jon. This time, it works and coffee is served.

Eventually the longed-for scheduled plane is on approach, the control tower and the coffee shop open and we are told it is now all right for us to get on our way.

We take off in two planes, our pilots, entering into the spirit of the adventure, are dressed as Superman and Batman. But all is not well. The first plane tries to land at Waterford but there is a heavy mist and it is too dangerous. We fly to Shannon Airport and land for a consultation.

We climb out of our planes but there is no one near us. So we stroll across the tarmac completely unchallenged and keep trying doors to the terminal until we find one open. We walk through and discover we have broken every security rule in the book. We get a right wigging, but counter that if the security people cannot pick up two blind people, a man in a black coat and top hat and a man in a wheelchair moving across a high security area, something is wrong. Our defence is not appreciated and I feel a night in jail coming on. Common sense prevails, we are escorted to a coffee shop and sit down to work out what to do.

It is decided that one plane, which has more instrumentation, can make the landing at Waterford, the other cannot. Miles, Mike and Caroline climb into the plane, Jon and I hire a car and hightail it to Leighlinbridge, our rendezvous point. Jon drives whilst I navigate. It is a great chance for me to get to know Jon better. We talk of the adventure, the journey passes quickly and we arrive just twenty minutes after Caroline, Miles and Mike. They have just experienced a spectacular helicopter flight from Waterford into Leighlinbridge. The pilot looks so young he could still be at school, but he flies excellently and they land safely.

Now it is time for the fancy dress. We are to ride with the Carlow hunt through the streets of the town, the first time this had ever happened, and it is decreed that we must do it properly dressed. Caroline is to ride side-saddle, Miles is to ride normally whilst for Mike the local organiser has found a saddle that had once been used by Kevin Kavanagh who had no legs, and this has been restored by the present Kavanagh family for him to use. Of course, what has been overlooked is that Mike is paralysed from the chest down, a handicap the owner of the saddle did not have to overcome. However, the saddle provides a platform for Mike to use and without it, he would be hard pushed to ride and stay up with the Carlow Hunt.

It is steam again as the team ride a road roller caravan towards carlow

Outside the Courthouse at Carlow, the team get ready to talk to the crowd

We change and set off for Carlow in a wonderful old steam-roller and halfway there, transfer to an ancient but much loved 1952 Ford car. We arrive in Carlow to a buzz of excitement. Mike, Miles and Caroline climb on board their horses, whilst I am taken to the town centre, to stand in front of the Court House to receive them as they arrive.

Like the coffee shop at Galway Airport, the streets of Carlow are closed, and crowds line them. First I hear the cheering, then furious clip-clopping as the horses approach. Caroline, all in red, is leading the procession, riding sidesaddle – I later learn that she had fallen off at the start! Next comes Miles, looking for all accounts like to country gentleman riding to hounds. A rider from the Carlow hunt is beside him but Miles can tell where he is going by the noise of the crowd. At times he has a sour expression on his face. He later explained that this rather pained expression was due to the fact that his trousers, hired for him, were too tight at the crotch and every time he bounced up and down ...

Then, to an enormous cheer, Mike arrives. Sitting proudly in his adapted saddle, dressed to kill, he bows his head to acknowledge the applause but tells me after that there were tears of emotion in his eyes as he did it. He confides he does not feel worthy of all the praise as all he is doing is living his life as best he can within the conditions imposed by his injuries. What is he supposed to do, he asks, lie down and die?

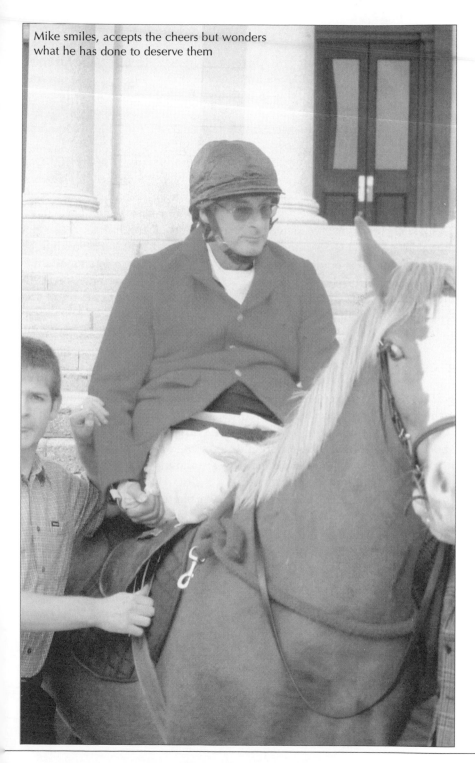

Mike smiles, accepts the cheers but wonders what he has done to deserve them

Mike is followed by the spectacular and colourful sight of the Carlow hunt, complete with their pack of hounds, yelping and barking. All assemble in front of me and the Mayor of Carlow welcomes us to his town and congratulates us on what we are doing. I follow with a speech but find the scene is too much and I am tongue-tied. It is an enormously emotional occasion. At that moment, I am surprised to realise that I have developed the strongest bond of affection, bordering on love, for Miles, Mike and Caroline.

After the ceremony, we proceed to the Delta Centre by horse and trap where we meet the inspirational Eileen Brophy who established at Delta the only full sensory centre for children who suffer from mental disabilities.

But the centre is also home to other children who suffer challenges. Adam is one and a half years old and has an unusual condition – he cannot metabolise fat. The resulting serious medical difficulties mean that he cannot walk or talk but he can laugh and smile. We meet him and Adam is enchanted by the sights, sounds and textures in the Delta Centre. It is his first visit and his enjoyment shows us just how important is the work and dedication of Eileen Brophy.

Carlow is Aoife's home town and it was she who had done much of the organisation for the day. Now, for the first time, I hear her speak at the dinner arranged for us at the centre.

It is a blockbuster. Emotion pours out as she talks of how she hated going out as a teenager because of her facial birthmark, how she fought her own battle to convince herself that she had an unusual kind of beauty. Words come faster and faster, each one an arrow that pierces the listeners and transfixes them to the emotional hot spot. She finishes, collapsing in tears and emotionally drained. She gets a standing ovation as people rush over to comfort and congratulate her.

Another day has ended. We have flown planes, travelled on a steam-roller, in a 1952 Ford, ridden horses with the Carlow Hunt and trotted by horse and trap. Two days into the Irish Republic and we have been to Dundalk, Roscommon, Clare Galway, Galway Town, and Carlow and are soon to reach Dublin. Not the most direct route between Dundalk and Ireland's capital, but who cares, we have seen a lot of Ireland, and met a lot of wonderfully warm people.

Tomorrow we strike out for the capital and that cardboard boat. I decide to take some glue and scissors just in case.

The omens are not good.

Some months before our adventure and through an introduction from Caroline, I had met Dermot Smurfit, head of the worldwide Smurfit organisation who are global leaders in the cardboard packaging industry. I had told him of our adventure. He decided to support us financially, making a very generous financial sponsorship towards our costs. In return, we agreed to sail up the Liffey from Jury's Hotel to the O'Connell Bridge in a cardboard boat!

At the time it had seemed simple, but now, as I stand at the docks in Dublin and look at the extraordinary vessel sitting in the water – two cardboard boxes with cardboard rolls between them – I have a strong wish to be somewhere else.

We had woken up in Carlow and had found our way to Dublin and the docks in the same 1952 Ford that brought us here yesterday.

Friday

13 September 2002
Carlow to Dublin

Forget that owl and the pussy-cat, we take to the sea in a cardboard boat and worry about it being Friday 13th!

In the company of Seamus Kelly from Smurfit's I approach the cardboard craft with apprehension.

'How long do you think it will float before it sinks?' I ask.

'No idea, we have never had it in the water before.'

I think of inviting him to make the trip with us, which would serve him right, but sadly there is only room for four in his floating contraption. I decide to take four water bottles on board to use as floats should we start to sink, but am delighted to find there are life-jackets.

I look around. Project Director Mary also takes a long hard look. Her full-time job is Group Health and Safety Manager for a major home construction company in the UK and she is wary of putting her charges into such an extraordinary craft.

In fact, this trip almost did not take place. Coman was aware that major crowds would gather to watch and the Water Commissionaires insisted on getting full public liability insurance. There was also the question of getting this sector insured for our own team of adventurers.

No insurance company would touch us, particularly when we told them we wished to undertake this precarious adventure on Friday 13th!

It seemed we would have to call it off. This was the problem that had arisen when we were at the Hollins Hall bonding weekend, and we thought had been solved.

Coman tried every contact he had ever made, pleaded with them, threatened them, but to no avail. With no insurance, there would be no trip on the Liffey on a cardboard boat.

Then Caroline decided to try her hand – and as we had learned, when Caroline decides to make something happen, anyone with doubts had better get out of the way, and fast.

She phoned the Deputy Taoiseach and fumed about the situation, the negative publicity that would arise and the general ridicule all round that would result. She also pointed out that any spectator would be standing on the banks of the river and not be in the boat, so why the public liability problem? Red tape gone mad, she said, it would make the Irish look silly.

Power is a wonderful thing, the man spoke the right words in the right ears and for the grand total of £100 the necessary insurance was obtained.

Back on the Liffey, Mary completes her risk assessment and gives me the go-ahead. She points to the fact that we would all be wearing life-jackets, that there were plenty of life savers in boats who would be around us, and she had satisfied herself that, although it looked extraordinary, the boat should be completely river-worthy and serve its purpose of getting the adventurers into the centre of Dublin, which is our destination for the day.

We climb on board. The boat is square, with a platform in the middle, and I go first and take my place on the left (or is it starboard?) rear corner. We load Mike into the other corner and he is propped up beside me, within easy reach should I need it. After all Mike might have to rescue me. Miles climbs on board and sits down in front of me, with Caroline pairing him. The crowd lines the bank, the television and other media boats circle us, quivering with anticipation and confident the boat will sink, complete with the four dafties in it.

The flag is dropped and we set off.

The boat designers have taken into consideration the fact that it is made of cardboard, and would have to float and be stable. What they had failed to cover was that it had to move through the water. Rapidly we discover that we might as well try to row a World War Two tank across the Irish Sea with the wind in the opposite direction. With its square bow, we can hardly move forward. Miles does not help by singing *For those in peril on the Liffey*. The crowd cheer . . . and cheer . . . and cheer but to our embarrassment, the unwieldy craft refuses to budge.

'Miles, when are you going to start paddling?' cries Caroline. I love the ribald rivalry between them.

I am doing my best, but as I pull on my home-made paddle – a stick with a piece of square wood nailed to it – it bends and creaks alarmingly and I realise that if I put any more strength on it, it will break and any rudiments of control will vanish. Then Miles and Caroline come to the rescue. Once again Mike can not put much punch into the paddling as he needs his hands to keep himself upright. As a veteran of sixty-plus and with a dodgy heart, there is a limit to my own contribution. My face has on a fierce expression, I have clenched all my arm muscles for the television cameras but truth to tell, I am not making a major contribution to the forwards direction of our craft and I know it. But Miles and Caroline are very, very fit. Realising the problem, and that the formerly cheering crowd has now subsided into puzzled silence and muted laughter, they both put in a superhuman effort, and to my great relief their paddles do not break and we begin to creep forward. Oxford and Cambridge it may not be, but even the most cynical must now agree that we are definitely moving forward.

Our task on this sector is to take the cardboard boat as far as the O'Connell Bridge right in the centre of Dublin. We struggle on, blisters boiling, crowds cheering, television cameras whirring, cameras flashing, our support team shouting. As each bridge approaches, I shout to the man in the nearby lifeboat and ask if it is O'Connell Bridge.

'Not yet' he replies.

'How far?'

'Just a little bit.'

I curse Daniel O'Connell for not having his bridge a bit more down river. I am not in the least interested in the information given to me by Miles at this time that it is the only square bridge in the world, as wide as it is long.

The team battle the River Liffey and make frantic efforts to get their cardboard boat moving

Nor could I care less that contrary to legend, the River Liffey that flows beneath the bridge has never yielded even one drop to make a pint of Guinness. All I want is to go home.

I look for signs of leaks but the craft is totally watertight and I realise that at least we will have to fall out to get wet.

'That is it ahead,' yells a man from the media boat and sure enough, right up front I see a bridge with a crowd hanging over it, pointing to us and shouting encouragement to the four fruitcakes crabbing sideways whilst going forwards, in their cardboard boat.

Then, greeted with an enormous cheer and a clamour of noise which irreverently includes sounds like laughter we reach the magic bridge. It is a moment of sheer triumph and we are elated. No explorer, on reaching the South Pole, has felt more elation. No yachtsman, on reaching land after sailing solo round the world, has felt more joy. No mountaineer, on attaining that elusive peak, has felt a greater sense of achievement.

What ever else is happening in the world, the moment is ours and we drink in the glory of achieving a goal.

We all throw our arms around John O'Loughlin and Bill Stevens from Smurfit Corrugated as a reward for building the un-buildable and helping us to do the impossible. But lads, stick to wrapping things in cardboard boxes and stop your nautical ambitions, it is not your style. The America's Cup is safe from your challenge. Seriously, you did a wonderful job and we love you for it.

We try to steer to the bank but the boat is now slightly waterlogged and even more impossible to move in any planned direction so we seek help. The lifeboat pulls us to the side. Coman and our blessed Mary have conspired, and there are bottles of champagne to be drunk. Jonathan Irwin of the Jack and Jill Foundation greets us, a quizzical grin on his face. The media go into frenzy of excitement and like demented firecrackers, fire their questions at us, hardly answered before the next fusillade hits us.

'Were you scared?'

'Shit scared.'

'Why did you go so slowly?'

'You try to row that contraption and see if you can make it move any faster.'

'Did you think it would sink?'

'It was a desperate race against time.'

'Did you think you might drown?'

Answer unprintable and luckily inaudible.

And so on. Interestingly, no questions were asked about disability and I and the team are delighted. We have been accepted simply as people, and not some kind of curiosity circus.

I check my adventurers. Miles and Caroline are in a furious but lighthearted argument as to which of them had finally got the craft moving. Mike is once again amazed at what he has done and is batting questions from the media with the confidence of a seasoned politician. After the strain of rowing I am totally exhausted but try to hide it.

I muse that in years to come, some Smurfit employee will look at a strange construction made out of tubes and boxes of cardboard.

'What on earth is that?' he or she will enquire.

'That is a boat that was once rowed down the Liffey by a man with a bad heart, two blind people and a man with no legs and paralysed from the chest down.'

'Why would they do that?'

'No idea. Must have been mad.'

But it is no time for future dreams for I and my adventurers require sustenance. Champagne is fine for fun, but no good for thirst. Time for the pub and a creamy expertly pulled Guinness. Now there is Ireland for you. Having just seen the Liffey water at close range, I am pleased with the information that Guinness is not made from it.

I write up the day's events in my diary but am suddenly stuck with an inability to spell the name of the river, for I cannot be sure if it is Liffy or Liffey. I ask a man called Patrick who is supping next to me in the bar.

'How do you spell Liffey?'

'With an L' he replies, as only an Irishman can.

We have reached the centre of Dublin and we are all still in fine fettle. Easy peasy. As the Guinness and champagne take their toll, I write a song to commemorate our great achievement.

A life on the ocean wave
A home on the rolling sea
Afloat on a cardboard boat
We row down the River Liffey

At the time I believe it is brilliant and sing it with enthusiasm. In daylight, I decide to stick with Jon's fish song.

DAY
Thirteen

Saturday
14 September 2002
Dublin

A glittering occasion that is crowned with a glittering speech from Miles

After our nautical adventure of yesterday, well covered on television, radio and the newspapers, today is a time for rest, reflection, minor patching up of paddling blisters and buying of essential supplies. Our experience with the Liffey has given us an aversion for water, but we find a pint of Guinness's most excellent stout to be a good alternative and we hold a review meeting in a Dublin bar.

In his packing list, issued to all of us before we set off, Jon, wanting to keep our kit as light as possible, has restricted the girls to three pairs of knickers, the boys to three pairs of underpants. The girls rebel and approval is given to increase their supply. Mary is also secretly briefed by the girls that when she joins them in the more exotic locations, could she please bring replacement knickers with her. Thus Mary adds knicker smuggling to her list of accomplishments.

The girls scurry off to Grafton Street to buy further supplies. The men remain content that three pairs of underpants is possibly one pair too many, though the spare pair could double as a handkerchief, a bandage or a water filter, suggests Mike.

But dark clouds are gathering and Mary and I go into a huddle. We have both realised that we are very short of money. We had planned two major functions, one in Monaco and one in Venice, at which funds would be raised to cover our costs. Sadly, due to illness, our organiser notified us that she was unable to set up the fund-raising functions. We do our sums and it is clear that things are tight. However, we are optimistic of the major fund-raising dinner to be held that evening in Dublin Castle, for the profits would be shared equally between the Jack and Jill Foundation and our own Around the World in 80 Ways Foundation. Estimates from the Irish organisation have given us hope of a significant sum.

Even with this, things would be very tight indeed and we decide to keep a very close check on expenditure. We share our worries with Jon. He tells me he tried the Around the World credit card in a cash machine today and it refused to pay. I realise my mistake. I had given Jon a card to use when he needed funds with a limit of £250 a day on it. I had also issued Mary with one. Today Mary had needed to draw funds and Jon's requirement would have put it over the limit so the card was refused. They agree to consult when funds are drawn to ensure this does not happen again. But it reminds us how important tight financial control is – running out of money in Dublin is hardly a problem, but if it happened in some remote corner of the world, then we would be in real trouble.

We prepare for the big night. The Jack and Jill Foundation have hired a professional events organiser and the all star gala dinner in support of both foundations is to be the social highlight of our week in Ireland.

Dublin Castle is the perfect venue. We arrive in the Lord Mayor's car – another means of transport – and as we enter the courtyard we are met by the drums and festival theatre tumblers. Upstairs, champagne flows and Mike checks out the waistlines of the guests. We do not think of this, but in a wheelchair, Mike's natural view is of waistlines and tummies. Whilst the rest of us look our guests in the eye, Mike tends to look them in the belly-button, thus avoiding a stiff neck. We have learned to crouch down when talking to him, but this simple courtesy is lacking in many who come up to him to converse.

Our dinner is held in the Grand Hall, which is stunningly laid out with candles and giant iced sculptures that literally take our breath away.

Tonight Miles makes one of the most moving speeches of the whole adventure. The story of Jonathan Irwin's son Jack has really touched him. Miles speaks about how this little person influences all those present at the dinner.

'Whilst baby Jack was not able to articulate during his short lifetime, he speaks very powerfully to us tonight' he says. 'But his life was not in vain: he has impacted on us all and will continue to enrich many others.'

Miles' speech is so powerful that many of the guests are crying. It is yet another emotion-packed moment in our adventure and another demonstration of the talent Miles has for public speaking.

There is a car waiting for us to take us back to our hotel, but Mary and I decide to walk. It is a fine warm evening, and we are both stunned at what has just happened – the spectacle, the food, the wine, the company – but most of all, the tremendous speech made by Miles and the way it impacted all of us. We are also cheered in that the event is obviously a major success and will help to provide us with sufficient funds to enable us to continue on our way.

Truly, baby Jack, who died so young, still lives a powerful life.

DAY
Fourteen

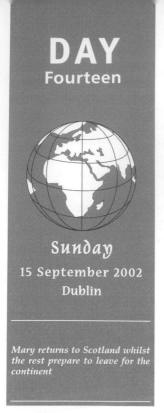

Sunday
15 September 2002
Dublin

Mary returns to Scotland whilst the rest prepare to leave for the continent

It is a day for preparation and goodbyes. We all feel we have been journeying in home territory, but now it is time to move on to mainland Europe and keep travelling east until we eventually return home to London.

We are all sad to say goodbye to our partners and friends – and it is also hard to say goodbye to Project Director Mary, who has taken holiday from her work to be with us from the Reform Club but now has to return both to her own job, and to masterminding the background support we so badly need as we journey around the world.

Mary too is sad, and later captures her feelings in her journal.

It is difficult to say goodbye, here I am in a taxi heading for Dublin Airport, a flight to London, back to my job and a feeling of excitement and foreboding. Robin wanted to come to the airport with me for I am laden down with Around the World stickers and postcards which have been printed in Dublin, these will be required in South Africa and Hong Kong. But, no, he needs to be with the adventurers and enjoy the afterglow of the night before. Too heavy for the adventurers to manage as they travel, I am left to get everything back to the UK, sorted and on route again to be sure that the supplies are there when they need them. I have five boxes in my cottage each labelled for the adventurers already beginning to fill up with 'things we don't now need', and 'presentation awards and gifts'.

Last night was truly amazing, as one who has managed 'sparkly events' all her life I can appreciate the show put on by the Jack and Jill Foundation was in a class of its own. How could I explain to Robin this morning, as he was on such a high, that I didn't believe any money was raised for the Jack and Jill Foundation and that means no percentage to help cover the costs for the Around the World.

Aoife is still a problem in that she has not raised the money to pay for joining the adventure and so Robin and I have decided to help her on a personal basis by covering any shortfall and thus ensure that Aoife would remain on the journey. Another young lady was on my mind as the taxi slowly made its way through the inevitable traffic jam to the airport – Mel – having spoken to her I knew how devastated she was about not being

64

part of the adventure. Stuart was now in contact with her, and it is his skill and compassion that has enabled Mel to walk away with dignity. Mel, if there was ever another adventure, I would want you there.

So early in the adventure, yet my mind is already working on the return to London. Andrew Woodward of Smurfit has promised the 'fantasy vehicle' the last means of transport to take the adventures to the Reform Club. Great, I really need the homecoming to be spectacular.

How lucky I am today to have one of those really great taxi drivers, helping me all the way to check in.

On the flight, I look out of the window, imagining how the adventurers would feel tomorrow as they fly out to Nice in a private jet – wish I was with them? Of course I do, but this is their adventure, not mine. I will soon be heading back to Edinburgh and a update meeting with Stuart and it is his turn to buy the chocolate cake.

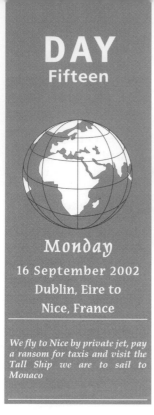

DAY
Fifteen

Monday
16 September 2002
Dublin, Eire to
Nice, France

We fly to Nice by private jet, pay a ransom for taxis and visit the Tall Ship we are to sail to Monaco

There is a tingle of excitement as we prepare to leave our Dublin hotel. Caroline's dad has arrived. A giant of a man, he should have played rugby for Ireland but as he himself says 'I thought I was so good it would just happen and I did not work hard enough.'

I size him up and although I am all of six foot tall, he still towers over me. He is warm, friendly, excited, a man with formidable presence, you do not miss him when he walks into a room. I like him very much.

He and Caroline's husband Fergal load our baggage into cars and we head off to Dublin airport. There we sample luxury for a Gulfstream 4SP executive jet powered by two beautiful Rolls-Royce Tay engines awaits us. There are hugs all round, we climb on board and head for Nice. Tracey plies us with tea, pastries, cooked breakfasts and drinks as we head for France on a wonderfully clear day. The windows are so much bigger than those on conventional planes and we get a fabulous view of Mont Blanc.

Executive jet bound for Nice, Carbonara examines Jon's camera while Aoife takes a back seat

Our feeling that we are in a perfect world is rudely shattered when we arrive in Nice. With all our baggage we need two taxis to take us to the hotel and each one costs us 90 Euros which makes a massive dent in our very limited budget. Jon buys a coke and it costs £3:50 in Sterling. Very quickly we decide to starve until we leave tomorrow.

Nice is nice, and we decide to walk rather than take a taxi to the harbour. *Tenacious*, our transport tomorrow to Monaco, is moored in the dock and we make ourselves known to the crew. Immediately they invite us on board. They are having a barbecue, and we tuck in. Free food! It helps to compensate for the money we have paid out for taxis and cokes.

The *Tenacious* is run by the Jubilee Sailing Trust and is kitted out to accommodate able-bodied and disabled crew. Currently en route to St Lucia via the Canary Islands, she has berthed in Nice to take us to Monaco. We explore and are delighted with all that we see. Mike is particularly enthusiastic about finding a lift that can take wheelchair people right up the mast and I know where he will want to be tomorrow.

We walk back to our hotel in high spirits – free food, some free drink and a lovely craft to sail tomorrow.

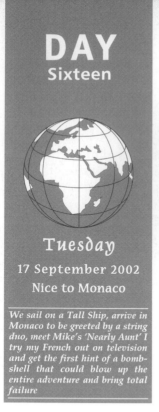

We sail on a Tall Ship, arrive in Monaco to be greeted by a string duo, meet Mike's 'Nearly Aunt' I try my French out on television and get the first hint of a bombshell that could blow up the entire adventure and bring total failure

Mike is in his element in France for he knows this area well. After his accident, he found a house for a company to purchase and for him to turn into a holiday home for disabled people, but it was frequently vandalised whilst he was away and equipment was stolen. On his most recent visit, he arrived to discover that his whole water system had been dismantled and taken away – even the water pump which was buried under ground had been dug up and removed. Clearly, someone nearby was building a home and was simply helping him or herself to Mike's property. The people in the local village were clearly ashamed at what had happened and tried to help, but it was too much for Mike and so to his sorrow, he decided to sell it.

Early in our planning he had introduced us to Monaco-based Brigitte Fossius whom he called his 'Nearly Aunt'. Brigitte was due to marry Mike's uncle, but tragically Nigel died before the wedding could take place. Brigitte and Mike have remained firm friends and thanks to this friendship, she worked tirelessly for Around the World in 80 Ways.

We rise to a warm sun, load our baggage, take an expensive taxi to the docks and board *Tenacious*. The sail to Monaco is a delight, with the sun shining upon us. Sadly, because of the shortness of the voyage and the lack of wind, we are unable to go under full sail – but that does not stop the Captain inviting us to climb up the mast and go out on the yardarm. Mike seeks to be included, using the special winch, but it is explained that the sail to Monaco is very short and there is just not enough time to get it fitted into position and working.

Caroline and Miles again show their prowess by nipping up the halyards and going out on the yardarms like monkeys, with a sheer drop of 90 feet between them and the water. For me, it is a different matter. Determined not to be shown up by them, I too struggle aloft, despite being terrified of heights. As we reach the crow's-nest, Caroline senses my fear and suggests that I remain there and do not try the yardarm. I later learned that she had been given strict orders from Mary not to let me do anything that she felt was beyond me!

I comment on their amazing courage in going up so high. It is Miles who points out to me that because they are blind, they cannot see the height and it is just as if they were only one foot above the deck. Probably the bravest of us all is Carbonara. Determined to get a good camera shot looking down

Above: *Tenacious*, lit dramatically, it makes a wonderful scene in Nice harbour.
Below: Miles and Caroline climb out on the yard arm

on the team, he climbs right up to the highest crow's-nest, pulls up his camera on a rope and fires away happily from there. He keeps the camera running as he lowers it again, thus obtaining some very spectacular shots.

Meanwhile, having got over his disappointment at not going aloft, Mike has persuaded the Captain to allow him to take the helm of *Tenacious* as we reach Monaco.

'It is a great privilege to take the helm to the port of Monaco ... and not bump into anything.'

I am having my moment. Being the leader of our group, the captain has asked me to hoist the Monaco flag as we manoeuvre into port. He tells me that I can be sure it is the right way up as long as I put the toggle with the short lead at the top, which I do. Recorded by Carbonara, I proudly hoist the flag as we enter the port in full view of the crowds standing on the dock. I hear string music and see two musicians, one on a cello and the other playing the violin. It is magic and I wave to the crowds.

Then I notice the pilot boat is flying its flag the other way up. Stricken with the terror that I have hoisted the national flag upside down in full view of the VIP reception group, the crowd and the media, I glance to the Palace for some reassurance. To my horror I notice that it too is flying the national flag the other way up. I seize the rope and furiously pull down our flag and rehoist it. The manufacturers had made it upside down!

We moor alongside to the applause of the crown and the musical greeting of the duo. Everyone is too polite to comment on my mistake. Though I have never met her, I instantly recognise Brigitte, a tall, distinguished and stylishly dressed woman. She too recognises me but that is not difficult for I am wearing my Phileas Fogg outfit complete with top hat. Her greeting is both warm and genuine and I can see why Mike is so fond of her.

The media rush to get on board. One of the adventurers – I never did find out which one was the joker – tells the television media that I am not only the leader, but I speak fluent French. The camera rolls and the interviewer spits out a long question in fluent and fast French. I wish him bonjour in my own schoolboy way, but I stopped learning French some 45 years ago and words, or mots, fail me. The adventurers are all laughing and I realise that I am being wound up.

Mike is fluent in French so he rescues me. Then Jon demonstrates an excellent command of the language, and he too, in a somewhat anglicised version reminiscent of Ted Heath trying to speak French, tells of our adventure.

It is time to go ashore and I, Miles, Mike, Caroline, Jon, Aoife and Carbonara climb down the gangway and join the furore of greeters and well-wishers who are on the dock.

They scrum around us, all seeking a part of the action. Once again, the questions come out like machinegun fire, but by now we are used to this. I look around and see them all, like veterans, handle the swarming crowd and am proud of them. But where is Jon?

Then he appears, grinning from ear to ear, triumphant with three taxis in tow. This gives us the excuse we need. I cry 'Follow me' yet again, people and baggage bundle into the vehicles, we are extricated from the friendly but still milling mob and are taken to our hotel.

But there is a problem. We all need visas to enter India and everyone, except Caroline and Aoife, has obtained them from London before leaving. They had assumed that when they reached Rome, they could pick them up from there. However, a phone call made from the *Tenacious* to check what time the embassy opens reveals that whilst the issue of the visa is almost immediate in their own country, it takes a minimum of four days for an Irish person to get a visa for India in Rome, presumably because of the checks that need to be made back in Ireland.

It is a new challenge. I had planned Monaco to Rome as the first of three adventure legs, during which I wanted to leave the adventurers to their own devices to make progress, and my only instruction to them is to arrive at Rome Airport in time for their flight to Cairo four days later, using as many different means of transport as they could. However, to get their visas, they would now have to leave the next day for Rome and spend the entire four days of the adventure section waiting for the documentation to be issued. Not what I planned.

I phone Mary who is back in Edinburgh and seek her advice. It is cold, clinical and as always, practical. She points out that there is no certainty that the visas will be ready within the four days, and that the only way to guarantee the safety of getting our flight to Cairo was for Caroline and Aoife to fly home to Dublin, where they would be in their own country and thus the visas could be ready within hours. They could then fly back to Rome in time for the flight to Cairo, complete with Indian visas.

I talk to Jon and he agrees that this is the best course of action. Caroline and Aoife are to fly home, Jon, Miles, Mike, and Carbonara will undertake the original plan.

Then Brigitte steps in. We find that she is a lady of some considerable influence. In Monaco, she has arranged for an hotel to provide us with sponsored accommodation and she has also arranged for us to dine with the French Consul to Monaco. Now a couple of phone calls from her and we have the guarantee that as long as Caroline and Aoife present themselves first thing Monday morning at the consulate in Rome, the visas will be ready before their departure four days later.

I am glad the problem has been solved, but angry to lose the adventure leg. To me they are a fundamental and important part of what we were trying to do. The idea, suggested and agreed by all of us at the Cross weekend, of telling the three adventurers that I was leaving them and would meet them in

Cairo in four days time, and they had to find their own way there, going through Rome and using as many improvised means of transport as they could, was exciting and challenging and added extra spice to our adventure. Now, because of a simple oversight we were in danger of ending up with a straightforward trip by public transport from Monaco to Rome and then days of tourist sightseeing as we waited for officialdom to take its course and the visas for Caroline and Aoife to enter India to be issued.

I call Jon to my hotel room and we discuss the problem. I find him upset at what has happened, understanding of my views, and determined to help. We decide that the spirit of our adventure can still be captured if I issue four challenges to the team to accomplish whilst in Rome; these being to obtain a major media piece about our adventure, to give at least one talk, to meet someone of influence and to visit at least one organisation involved with looking after underprivileged people. Oh yes, and to do it all at minimum cost.

I leave the mission to Jon to handle for I have another challenge to meet. More warnings from Mary indicate that we are fast running out of money. She is not happy that the Irish event would deliver the funding that is essential to meet our costs in getting to Hong Kong.

I ask her the basis of her feelings.

'They keep me at a distance from the organisation and I feel they are hiding something from me' she says. 'They did this on the run-up to our visit to Ireland and all the time I was there, I did not feel welcome behind the scenes, when I tried to find out what was going on.'

It is true that all around the world, Mary's help and advice was welcomed, but in Ireland it was made clear to her that the team there were in control and she had to keep her distance. In the run-up it was a problem she mentioned to me many times, and each time I told her that it was the way things had to be handled in Ireland, she was to leave it to them and concentrate on the other areas, an instruction she was prepared, but not happy, to accept.

But the visa incident has shaken me. Mary would have caught that and I allow myself the thought that she might be right about the funds. Without the fund-raising events for the Around the World Foundation in Monaco and Venice, I was now depending on the Irish dinner contribution to get the team to Hong Kong. What if the contribution from Ireland did not come up to forecast expectations? How would we make up the missing funds?

I sleep uneasily that night. I would have got no sleep at all had I known that the Irish event had been run at a loss, and that far from getting the expected contribution towards out total costs, no funds at all were available to us.

I wake up depressed. I am worried about money, and worried about the loss of the adventure sector. My depression eases somewhat with the realisation that it will be a real test of Jon's character, initiative and ability to lead the team and would give me pointers for the rest of the journey. In fact, subsequent events are to show it is to be an even sterner test of Jon's ability than I had thought and he passes superbly.

On which the leader returns home to find some more money and the adventurers start their first adventure leg

For the first time since day two, I leave the adventurers in Jon's hand and turn my attention to other challenges. If Mary is right and we do not get a significant donation from the Irish programme to go towards our costs, then we are in major trouble. Without it, we are going nowhere. Something drastic is needed and I am the only one who can do it, the rest are busy. I will take the chance of being back home to talk to Route Director Stuart Nussey to see how many of the means we have used have been approved and how his side of the project is going. Back in Monte Carlo the team, deciding to make the most of their stay, hit the town once they have attended to the usual routine of e-mails, phone calls, laundry and record keeping.

Now it is 7 p.m. in the evening and the adventurers set off for Rome. They have had a great time enjoying the streets and Mike has taken the opportunity to taxi round the Grand Prix circuit. But they are about to pay for having had a good time.

A taxi is ordered but the driver has obviously had a bad day for he refuses to take all the bags. So a couple of the adventurers rolled, walked and tripped their way to the station as a second taxi is organised. Then the fun begins.

When the train tickets were booked, wheelchair access was confirmed as 'no problem'. The guy must have been on drugs! With Jon and Caroline lifting the chair from front and back, Mike still has to remove both wheels before he can be squeezed through the train door, which is three feet off the platform. Once inside, Mike finds that he cannot get his wheelchair around the corner, let alone down the corridor. The adventurers swap Mike into his special wheelchair which he uses to have a shower, as it is narrower, and this does the trick. Thus, Mike in his wheelchair, two blind people, Jon, ife and Carbonara stagger through the crowded corridors until they reach their sleeper compartment, only to find it has been double booked.

Two hours later, the mess has been sorted out and the group settle down for what is not very likely to be sleep, with Carbonara in the next compartment with his camera and some other equipment as there is not enough room for it all in the first compartment.

The team cram into the tiny sleeper and prepare for the trip to Rome from Monaco. They share a picnic in the shabby and evil-smelling cabin. Jon leans out the window and buys two bottles of Chianti from a passing vendor. They drink from paper cups and share loaves of bread, cheese, ham and chocolates. They think about the contrasting means of transport they have used, from luxury private executive jet to Mattie's tipper truck. They wonder if putting up with their conditions on the overnight Rome express will be balanced by a later trip of the Orient Express in Malaysia.

They tuck themselves into their cramped quarters and prepare to watch the night go by. They do not notice the evil that has joined their company.

It is morning and Carbonara is darting in and out of both cabins. It is obvious that something is wrong. Before coming on the expedition he had spent £14,000 on a state of the art camera. Overnight, along with other recording and photographic equipment, it has been stolen.

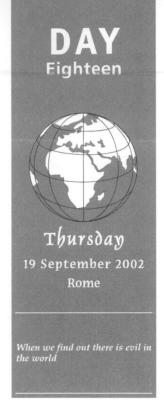

Thursday

19 September 2002
Rome

When we find out there is evil in the world

There is still some time to go before reaching Rome and all the team can do is to sit and think about the person who has stolen from them and who is still on board. As Aoife writes in her diary:

The sickening thing about the crime is that we were marked out from the start as vulnerable. We were obvious. We had white sticks, cameras, wheelchairs, equipment and of course disability. We are sure it was not just one opportunist on that train that night but a coven or band of thieves that spotted us as lambs for the slaughter.

Revenge and retribution are not the answer. As a Karma, what comes around goes around is a worn-out and often ridiculed idea, but it has been around long enough to convince me these people will get what is coming to them.

Carbonara feels as though everything he had worked for has been destroyed. I am sure he reflects about the justice of taking a chance on a charity and then being robbed; giving money and energy to help spread a positive message and then have it taken away in such a negative malevolent way is the greatest wrong.

Carbonara is not to be comforted. He feels that everything he has worked for has been destroyed in one instant. It is clear that the team's innocent idea that everyone is on our side went with the camera and the bag. Not everyone is positive, not everyone wants to help.

It is a devastating blow and the team arrive in Rome totally dejected. Jon's ability to pull morale around and provide leadership is tested to the fullest extent. The police prove to be useless, saying that gangs work the trains every night. We might at least have been warned and it is time someone does something about it.

Without his camera there is nothing Carbonara can do so he decides to fly home to confront his insurance company quickly, get a replacement camera and return as soon as he can to the adventure. By now, the team have become really fond of him, and his disaster, accompanied by his departure, leave morale at rock bottom. It is the lowest point of the adventure so far.

But there is work to do and Jon sets about repairing the damage.

The first need for his demoralised team is accommodation. Jon talks to Rolls-Royce, his employers, and in no time has fixed up a van for the team to use. Then Miles tells him of his good friend Roman Pryjomko, who had previously offered to help us. Jon phones him and to all our delight, he fixes up accommodation in a wonderful and luxurious villa in Todi, a good step in repairing morale.

The rest of the day is spent in visits and on the phone, trying to make the arrangements to meet the challenges laid down for the adventurers, talking to contacts, embassies, hotels – and the insurers of the equipment are also contacted. Despite the camera being brand-new, their offer is derisory and Jon decides to let Carbonara tackle it in person.

So he is driven to Rome airport and goes home. It is a sad moment, for he is totally dejected both at the loss of his equipment and at the early return home from the team. We do not know if he will be able, or indeed have the spirit, to rejoin us.

We should have known better. Carbonarra is made of stern stuff.

Jon has told me of the catastrophe on the Monaco to Rome train, I reflect that it would never have happened had the adventure sector gone as planned, as they would not have been on the train – but then, they could have been involved in a car crash instead, so I realise it is a negative and undeserving thought and take it out of my mind.

Instead, I think of my task, which is to find more money.

My first estimate was that we needed around £200,000 to cover our costs. It was a very small budget to cover 100 days of travel, accommodation and food for four people, plus my own travel, accommodation and food costs, and the costs for Mary, Stuart, Carbonara, Aoife plus our equipment, insurance, printing, and administration. However, I also felt that we could get most of the accommodation, and some of the food and travel, sponsored. In addition, I made a rule that no one working on Around the World anywhere in the world was to receive any personal payment for so doing, they all had to volunteer their services.

To make sure things were kept right, I hired a highly prestigious legal firm of Turcan Connell who are based in Edinburgh. They are the leading firm in Scotland dealing with charities and I was honoured that Douglas Connell himself gave his attention to our project. He also enlisted the help of Gavin McEwan, a Senior Solicitor and now an Associate. They undertook our many legal requirements, including registering us as a charity, provided friendship, help and encouragement throughout the entire project and never sent us a bill for their services.

Two trustees were enlisted, in addition to myself. Alistair McLean had worked with me for fourteen years. He was now working with two colleagues in their own firm, Acumen Public Relations of Edinburgh, and I knew him to be a man of the utmost integrity. I had known of John Moorehouse for almost as long, mainly during this time with Business in the Community and then as the driving force behind The Big Idea, a scientific interactive educational experience located at Irvine in Ayrshire Scotland. Both agreed to serve as trustees and provided much help and support.

Thanks to the generosity of Smurfit and many of Mike's friends, a major hole in our cash requirements had been made before we set out. I planned that the rest should be raised by asking for a voluntary donation of at least 15 per cent from charities that were to benefit from fund-raising dinners held as part of our adventure. There were three that seemed to promise major contributions, these being in Monaco, Dublin and Hong Kong. Now I was confronted by the fact that due to illness of the organiser, Monaco had fallen through, Dublin was likely to make a nil contribution and only Hong Kong of the big ones remained. Urgently I needed some £50,000.00 to feel safe.

Borrowing from a bank was not a workable option. Understandably banks only lend you money when they know there is little risk, and when you have enough guarantees to offer to ensure that if things go wrong, they will be the first to be on the lifeboat. Getting more sponsorship at this late stage was also not a workable option.

But it seemed the only way. So I hit the phones. I phone and phone, e-mail and e-mail. But finding a sponsor for an event that is already under way is not easy and the put-downs are everywhere.

It has been a depressing day. The feeling of elation all of us experienced yesterday has been well and truly punctured. Miles, Mike and Caroline are deflated by finding out that not everyone is for them and the adventure, I am growing increasingly worried about the lack of finance. I know the adventurers will tell me they will go on no matter what, but I know that without having enough money to cope with emergencies, I will have to recall them when I hit a level at which there is just enough money to get them home safely.

I wonder if they will obey me if I have to put out that order!

DAY
Nineteen

Friday
20 September 2002
Rome

Technology and the team – a day in the life of the tech team. To keep in touch and plan our routes, the team use many technical devices

Technology and the team – a day in the life of the tech team. To keep in touch and plan our routes, the team used many technical devices – however, these have their frustrations, as Aoife O'Connell records in her diary for this day:

I am firmly of the opinion our bags would be about twenty-two stone lighter if it were not for technology. We are like walking techi's. People who pass us must imagine we are piloting new phones, or testing new walkie talkies or that we are all from a television station, radio station or newspaper.

Everywhere we go each team member has a phone stuck to their ears, phone whirling, the camera rolling or the mini-disc recording. Each piece of kit, together with laptops, chargers, extension leads, adapters and other gadgets are loaded in to the transport or vehicle of choice. Of course it is wonderful to have all these thingamajigs until they start to play up or have temperamental lapses of good behaviour.

So far something as 'simple' as accessing the internet has meant major trouble for the team. You start off plugging your modem into the phone line, cross your fingers and hope for the best. Then the rotten little message pops up on your laptop delightedly telling you 'Sorry but your modem isn't working, your phone line isn't plugged in' or some other useless piece of information, as you stare dumbly at the screen.

Keeping in mind it is now probably well after 10 p.m., you have been up signing autographs, gone jogging, met 57 people, drank 6 coffees, had lunch with some VIP, have 3 modes of transport under your belt, bumped into a pole, been hoisted from vehicle to vehicle, talked about disability for half an hour to some group, smiled till your cheeks ached, posed for your photograph 36 times, carried the 11 suitcases up 4 flights of stairs and after all this you sit down to a few bloody e-mails and do you think the state of the art technology will work? Not on your life.

A deep breath, perhaps a glass of wine later, you try connecting to the phone and if you finally connect to the damn thing you are guaranteed to be in front of your laptop for at least two hours trying to send one e-mail. Instead you could get very excited when you walk into your hotel room and there is an internet on your television. You trip over yourself trying to find the remote control and the keyboard but alas there are no batteries, or perhaps the keyboard is just having an off day.

It is then, and only then, you reach the point where you are clutching things with white knuckles, in a tight little voice you are whispering foul language into the data ports and vowing to throw the thing against the nearest wall if it does not behave itself and send the damn e-mail that it sends it. Unfortunately for you the tiny terrorists are far too absorbed in their work to notice your mini heart attack and the subsequent collapse on the floor!

The joy that is technology will be with us as we travel around the world – lucky us!

DAY
Twenty

Saturday
21 September 2002
Rome

A day in the sun

It is time for reflection. There is no doubt that a lot of steam has been knocked out of the adventurers. Until the fateful train trip from Monaco to Rome, everything had been glorious. Everywhere we travelled, people had gone out of their way to help and the kindness and admiration to us had been immense.

But the theft on the train has undermined the feeling that people everywhere are cheering our adventure on, and are keen to help when they can. Fully aware of our special challenges, someone on that train has still taken advantage of us and has stolen, not just our cameras and equipment which are replaceable, but some footage of our adventure so far, which is irreplaceable. In so doing, they have introduced evil into our adventure, where only kindness, warmth, help and goodwill had previously existed.

Monaco, and the trip to get there has lulled us into a sense of false security. Now, the visa problem, the loss of the adventure sector, the difficulty in getting Mike on the train, the double booking, the smelly cabin on the train and the theft have given us a reminder that we are facing a challenge, not a jaunt.

Weekends are taken pretty seriously in Italy so Jon decides it is a day for rebuilding spirits, washing clothes, reorganising kit and carrying out running repairs. Caroline continues with her keep fit routine and manages to persuade Miles to go out running with her. The concept of Caroline who is registered blind, taking Miles, who is totally blind, for a run in countrywide with which they are totally unfamiliar is a worrying one but Jon decides to let them go. To his enormous relief, they return safely.

Mike uses the morning to get his pills right. Every weekend, Mike has to mix up his quota of medication for the week ahead. The actual quantity and composition may vary depending on blood tests that he administers to himself; he then e-mails the results back to England for doctors to calculate any revised dosages. He takes around 27 tablets a day and prefers to wash them down with a wee dram.

The rest of the day is spent lazing in the sun, then going out in the evening for a meal.

In Edinburgh, it is a time for more sums. I am determined that the adventure should not come to an early end through the lack of funds and decide to put the emergency plan into action on the assumption that no funds would come to us from the event in Dublin.

My beloved mother had died early in the year and in her will, she had left me half of her house, the other half going to my elder brother David. The house was up for sale and I realised that on the strength of these forthcoming funds, I could get a loan from a bank against the time when the property was sold. My half would just about fund the trip to Hong Kong. We had a major fund-raising event there and my belief was that it would generate the funds to get home again and repay some of the costs of getting there.

But I have a problem in doing this. What would my mother have thought, I wonder, about my giving my inheritance from her to fund such an adventure?

In the end, I realise I have no choice. I either have to go that route, or bring back the adventurers. I knew she would not have wanted me to do that. The decision is taken and the future of the adventure as far as Hong Kong is underwritten, if not assured.

But I have not spent all the time back in Edinburgh worrying about money.

When we were learning to scuba dive in Nottingham, I was aware that I had not put up a good show. I knew the problem was the weighting.

I am totally at home in the water. David and I grew up right on a shore and as small children, had gone for swims at least three times a day in the giant rollercoaster waves that smash on the glorious beach at Whiterocks, near Portrush in Northern Ireland. David went on to represent his country at swimming in what were then the Empire and are now the Commonwealth Games. I lacked his talent but not his love of the water and it has remained with me ever since.

But I have a natural but disconcerting list to starboard whilst floating, and unless I make correcting moves, I turn over. At Nottingham, I found it impossible to sit on the bottom of the pool without making these correcting moves, and without them, I simply turned turtle. This caused a problem with the instructors who were trying to line us up on the bottom of the pool and teach us how to get regulators out of our mouths. Whilst Miles and Caroline were able to stay rock steady, I simply couped sidewards unless I flapped my arms.

So, back at base I take some sneaky lessons and as I thought, being able to do them one to one, I soon get the hang of floating weightless in the water. As I climb out of the pool, I know that when we get to the Red Sea in a few days, I will be able to hold my own with Caroline, Miles and Mike.

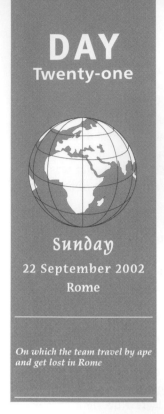

DAY
Twenty-one

Sunday
22 September 2002
Rome

On which the team travel by ape and get lost in Rome

This is the third Sunday of the adventure and it is time to review the progress of the assigned tasks which have replaced the adventure sector.

'What about meeting the VIPs, Jon, what have you done there?' I ask.

His answer is dramatic – he has contacted the Vatican to see if they can meet the Pope! Rolls-Royce people locally are using their influence to see if such a visit can be accomplished.

Jon tells me about the villa where they are staying and the lack of progress on the other assignments, though he is confident that they will all be achieved. I am relieved that the visa problem is to be solved, and delighted in the way that Jon is tackling the assignments. However, two days in a luxury villa in Tuscany was never a part of my plan for the adventurers and I am anxious to get the group back on track.

The team know that their short unplanned stop at Todi in the luxury villa owned by Daniella and Maria has been heaven-sent and they have all rebuilt their morale after the demoralising theft of the camera and broadcast equipment. Now it is time to get back into the adventure.

Three hours later than planned, they hit the road for Rome. Daniella and Maria slash their costs for the villa. It is wonderfully generous of them, and is their contribution to our adventure. For Jon it is also a move to achieve one of his tasks – that of keeping the costs down to a minimum.

The adventurers set off and at once notice a very strange vehicle at the side of the road – a three-wheeled agricultural vehicle belonging to a man called Cirri who works at a nearby guesthouse with his wife.

Jon leaps off the official car, explains our adventure and

The Trio ride the Ape car

Cirri invites the adventurers on board. He explains it is called an Ape Car and the team are certain that Stuart will allow it as another means of transport.

And so, the Ape Car sets off towards Rome, straining under the weight of the wheelchair and the gang leaning and bouncing around in the back. Another means of transport is claimed and another of the assignments completed.

Back in a more conventional car, it takes Jon and the rest some five hours to reach the hostel which Jon has arranged to be their home for the rest of their stay, the Sisters of Mercy Hostel.

Trying to find lunch on the route poses an unexpected problem. On Sunday, everywhere shuts up shop, but Jon manages to find one small place that is open and stocks up with chocolates and crisps, fine healthy food.

The hostel is not easy to find. Jon drives whilst Mike navigates, a James Bond soundtrack booming out from the car radio. Each road seems to have a policeman blocking it, who sends them back the way they came. They pass the same railway station three times before finally finding the hostel. It is charming but an enormous contrast to the villa at Todi. For the Irish contingent it is just like being back in school. Linoleum floors and white walls adorned with holy pictures bring back strange and haunting memories. Walking down the corridors, they expect the doors to be flung open and the corridors to fill with schoolgirls in matching uniforms.

The group have a pizza and an ice cream and retire to bed.

Jon reports that he has not yet heard if the Pope will see them, I do not tell him of my own efforts to help – but behind the scenes, I am pulling a very influential piece of string.

Sir Tom Farmer is one of our greatest supporters. He is also a devout Catholic and is held in considerable respect by the higher echelons of the Catholic Church. I speak to him and he tells me he will make a couple of phone calls and will come back to me. Give it a day or two.

I retire but it is hard to get to sleep. The first adventure leg bears no resemblance to what we had planned. Caroline and Aoife still do not have their visas. And we are running out of money.

I decide the biggest danger is still the lack of funding and that this must be my priority. I have arranged a loan, with the guarantee of my mother's house against it, but the loan has to be repaid and so it is only a short respite that I have won. In Mary and Stuart, I have more than enough talent to keep the adventure on course and Jon is putting in a strong performance on the ground. My immediate priority is to find money to replace the budgeted contribution from the Irish programme which does not look like – materialising.

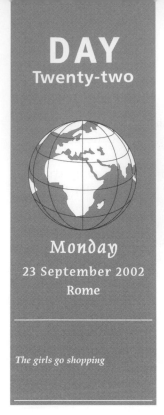

It is the first day in Rome. The team, now safely making themselves at home in the hostel, know they are there under false pretences, as they are simply waiting for the Indian visas to be issued. They decided to make the best of it and so some sightseeing.

The girls set off to check if the visa problem has been solved and are told that satisfactory progress is being made and the visas will be ready on time. They rejoin the others.

Heads turn as the unusual group make their way through the cobbled streets of Rome. Bus and taxi drivers enjoy it most, tooting their horns in welcome. Jon spends most of this time setting up the final assignments and dealing with the many management problems.

Jon also proves he is a man of some steel. Determined not to be beaten by the prehistoric streets, he manages to take the wheelchaired Mike through narrow doorways, push him up slopes, over cobbles whilst at the same time leading Miles and giving him a running commentary of where they are and what they are doing, so he does not miss out. He manages to navigate the psychotic traffic with a wheelchair and even has the good humour to laugh about it all.

'It was really funny, you could see all the drivers staring at me, totally bemused, they must have been wondering what this guy is at' is how he later described it.

In her diary, Aoife captures their feelings towards Jon.

The truth of the matter is what Jon is at is probably one of the most difficult things any one can be at. It is hard work, it is tiring and it can be demanding, but he is always there for Miles and Mike in particular. He never gets angry or raises his voice, he never says no. He is a truly brave and gutsy person, he keeps pushing the boundaries, he does not accept that people with disabilities cannot do what they want.

Bob Huddie is the Regional Director for Rolls-Royce plc in Italy and he takes the adventurers out in the evening for a meal in a little restaurant next to the Pantheon. Rolls-Royce have been magnificent helpers to us providing us with our uniforms but more importantly with local knowledge support. It is wonderful to have their involvement.

The team has turned the Sisters of Mercy hostel into an office and the morning is spent phoning the Indian Embassy, The British Embassy to the Vatican, the Scottish College in Rome who had phoned as a result of being contacted by Sir Tom Farmer, and umpteen disability organisations in a bid to fulfil another of the set tasks.

Mike takes his wheelchair ride down the Spanish Steps, morale slips a bit but a magic phone call makes the day end in delight

They decide to dump the hire car and to tackle one major challenge.

'Why not go down the Spanish Steps?' suggests Jon. With two blind people and a third in a wheelchair this is an impossible task. Just what is needed.

With wicked grins on their faces, Caroline and Jon take either end of the wheelchair and start to bump Mike gently down the first of the 100 steps.

As always the steps are packed with tourists. Some refuse to get out of the way, some jump up and offer to help. Others seem baffled as to why Mike bothers particularly as there are alternative means of getting down ideally suited to disabled people.

The team start to talk about the whole adventure and morale slips. Some talk about going home. It is not just the challenge of getting Mike down the Spanish Steps, it is all the challenges that have to be faced by them.

I realise that everyday challenges and experiences we take for granted are just that bit different for the three adventurers. Simple things like trying to check in at an airport when the desk is way above your eye level, struggling to fill in a form you cannot see properly, choosing what to serve yourself at a self-service café.

For some reason the trip down the Spanish Steps seems to trigger off pressures and problems that have been kept in check. It is a good thing, for the steam escapes and by the time the bottom is reached, things are back to normal. The team, by now covered in sweat, have overcome yet another challenge.

They are rewarded by a spectacular phone call. Whether it was Sir Tom, Mark Rudd from Rolls-Royce, or the Scottish College, the fact is that tomorrow, the Pope has agreed to see and bless the team.

The day ends in a high, with morale totally restored. But thoughts are still with Carbonara, who is fighting to get compensation for his camera loss.

The day also ends in a high for me back in the UK. Formalities to borrow against my mother's house have been completed. Funds will be

Halfway down the Spanish steps the team wonder if it was such a good idea after all!

available if needed. Also my scuba diving is now of an acceptable standard, having cracked the floatation problem and I am ready for the Red Sea. Except I am now fighting a cold and I know that with a cold, there will be no scuba diving for me.

It is the big day. The team have been invited to do an interview on the adventure with Vatican Radio and Jon calls me triumphantly to point out he has now completed all his assignments, with meeting the Pope and doing the broadcast being the final two. I congratulate him but remind him that he still has to visit a group or organisation involved with the disabled to achieve total success.

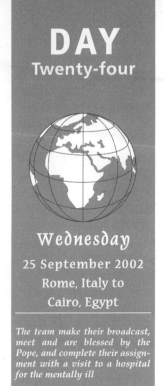

The team complete their broadcast and move on to the Vatican and the meeting with the Pope. They join the thousands of others assembled for the same purpose but are astonished when they are invited right up to the front, just a few feet from the Pope, rather than be kept with the thousands of pilgrims roped off in St Peter's Square. But a greater honour is to come, for at the end, each of the adventurers is asked to go forward to be blessed individually by the Pope.

The team make their broadcast, meet and are blessed by the Pope, and complete their assignment with a visit to a hospital for the mentally ill

Whilst passing through Ireland, a miraculous medal was pressed into Caroline's hand to keep her safe on her journey. She brought the medal with her and this time pressed it into the Pope's hand, who blessed it and returned it to her. Caroline eventually returned the medal to the person who had given it to her, when she returned safe and sound from the adventure.

'The energy was incredible,' writes Aoife:

> People were singing and whooping with joy, flags were flying the colours of countless different countries throughout the world. Religious orders made up only a fraction of the crowd which included many nationalities. Nuns were bursting into song, people were screaming at the top of their voices. Various organisations, Catholic and other groups would howl with glee when their names were called out by the cardinals.
>
> Amid all this zealous worship, members of the Eighty Ways team were transfixed. It is strange how this adventure takes in all churches, community groups, charities and is then suddenly affirmed by one of the most powerful figureheads in the world.

For Jon there is another triumph for he has arranged for the adventurers to visit a state of the art rehabilitation centre for the mentally and physically ill, thus completing the final assignment.

The first adventure sector is over, all assignments have been accomplished. It is time for the adventurers to be reunited with their leader at Cairo Airport.

DAY
Twenty-five to Twenty-six

Thursday–Friday

26–27 September 2002

Cairo to Hurghada

A week in which Mike shows it is not impossible for him to scuba dive, he and Miles go for a walk at the bottom of the Red Sea and I have heart failure

I am in Cairo International Airport, it is half past midnight and I have lost the team. We are in Egypt to undertake one of our most challenging means of transport – scuba diving in the Red Sea. Thanks to my extra lessons, I am now ready to take part with them. But they have gone missing – all of them – Miles, Mike, Caroline, Jon and Aoife have disappeared.

I last heard from them in Rome, where, despite the gloomy start, they had managed to fulfil the spirit of the adventure after all. I had spoken to them by phone, congratulated them and said I would be arriving in Cairo one hour before them and we would then continue with our adventure.

Now, I am in the arrivals lounge, surrounded by hawkers, greeters and meeters. Their plane has arrived but they are not on it.

Not a funny situation. How the hell can you lose two blind people, a man in a wheelchair, a girl with a facial birthmark and an Indiana Jones look-alike? The situation is stupid.

I have planned a warm welcome for them and transport for us and the baggage to the terminal for internal flights some distance away, for we are bound for Hurghada and one of our most difficult means of transport – scuba diving from one location to another.

I think they must breed taxi drivers like rabbits in Cairo. Everyone, no matter what they are driving, is a taxi and they pull and push me, shouting out how theirs is the very best taxi in the entire region, if not the world – and is the driver not the safest driver in the world as well? I try to make it understood that I am trying to arrange transport for two people who are registered blind, and one in a wheelchair. Oh yes, there is also the manager, the journalist and about twenty pieces of luggage. I try to tell them it is best if Mike can stay in his wheelchair and does anyone have such a vehicle? They all have, they scream, begging me to go with them to see their chariots. One man even offers to drive us all to Hurghada, a distance of some 300 miles.

I am not amused. I spot a man with an official photograph on his chest, which says Airport Guide and it is signed. The photograph looks like him, which is good news. He chases off the crowd, organises three taxis, one 'most suitable' for a man in a wheelchair, and then sets up a reception committee to go airside and meet my team as they come into the airport. I sigh, think I have done a good job, though something tells me I am being cheated. I put the thought out of my mind and have a coke. I usually drink it with whisky to hide the taste but at this moment I think it unwise to do anything that might befuddle my already fuddled brain.

Now it is one hour after their plane arrived, all the passengers have alighted, and my official friend with the photograph announces that the team are not on board and have therefore been lost!

I wonder what has happened and try to phone Jon but there is no answer. Clearly they have either missed the plane or something else has gone wrong at the Rome end. The airport is now empty and some suspicious people are greedily eyeing me and my baggage, so I decide to leg it to the internal terminal some miles away and work it out from there.

As I arrive there at 2 a.m. my mobile rings.

'Hey Robin' says Jon, 'Where are you? We are at the airport and there is a bloke here waving one of your cards in my face and telling me I and the team have to go with him.'

I had given Mustapha – not his real name which I have forgotten – my card. It seems that the team had been kept on the plane for ages whilst they let off all the other passengers and assembled the people handlers. They were then taken, not through the official channels, but around some back corridors – so my reception committee had missed them entirely!

'Put him on, Jon.'

I recognise the voice and tell Jon to get himself, the team and the baggage on board – but not to pay as I have agreed the sum and would only pay on safe delivery of the goods and their baggage.

They arrive an hour later. Mustapha demands more money before he will open the boot and unload our baggage.

'There is the overtime, the waiting time, the parking time, the missed other journeys, they must all be paid for.'

We haggle and agree a sum.

'Now, there is the reception committee. They had to pay to go airside.'

We haggle and agree a sum.

'That is good. Now that is everyone paid except me. I need my fee for all the work I have done.'

I notice an airport guard has come to the door and is watching us. I look his way and motion him over. Magic! Mustapha immediately releases our baggage and takes off at speed. We are free!

I feel a sense of triumph, I know I have been 'done' but at least I have won the last round and maybe that is all that counts.

We sit in the airport for five hours to get our early morning flight. I detect that morale is flagging. The team have had a wonderful time in Rome and I think that they have tired each other out. I also feel a stranger to them, which is odd, but I decide it is because I was not with them in

Rome where they had to sort out many problems on their own, working as a team. I wonder what lies ahead and feel some apprehension.

All that changes as we reach Hurghada. It is staggeringly hot, and we are glad to reach our hotel. I feel a stuffiness in my nose and am breathless, but assume it is all to do with the heat.

The Red Sea Five Mile Challenge would not have taken place but for a chance meeting between Miles and Darren Brookes.

Miles speaks regularly at corporate functions and he usually talks about how we all live in our own circles of familiarity and we need to step out of these circles to expand our experiences.

Darren Brookes was in the audience at one talk to Round Table, became spellbound with the message and wondered how he could step out of his circle.

After his speech, Miles was approached by Darren, and told him about Eighty Ways. In turn Darren told Miles about his passion, scuba diving. A wicked grin spread across Miles' face as he said 'I would love to try that'.

No further encouragement was needed for Darren, who refused to believe that a blind man could not scuba dive. In a few weeks, Miles was scuba diving and suggested that the Around the World adventurers could scuba dive as one of their means of transport.

Darren hit the phone and for the next nine months it never stopped ringing. Mary Munley from Regal Dive came on board and offered to sponsor all flights and accommodation. The Round Table paid for all training and equipment was sourced and obtained. A dive boat was needed and Emperor Divers pledged their support. In the end, Darren and his friends raised some £20,000 in sponsorship to enable the adventurers to scuba dive one sector in the Red Sea. Darren became so involved in the project that he decided to launch a new charity, Dive-Able, with Mike and Miles as Trustees, and with the purpose of teaching disabled people to scuba dive.

Having taught Miles to scuba dive, Darren turned his attention to me, Caroline, Jon and Miles. Caroline presented no problem other than her eyesight; my doctor had cautioned me against scuba diving with my heart condition but I ignored him. Jon was fine but Mike presented us with the biggest problem.

Having no legs, his balance was all wrong. Being paralysed he had no control over his body temperature to counteract the changes in temperature of the water. Nor could he swim in any conventional way. Teaching him to scuba dive was impossible – but not to Darren who was prepared to step outside the conventional circle and try.

I think back to one day in a swimming pool in Nottingham. Darren Brookes and Jim Corbally from the Nottingham Dive Centre take us through the land-based tuition exercises and exams and then we all put on our scuba diving equipment. Mike has a problem for they do not make wet suits with no legs, but some clothes pegs provide an improvised solution. Mary gets into the pool with Mike and Darren. 'If you need me to do anything to help Mike, just tell me what to do. You will only have to tell me once' she says.

Slowly Mike is lowered into the pool and he holds Mary's hand as he starts to move forward using this upper body strength. Without lower legs his position in the water is mainly vertical and not horizontal. Darren plays around with the weights, trying to get more weight on Mike's chest to pull it down and the lower end up but it is only partially successful. But the moment has arrived, Mary and Darren let go, Mike submerges, breathes through his regulator, pushes himself forward with his arms and hands. He is scuba diving.

Later Mike tells us of how he felt when, for the first time since his accident, he found that he could move forward unaided by anyone else and without using his wheelchair. In addition, because of his upper body strength, he could match the efforts of able-bodied divers. We all cried.

Back in the pool, Caroline and Miles soon followed. Ten years ago Caroline had been told that because of her eye problem she would never be allowed to dive. She had spent the whole summer picking mandarin oranges in Australia only to fail the medical when she went to learn. Now, Darren and Jim proved that she could scuba dive with safety, on the well-worn buddy principle. Caroline proved herself to be a natural, Miles had already qualified and was our best scuba diver. I found difficulty in getting my weights right and either sank like a stone or floated around out of control, bobbing up and down in a most undignified manner for the leader of the adventure and using up great gulps and burps of valuable air. But I know that with my secret lessons, these problems have been overcome.

Now we are in the Red Sea and ready to complete our scuba diving sector of Around the World in Eighty Ways – two registered blind people and a man with no legs, paralysed from the chest down, and with no internal temperature control, and a man with a heart condition.

DAY
Twenty-seven

Saturday

28 September 2002
Red Sea, Hurghada

In which the team go scuba diving and I begin to feel unwell

We wake up and there is excitement in the team. The group from the Nottingham Dive Team arrived last night and are up early ready for action. They have put so much into the scuba diving sector and now it is time for them to fulfil the programme.

We are in the Hilton Hotel and breakfast is served upstairs. There is no lift nor is there an easy way to get Mike up the stairs. Mike is told he can sit downstairs and someone can bring his breakfast to him. It is a bad start. We all sit with Mike downstairs and order our breakfasts. We are surprised that as formidable an organisation as the Hilton Hotels does not provide disabled access to the breakfast room.

After breakfast, I return to my room, but I do not feel well.

Dizzy spells alternate with breathlessness. I recall the warning given to me by Dr Joliffe, of Edinburgh, not to scuba dive unless I felt right on top of my form. I make a decision not to tell the adventurers that I do not feel well, but that I have some administration to attend to, and that they should spend the first day with the Nottingham team on their own.

Jon gives me a deep look and I think he suspects something but he says nothing. I help them load the boat which has been provided for us by Regal Diving, one of the foremost scuba diving operators in the Red Sea and with a very heavy heart I watch them set off.

Miles writes about the first dive.

I suppose as a blind person I am constantly trying to become aware of my environment, like on the boat – where is my cylinder, where is my equipment? It always feels a bit strange strapping on about seventy pounds of lead, putting on all the equipment and then jumping off the back of a boat and expecting to be caught. Because I cannot see what is going on around me, it is like a leap of faith.

I jump into the Red Sea. The sound is amplified under the water, as soon as we get down around the coral reef with Darren as my buddy, I am very aware of the light tinkling coral sound all around me. I can hear things like parrot fish chewing the coral and all the different forms of sea life crawling around. I love that – I hold my breath and listen to it. As a blind diver I hold on lightly to my buddy Darren's wrist – it gives me some sense of spatial awareness and the direction in which we are moving. My little dive computer strapped against my ear speaks to me and tells me things like my depth, how long I have been underwater and when I need a safety stop.

For Mike too the first dive in the Red Sea is memorable.

It was my first open water dive after doing the pool sessions in Nottingham, I was a little bit unsure of what I was going to meet, and being thrown from a boat for the first time was perhaps a little worrying. As it turned out, I rolled into the water and bobbed up to the surface. I felt totally relaxed, perfectly safe, and from then on I felt totally at home in the sea.

The boat returns late afternoon and it is clear that it has been a success. All of them have been in the water, and all have shown wonder at what they have seen. Mike has found a new skill, and has proved himself to be an adept scuba diver, bearing in mind the special challenges he has to face. Caroline is a natural and Miles, by far our most experienced scuba diver, has shown excellent leadership skills to the group.

The Nottingham dive team are elated. Mary Munley, Jim Corbally, and Darren Brookes tell me that it went like a dream for them. I am well satisfied but ask Darren if he thinks they will accomplish the five and a half miles scuba dive that the task demands of them.

'No problem' he tells me, and when Darren says he will do something, then it gets done.

In the true tradition of scuba diving, the night ends in a pub, but I do not join them. I am still suffering from breathless spells and I can feel my heart bumping about. A good night's sleep will settle it all, I tell myself.

DAY
Twenty-eight

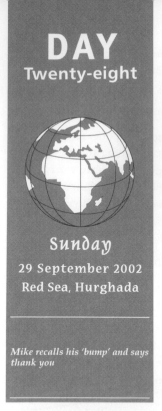

Sunday

29 September 2002
Red Sea, Hurghada

Mike recalls his 'bump' and says thank you

Once again I wake up feeling ill. I drink half a litre of water in one go to counter the effects of dehydration and set off for breakfast. My room is some distance away from the restaurant and getting there becomes a nightmare. The heat is horrendous and I have to stop every few yards to get my breath back and recover in some shade. Crossing the road to the restaurant is a major hurdle. I realise that it is still early morning and the peak temperatures lie ahead.

Once in the shade of the hotel, I review my position. Clearly, I cannot scuba dive. The adventurers are in the safe hands of the Nottingham Dive Centre and I realise that it would be best if I were to return to the comparative coolness of Cairo and recover myself in time to move on to South Africa.

I have breakfast with Mike who is still unable to get to the restaurant. It is a significant date for him, for it is the ninth anniversary of the day he had his 'bump' in Bosnia.

At the time Mike, who had been in the wine trade for 21 years before changing his career and becoming the Director of Operations for Scottish European Aid, was in Sarajevo working with the charity to restore water supplies in Tusla, in the north of Bosnia. One night he and his two companions were struck by a car driven by a Croation. Mike survived, the others were killed.

He spent two days in a Sarajevo hospital, where they diagnosed many injuries, including a serious brain-threatening injury to his head, internal injuries, injuries to his hands and legs, one of which was amputated. He subsequently lost the other as a direct result of the accident. He was flown home to the UK where they discovered that he had severed the nerves in his spine at the top of his chest and that he would be paralysed for the rest of his life.

His recovery was long and tortuous. Divorced at the time, he enjoyed loyal support from his father and mother and his son. At first he tried to live back amongst his folk in Scotland, making his home at Inver in Perthshire. However it soon became obvious that he needed to be close to the National Spinal Injuries Centre at Stoke Mandeville, near London, so he found a place to rent in the attractive village of Thame.

Mike became active in the rehabilitation of people suffering similar injuries, and it was largely due to his efforts that Spinal Injuries Together

(SIT) was set up as a single body representing five separate charities working in the field of spinal injuries.

Now the bump is behind him and he is sitting with me in Hurghada on the Red Sea, preparing to spend the day scuba diving. A miraculous recovery indeed!

Once more, I accompany Miles, Mike and Caroline down to the boat. I notice that Aoife is also boarding and this disturbs me. I have become aware that our diaries and daily web site entries, which Aoife compiles, have fallen well behind schedule. I make a note to ask Jon if her time might not be better spent staying on shore catching up with her paper work rather then spending the day with the scuba divers. I then think I am being unfair to her. How can you take someone to Hurghada and be upset with them for wanting to spend their time on the water? Still, she has a job to do and that must get priority.

For Miles, Mike and Caroline the day is spent scuba diving with the wonderful Nottingham Scuba Diving team. I travel into the town and visit the airline. I am feeling much better but decide to stick to my plan of an early departure and book myself to Cairo in two days time. Before I leave I am determined to spend one day on the boat with the team.

When the boat returns at 4 p.m., I am at the docks to greet them. Mike is elated at his skill in scuba diving. As it is the anniversary of his accident, he is asked what he would do if he met the person who had caused his injuries.

'I think I might shake his hand and thank him for giving me so many opportunities which I have grabbed,' he replies.

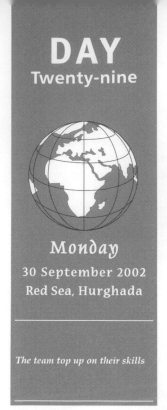

First we pay a visit to the shop in the hotel. Miles has decided that he would cut a more dashing figure in the swimming pool if he were to purchase a new pair of trunks, so he, Jon and I take a look at the stock.

Miles has a wonderful feeling for clothes and being smartly dressed. Whilst all of us look somewhat dilapidated in our Round the World outfits, by now badly worn, Miles always manages to look as though he has just stepped out of a boutique.

First he tells the assistant about the style he requires, and samples are brought to him. These he feels minutely – the stitching, the seams, the band, the upholstery inside, the material. It is a meticulous performance and it takes time, careful thought and consultation with us before he makes a choice of style.

Now we are on a decision about colour. Miles asks us to describe in detail the colour. How do you describe colour to a blind man? But Miles has not always been blind, so the problem is not as acute as we think it might be. Miles decides that a red would suit and one is found.

'What shade of red it is?' he asks. Flummoxed for a bit, we end up telling him it is not as red as a brilliant sunset. Miles wants a bright red, and asks the assistant if he can get him one. The assistant has nothing in stock, but promises to try to find one that is suitable.

We leave for another day with the Nottingham Dive team, to build up our experience and to get more scuba diving yardage under our belts.

Once again, the sun beats down relentlessly, I hope I am getting more used to it, but still feel that things are not right.

Today's plan is to return to the dive centre and get in more mileage towards our target of scuba diving for over five and a half miles. In fact, this target has now almost been reached and the team determine to continue to see how far they can get in the allocated time.

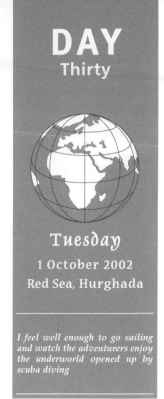

I feel well enough to go sailing and watch the adventurers enjoy the underworld opened up by scuba diving

I am feeling better and decide to spend my last day on the Red Sea out on the scuba diving boat. So at last I join the team and share the excitement with them of putting to sea and sailing for the one and a half hours to the dive site.

Once we reach the site, I sense the excitement. Although I have brought along my gear, I decide not to join them in the water. We are still only a third of the way along our adventure and it is no time to take any health risks.

So I stand and watch.

I watch Miles put on his diving gear and notice it is impossible to tell he is blind. His hands reach out unerringly for his equipment, buckles are fixed without fumbles, tests are completed on his equipment without hesitation. Never for one moment does he look uncertain. He is confident, enthusiastic, bursting with energy, and a superb example to the rest of us.

It is the same for Caroline, who slips into her wet suit with ease and who simply looks totally at home in the scuba diving kit.

Mike too has learned how to put on his kit. Wet suits are something of a challenge for him, as they have full legs and he has none, and being paralysed he cannot feel when things are on all right. Naturally his first attempts were clumsy, but now he too slips into his wet suit with ease.

Then it is time for the water. First Miles stands at the edge of the deck and on the word of command from Darren, he leaps into the air. It is an act of faith. He knows there are people in the water and that they will pick him up. But he cannot see them. He just trusts them.

For Caroline it is different. Though registered blind, she can see a metre or two in front of her so when she goes over, she can see her buddy waiting for the link up. Nevertheless with her lack of vision, I realise it still takes some courage to take that leap into the water.

Mike has to adopt a different technique. It would be easy simply to pick him up and drop him overboard but Mike is determined to do it himself. Slowly he edges himself to the side of the boat and then, with an almighty

Miles and Caroline getting ready for a dive

splash, he heaves himself into the water, confident that someone will catch him and not let him drown.

It is he that inspires me most. Both Miles and Caroline can move freely and thus swim out of trouble if anything goes wrong. For Mike, when he rolls into the water, he is helpless unless someone is there and locks on to him immediately. I recall his comment to me that he is simply living his life the way he has to. No way, Mike, you could be stuck in a very limited circle, the fact that you are doing what you are doing with the team is due to your determination to step outside of your circle.

A few minutes are spent on the surface carrying out checks and then Miles, Mike and Caroline submerge.

I watch them below water. Miles is moving under the boat, holding Darren's wrist to give him a 'feel' of where he is. Caroline is with her buddy setting out for the shoals of fish which she has been told lie ahead. Mike is driving powerfully with his upper arm strength, with Jim Corbally near to him keeping a watchful eye.

I am jealous but try to hide it. Later I read Aoife's diary and am deeply moved by what she says. I realise that the team understand just how difficult it is for me to have passed up my personal dream of doing the eighty ways adventure on my own, sharing it instead with others and then finding that I am the one who has to sit on the sidelines.

To Robin's great credit,

she wrote

he kept his head high. Dignified as always, he complimented his adventurers on their diving prowess. At the team meeting, he admitted that he was jealous as hell.

Now Caroline Miles and Mike are putting in some more distance on their scuba diving marathon, whilst Aoife has jumped overboard and is yelping with excitement at the joys of swimming in the Red Sea. I sit in the shade, drink water and munch sandwiches, feeling miserable and with nothing to do. I decide I am glad to be going to Cairo tomorrow where I can recover my health.

We return triumphant to the dock with another two miles under our belts. We go to the swimming pool and relax.

Once again I am feeling increasingly ill, so I tell Jon of my plan for him to see the sector out. I will get out of Hurghada and go to an air-conditioned hotel in cooler Cairo.

I get up to leave him and the rest, who are splashing around in the swimming pool. The hot air starts to strangle me. My legs go weak. I struggle into my room and within seconds, there is a knock on the door. It is Jon, complete with Doctor Chris Calton from the Nottingham Diving Team.

'Robin, I have seen dead people look better than you do' says Jon, who had watched me walk away and immediately sent for the Nottingham Scuba Diving Centre doctor. At that moment, I share the confidence the team have in Jon.

Chris gives me a full check and asked about the drugs that I take. His verdict is that I am suffering from extreme heat, am not drinking enough water and that I should certainly get out of Hurghada and into the cooler climate of Cairo.

So the die is cast. I will go to Cairo, spend a couple of days there and then get down to Cape Town in time for the pre-publicity for the arrival of Mike, Caroline and Miles.

Jon will complete the scuba marathon and then bring the team down to Cape Town.

DAY
Thirty-one

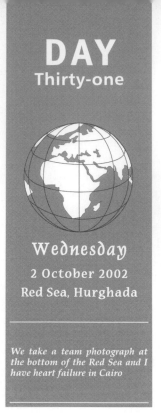

Wednesday
2 October 2002
Red Sea, Hurghada

We take a team photograph at the bottom of the Red Sea and I have heart failure in Cairo

There is more mileage to do today but first, it is time for the official photograph and Miles has the idea, which he shares with Mike – why not take one of him pushing Mike along the bottom of the Red Sea in his wheelchair?

Mike is willing, but points out that his chair is very expensive and he does not want it to be corroded by the salt in the Red Sea. He goes to hotel reception.

'My wheelchair has to have a servicing tomorrow, can you lend me one for the day?'

The hotel duly obliges, Mike hides his own chair away and sets off to the photoshoot grounds.

Darren and Jim lower the hotel wheelchair to the bottom of the Red Sea. Mike takes up his position in the chair and Miles, plus his white stick, takes up his pushing position.

Miles, having much more lung capacity than Mike, decides to hold his breath and so takes off his regulator and mask for the photo. Mike is given the job of hitting Miles on the leg when the photo has been taken, so Miles can replace the mask and regulator.

Mike descending

Miles walks Mike along the bottom of the Red Sea. 'Hey Mike, how did you say that trick about parting the Red Sea worked?'

Unfortunately, once the photograph has been taken, Mike is distracted by the beautiful coral fish in the area and forgets about the signal. Miles' smile slowly turns into a grimace as he wonders why the photographer is being so slow. Just in time, Mike remembers and bangs Miles on the leg, just as Darren decides it is time to swim to the rescue!

When developed, the picture is a classic – a blind man using his white stick to guide a legless man in a wheelchair along the bottom of the Red Sea. It was taken by Dr Chris Calton of the Nottingham Dive Team.

We return to the dock. The crew are clearing up and there is a pair of unclaimed fins. A crew member asks Mike if they are his and then realising that Mike has no legs, goes puce with embarrassment.

But for Mike it is a wonderful moment. He knows that he has been taken as a scuba diver and not a man with no legs. We are winning.

The adventurers are now in full flight and believe that nothing can beat them. I have let them enjoy the feeling, but think about the rest of the journey – will they overdo it in Hurghada, and have enough energy for the rest of the adventure? I think of the hundreds of volunteers who have given up their time, money and talent and whose turn lies ahead, and wonder what I would say to them if one act of carelessness amongst the three main members of the team makes it necessary to stop.

I have confided this view to Jon but he tells me not to worry, he is keeping a close eye on them all. I know that he has now won their complete confidence, and I allow myself the luxury of turning to my own problem.

I take a flight to Cairo and book into the Hilton Hotel.

I visit a museum and then as evening approaches, I go back to my room. But I realise that, even though I am cool, I am again unwell. I have to suck each breath into my lungs, my head is light and my heart is trying to jump out of my chest. I grab the phone and the hotel doctor is summoned.

'You have heart failure' he says.

I panic.

'But you are not dying.'

I unpanic.

He explains that affected by the heat, the stress of the journey and the physical exertion of the past few days, my heart was having some difficulty in finding its rhythm. He recommends that I spend a week in the local hospital.

I decide that I would rather be treated back in Edinburgh where Dr Shaw, my own heart doctor, could deal with me. I am assured that I can be given drugs to provide an emergency treatment to get me home safely.

I phone Mary and within an hour she has me on a British Airways flight, with take-off time early the next morning.

The journey is difficult, and oxygen is needed. I reflect I should have stayed in Cairo, at the hospital there.

Once home, Dr Shaw listens deeply to my account of what has happened and the drugs I have been given to get home.

'He did exactly the right thing in his treatment' he assures me about the doctor, adding that Cairo has wonderful facilities for treatment of heart condition. I think of how the initial impression formed by those money-grabbing thieves at the airport has conditioned my response to staying in a Cairo hospital and remind myself to learn the lesson.

I am glad that if anyone had to fly home for a problem, it was me and not one of Caroline, Miles and Mike. Without each of them doing each and every means of transport, the concept would not hold up. I realise what a massive challenge and responsibility I have given them – and Jon and Stuart, let alone Mary, the anchor for the adventure.

Thursday

3 October 2002
Red Sea, Hurghada

I fly home and the team finish their scuba diving marathon

Back on the Red Sea, it is time for the last dive. By now the Nottingham scuba divers and the Around the World adventurers are as one.

As Aoife writes in her diary:

In many ways the Red Sea Diving adventure leg was like the beginning of Eighty Ways over again. As soon as we met the Dive team, everyone clicked into place. On board our boat we had the diving instructor Jim Corbally, our dive master Darren Brookes, our creative director, which is what our underwater leader Jon Blackwell liked to call himself, Nick Evans from *Diving Magazine*, Mary Munley from sponsors Regal Dive, the team doctor Chris Calton, our instructor Stella and co-divers Naill and Sally.

Everyone looked out for each other. Always ready with mock sarcastic comments, the boys had us all in stitches. It was so refreshing to hear the team laughing and enjoying the challenge. I could feel the goodwill of everyone on board the dive boat. Amazing to think that these people have spent so much of their time, money and effort to create this underwater adventure. Their dedication to us was extreme, caring for our welfare, tending to our special needs. Whether it be picking up sea cucumbers for Miles or getting a wheelchair along the bottom of the Red Sea, or helping

Mike to kit up, at the end of the day we were able to say that the time spent in the Red Sea was one of the most remarkable periods of our journey.

I imagine that if times are hard over the next two months, the team will always remember how much they accomplished in the Red Sea. The 11.5 mile dive will remind them how capable and able they truly are.

In Edinburgh, Dr Shaw examines me and his advice is reassuring.

A couple of days in the cool of the UK, a change of drugs, and I feel fine. I decide to stay in the UK for a week to make a full recovery and then catch up again with the team when I am well again.

Often we think that airports must be the worst places on earth. Stressful and busy at the best of times, they become a nightmare when you have three people, two of whom are registered blind and the third is in a wheelchair.

The adventurers say goodbye to Hurghada and set off for South Africa

It is time to move on to South Africa and the team order their taxi to take them to their flight from Hurghada to Cairo – which brings the first stress of the day. By now, well used to the tipping culture, there is no surprise when it takes someone to open the door, another person to carry the luggage, another to help everyone get in and another to drive and none of them will work without a tip. Also they all gang together, so that if you do not tip them all, the taxi goes nowhere and probably develops engine trouble which will need the services of twenty-six mechanics plus a breakdown lorry, and you will need to pay for the mechanics and of course for the hire of the lorry.

It is worse on arrival at the airport. A sweaty swarm of happy helpers arrive, surround the taxi, shout a lot, move a lot but with little purpose, unload bags, wheelchairs, cameras and people, and then demand large tips or they will run off with the lot!

Poor Mike is seized by an over-enthusiastic attendant and to the alarm of everyone, is pushed off by him. At pains to explain that his hands are working perfectly and that he is totally capable of moving along on his own, Mike is ignored. In the end, rescue comes when the cavalry, made up of the whole team, surrounds the so-called helper and shouts at him to let Mike go.

He does so, demanding his tip at the same time. However a short study of the team's expressions is sufficient for him to change his mind and hightail it out of our presence.

The flight from Hurghada to Cairo is uneventful and the team have time to shop and sightsee, still unaware – because Mary has kept the news from them – that their leader has been stricken by heart failure in Cairo no less than twenty-four hours previously and is now back in the UK for medical treatment.

DAY
Thirty-four

Saturday
5 October 2002

Cairo

Miles shops in Cairo to get his computer working again

The day is spent sightseeing and renewing worn-out computer parts. Early in the morning, Miles and Jon leave the hotel in search of modems to pacify Miles' pouting laptop. To Miles, his laptop opens the door to his very hectic lifestyle. It helps him to communicate, it keeps his life organised, it speaks to him and tells him his timetable, in many ways it is a part of his body and is completely indispensable to him. So when it is ill, Miles is ill.

To their delight, their mission is successful and by mid afternoon, the new modem is safely tucked in to its port. Miles discovers that there are eighty new e-mails awaiting his attention!

With that, the team board their plane and head off for South Africa.

I have decided to take time off to recover from my illness and rejoin the team at the end of the South African sector and be with them for the trip across India. The time at home could best be used by getting better, and trying to sort out the by now chronic shortage of funds. But the explosion of a problem that had been simmering for some time caused me to change my mind and get out to South Africa as soon as possible.

The South African sector is organised by the South African District of Rotary International, under the direction of Linda and Aldo Girola who had heard about Around the World from the South Queensferry Rotary Club in Edinburgh.

DAY
Thirty-five

Sunday
6 October 2002
Cairo, Egypt to
Georgia, S. Africa

A split looks serious, and causes much worry

We had been attending a news reception in Dublin announcing the adventure when my mobile phone rang. It was Linda, phoning from Cape Town to say she had heard about us from Gordon McNally of the South Queensferry Rotary Club and a former District Governor for Scotland, and would like to help by organising the South African sector from George to Cape Town using the local Rotary Clubs.

We were overjoyed. I had paid a reconnaissance visit to Cape Town some time ago to see if I could find a project manger. Knowing that Harley Davidson people tend to be that little bit different, I walked into the main Harley Davidson dealership and met Ad Keukelaar. I told him what we planned to do and when he had stopped laughing, he immediately offered to help.

But Ad's influence only extended in the Cape Town area so it was a great relief when I received Linda's call.

It was also on that reconnaissance visit to South Africa that I learned a lesson. I had spoken at a public meeting and the usual question came up.

'Who thought up this great idea?'

'I did,' I replied in my usual modest manner.

After the meeting a large and formidable-looking lady called me over.

'My son, it is not your idea, it is the Lord working through you.'

It made me think – often – and still does, as I look back on all that we achieved. If it is true, he chose a very unlikely character. The Lord may indeed work in mysterious ways.

However because of the enormous trouble to which Ad and Linda have gone, I am not happy that through my illness, I will not be there. I ask Mary if she can fly out and lead in my absence.

Meanwhile the adventurers are facing an epic journey from the Red Sea to George in South Africa, a journey that will take 24 hours.

They had spent the previous day in Cairo. Sightseeing had been planned, but after the heavy schedule in Hurghada, they decided to rest up.

Today the team head for Cairo Airport. The first sector to Dubai is by Emirates Airlines who kindly upgrade everyone and they enjoy a very comfortable three hour flight, treated as VIPs. At Dubai, they are made to feel like a danger to society. They are made to feel like public enemy no 1, with each one having an escort to take the 'cripple' as they called Mike to the disability lounge. This turns out to be more like an old folks' home, with no bar, which Mike finds disgraceful. The lounge is far away from the shops and bars. Mike wonders why people always see disabled people as weak and feeble. Does being disabled mean you cannot have a drink? Does being in a wheelchair affect your ability to buy nice things? Aoife sums it up with biting satire.

'Silly me, I forgot, disabled people cannot possibly be fashionable, after all they are too busy looking frail and dependent.'

Next the team endure what becomes known as the flight from hell, Dubai to George, our entry point to South Africa. Mike has a very serious tummy upset and trapped on a plane for six hours, it is no time to discover his colostomy bag is leaking. All attempts at sealing the bag fail and Mike spends the flight with his bowels emptying all over his clothing. With a full plane the team are unable to clean and change the bag and understandably Mike feels more and more miserable.

On arrival at Johannesburg Jon and Caroline take Mike into a washroom, and manage to clean and change him, before, with much support of the airport ground staff, they transfer to the flight to Georgia.

On arrival, they are met by members of the Knysna Rotary Club, but they discover that Mike's spare wheelchair has not arrived, and that his main wheelchair has been damaged. At the hotel, another colostomy bag fails, ruining another set of clothes and a set of bedding.

Not a good day at all.

In Scotland, Mary, Stuart and I have a conference. Stuart outlines that we are well on our way to our target of 80 means of transport. He is very confident that South Africa will produce some splendid additions to our portfolio, for each of the Rotary Clubs is determined to outdo the other. Mary puts a damper on the proceedings. She has been talking to our accountant Mike Thomson who has warned that we are almost out of money.

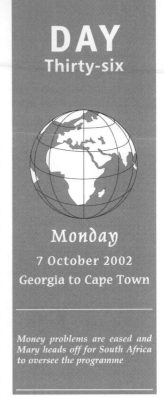

Money problems are eased and Mary heads off for South Africa to oversee the programme

'When you get to the middle of the South African programme, you will be totally out of money and will have to bring the team home.'

The news becomes worse when I decide I will have to implement my emergency plan. I discover that the proposed sale of my mother's house has fallen through and that the loan I though I had arranged is not to be made available.

I phone Sir Tom Farmer who agrees to see me at once. My new drugs have sorted out the heart problem and I am full of beans and raring to get back to South Africa, but have been told to take a few days rest before returning to the front line action.

I put the facts on the table.

'How short are you?' asks Sir Tom.

I tell him that funds will come in from Hong Kong, but there is an acute cash flow problem.

'I need fifty thousand pounds to be sure to get the team down South Africa, across India, down the Malaysian Peninsula, through Singapore and to Hong Kong.'

Sir Tom writes out a cheque for the full amount and hands it over.

'You will get it all back,' I promise him.

I phone Mary, who is at the airport leaving for South Africa and she can tell from my voice that I am ecstatic. Sir Tom has been a wonderful friend to us all the way along. In the planning stage he had donated an office and equipment for us to use and now without him, we would not have got further than South Africa.

Meanwhile in South Africa, the adventurers have arrived in Knysna, completely unaware of the drama that has been played out at home to ensure the continuation of the adventure.

Mary has set off from Scotland to supervise the arrangements. In her journal she writes:

Africa, I had a farm in Africa, at the foot of the Ngong Hills – the opening lines of Karen Blixen's book are going round and round in my brain, gosh what is wrong with me? Stress, a heavy cold and impending jet lag, yet here I am on my way not to Kenya but South Africa and have just flown over the Equator. Perhaps it is the responsibility of carrying the Phileas Fogg top hat!! Muppet – a word used by Caroline when she is not on form sounds loud in my brain. Pull yourself together Mary, you have work to do.

Working full-time I only have a certain amount of holiday days, so in the beginning Robin, Stuart and I sat down to see where the best use of my time would be. In this instance the decision had been between the Red Sea or South Africa. How I wished now I had chosen the Red Sea so that I could have been there when Phileas Fogg needed me most.

The original plan had been that Robin would fly from the Red Sea to Cape Town, I would time my flight down to meet his and would have time in Cape Town to prepare for the very heavy South African sector, before the other adventurers arrived. This would enable us to ensure that the media coverage was in place, meet members of the Rotary Clubs and appear on local television and radio. Robin had already achieved major coverage in the South African Times when he first went out and met Ad Keukelaar from Harley Davidson.

This all went haywire when I had the call from Robin from Cairo to say that he had heart failure – such a calm voice he had on, too – and could I get him back at once to the UK and to his own heart specialist Doctor Shaw. Thank you British Airways, the speed with which you reacted was wonderful and within hours Robin was on his way home.

I didn't recognise the man stumbling towards me in Edinburgh now being able to let his guard down. I could see he was very ill indeed. 'Looks like you are off to South Africa without me,' he said. 'No way' said I. But, all adventures have points when tough decisions have to be made and this was one of them. Robin would stay behind for a couple of days, get his heart working right again with some new drugs, and I would head for South Africa, fulfil the media commitments, catch up with the team and make ready for his arrival, for I knew he would come out later – after all, there isn't much that can keep a man from a ride into Cape Town in a convoy of Harley Davidsons.

Africa here I come.

For Caroline, Miles and Mike it is time to start the South African programme which Mary has constructed to include the means of transport, but in conjunction with each Rotary Club, she has built in a social purpose to each day.

So Caroline, Mike and Miles wake up and head off on a visit to a residential care home for people suffering from epilepsy. Run by a small but highly dedicated team, the centre provides work and care for those who suffer from this debilitating illness. As always, the visit is inspirational, both for those visited and for the adventurers.

The first means of travel is by oyster barge, and then by the Choo-Tjoe, a steam train that travels from George to Cape Town. The team disembark at Outshoorn and are met by Harve of the Outshoorn Rotary Club and sample their first braai or bar-b-que.

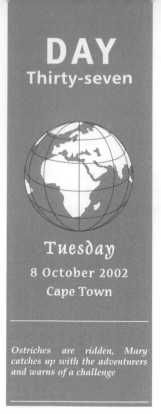

Tuesday
8 October 2002
Cape Town

Ostriches are ridden, Mary catches up with the adventurers and warns of a challenge

One of the ways of transport we have all been talking about is riding ostriches and today the adventurers are at the Highgate Ostrich farm.

Could Mike stay on an ostrich? In pre-publicity I had spoken about trials using Velcro, but now it is for real. Of course, not to be beaten, he rides the ostrich but with a little extra help.

Miles, Caroline and Jon also have a go. Holding on to the wings and gripping tightly round the body, the birds are ridden as they set off in random directions with erratic movements and there is no hope of steering them. Jon is the only one to fall off!

Then the Mossel Bay Rotary club take over. They invite the adventurers to a retirement home which they fund. Local disabled athletes join in, and everyone tucks in to a fish braai. In the middle of the dinner, Mary arrives, bringing with her a stinking cold and feeling rotten.

Racing an Ostrich is not for the foolhardy – or for those who get sea sick!

I am back in Edinburgh waiting for her call to tell me she has joined up safely with the adventurers.

She phones and it is not good news. She relates that when she caught up with the team they are in Mossel Bay. Jon is on his feet making a speech but fails to acknowledge her arrival. He asks all the party – even Carbonara our cameraman – to make a speech but does not ask Mary or even say who she is or that she has just arrived from the UK to be with the team. It is left for the President of the local Rotary Club, who has met Mary at the airport, to get on stage and introduce her. Later she learns that the team are having a birthday party for Carbonara, but they do not invite her. Taking her courage in her hands, she goes along uninvited and provides a bottle of champagne.

'Robin, we could lose them if we do not act quickly' she tells me. 'They virtually ignored me, they have been bonded together so closely by what they have done so far, they now see us as outsiders. You are going to lose control if you do not do something.'

Mary is a tough nut who has tackled some very big problems in her life, but I sense a real possibility of a split. I decide the situation is sufficiently serious and has a potential for disaster and make arrangements to fly immediately to South Africa.

Meanwhile Mary is asked to go into the local radio station and do a ten minute spot on Around the World. As she talks, phone calls come in live and she chats to those making them, answering their questions, sharing their own challenges. What was to have been a ten minute spot is only stopped after one full hour by the ending of the programme. It is a barnstorming performance from her and the reaction from the listeners is enourmous.

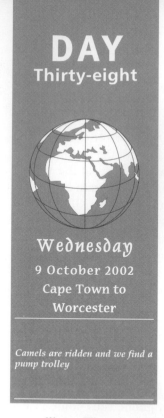

Camels are ridden and we find a pump trolley

Now it is the turn of the Worcester Rotary Club and the adventurers, Jon, Carbonara and Mary are driven first to Riversdale and then on to Swellendam.

During the car journey, Mary and Jon talk about the previous night and my fear that a split is developing. It is a long and deep conversation. Jon explains that because he is with the team all the time, looking after them and ensuring that they are safe and well, it is very hard for them when someone else joins the group – they do not mean to be rude, but they just want to be together. Mary understands, but points out that his job is not just to look after the progress on the ground but to keep close to the support team as well. It is a good conversation, with both acknowledging that each has a point of view that merits consideration and they agree to work together to ensure that all the team feel as one, for that was the purpose of the bonding weekends.

On arrival at Swellendam they transfer to vintage cars and have lunch with the town councillors. Then it is the turn of the camels.

The South African police used camels for transport right up until 1948 but now few remain this far south. Once again, riding camels is one of the forms of transport we often talk about, and the adventurers climb on board. Caroline having cracked elephants, has no trouble, whilst Miles simply looks like Lawrence of Arabia. Is there anything that this man cannot do?

For Mike it is a different story. With no stomach muscles to compensate for the lurching forward and to hold on when the camel stands up, or to stay stabilised when the camel moves from side to side swaying as it walks, he has to ask Jon to sit behind him and hold him firmly in the saddle. It is an enormous demonstration of the bond of trust that has developed between Jon and the team that he does this with confidence, though he is later to tell me that riding the camel was one of his most frightening experiences. He does not know that another camel ride lies ahead of him!

Mike captures his fear of camel riding in his diary.

I had not anticipated being genuinely frightened in attempting the ways. Not having the use of any abdominal or tummy muscles is a problem that gave me some terrifying moments. The first time was riding a camel in South Africa. Getting on the beast was not a problem as Jon simply lifted me on. The difficulty was that it was lying down as low as possible and

Above: Caroline reflects that if she can drive an elephant, a camel should be no bother

Below: Have we left someone behind?

there was little to hold on to other than a couple of very small handles on the saddle. A camel has an alarming way of getting up which involves tilting backwards then forwards at an acute angle. Fortunately Jon held me but even so it seemed like a very long way to fall. Having survived, the strange gait of it walking was equally designed to make me feel fear and my mouth went instantly dry with anxiety. After a short while, I was asked by the lead camel driver if I wanted to go further or stop. It was hardly a split second before I volunteered to stop. The worry then was the camel's lurch as it lay down but there was no choice but to grit my teeth and go for it.

The Worcester Rotary Club take over and their challenge to the team is immense. Somehow they have commandeered a pump trolley. Most people have seen one in old films but they still exist. A four-wheeled vehicle on rail tracks, it is powered by two people pumping a sea-saw up and down, which generates movement in the wheels.

The adventurers clamber on board and do a thirty minute shift to their allocated destination, long enough for Stuart to be satisfied that they have undertaken a genuine journey, long enough for them all to be totally exhausted.

But there is no time to rest, for Mary has organised another item for the social work. This time it is at Pioneers for the Blind, and the team give a presentation on their adventure so far.

It is well received and Mary is delighted with her insistence that each day should include some social and inspirational work as well as forms of transport. Being a Rotarian herself, she has established enormous rapport with the Rotarians in South Africa, and this has resulted in a really packed programme with a purpose more than simply using means of transport.

Travel by rail dolly goes into the records as another means of transport

I remember the story that when Sir John Harvey Jones was to make a speech, an inexperienced organiser phoned to tell him how to find the route from his plane to the taxi rank.

I rejoin the adventurers, we ride in a wagon to sample wine, visit a craft shop run by disabled people and meet a girl who eats ice cream from her toes and a boy with an odd name

'I do not think you understand,' huffed Sir John. 'I do not do that. I am met.'

Linda meets me at Cape Town Airport – wonderfully warm, bubbly, friendly, efficient, loving, no one could have made me feel more welcome. She introduces me to Peter Vergerlis, President of the South Africa Rotary District. who shakes my hand in a funny way. Then I realise that Mary has briefed them and he is taking a sneaky check on my pulse rate. There is water in the car and he insists that I drink some. I am in safe and loving hands.

Now I am standing in a car park in Paarl waiting for the adventurers who are being driven over the mountains to join me.

We reunite and then set off for wine. We are of course in wine country and the Paarl Rotary Club have commandeered an old horse-drawn wagon, used by settlers in days gone by.

It is a wonderful journey. Mary, Mike, Caroline, Miles, Jon, Aoife and I sit comfortably in the wagon. Now we are once again together as a unit, the difficulties I feared to be developing seem not to exist. We pass people picking grapes, they wave to us and we return their greetings. We also have an accident. We have been rejoined by Carbonara who has bought a new camera. In his bid to get some spectacular film, he leaves the track and climbs up into some scrub. We ride past and he runs after us, filming all the time. But Carbonara only has one eye and it is clamped to the lens of his camera. He takes a massive purler and injures his ankle. We pull him on board the wagon and pour cold water on the injured limb.

' I think I have broken my ankle' he gasps.

We arrive at the winery and sample their wares. Being in the trade, we all take our lead from Mike and benefit enormously from his specialist knowledge. Carbonara manages to join in. After all, you do not drink through your ankle.

It is time to move on, for we have our social visit to undertake. But where is Miles? We soon get the answer. There is the thunder of hooves and around the corner, and at full speed, Miles arrives at full flashing gallop on a magnificent snorting steed, accompanied by its owner on another such

The finest of horses trot us through South Africa

beast. His face is alight with excitement and there are no clues at all that he is blind. He trusts the horse and is happy to ride at full speed, even though he can see nothing. The horse knows where he is going. It is another wonderfully inspiring moment and I forgive him for holding us all up!

We head into town and find a small business that sells craft goods made by disabled people. As we are to talk in an adjoining hall, we take a look at the items in the shop,

Caroline is there before us for she has been asked to do a radio interview. Having checked out that the radio lines are working and completed the interview, she finds a corner and lies down for a snooze, waiting for us to arrive. She does not realise that all the guests coming to our presentation pass by her and their first sight of the dynamic and wonderful adventurer they have been told so much about is an unconscious snoring Caroline. She is not amused when she wakes up.

We talk and then walk around the factory, chatting with the disabled people who work there. Caroline, Mike and Miles tour the factory and once again I feel that these visits can contribute more to our adventure than the means of travel.

Then the Somerset Rotary Club host us to another wine tasting session before we are taken to The Strand where all the Rotary Clubs involved in the sector have been invited to attend a meal and meet us.

We go in and the first thing I notice is a girl, Nikki, eating an ice cream with her toes. She has no arms, but has driven to the event. She is as remarkable as our adventurers and I realise it would have been a good idea if in each sector I had invited local people as inspirational as the adventurers to join us as we passed through. Then I remember the wonderful contribution that Cameron Sharpe had made in Scotland and Tim Haddock in Northern Ireland. I should have taken up the idea then.

Mary is talking to a young boy.

'What is your name?' she asks and he replies in a local dialect.

'Can you translate that into English for me?'

The boy relates how his parents, having only managed to produce boys and wanting a girl, named him after a remark made by his mother on his birth.

In English his name translates as *'Not Another One'*.

It is time to speak, I ask Miles to go first to warm up the audience, which he does. Then it is Mike's turn but there is something wrong. He starts but then falters.

He asks for a glass of water which is poured and devoured.

He starts again but it is clear that he is in trouble. He is struggling for breath and there is no strength in his voice.

I ask Caroline to take over and check on Mike. He is all right, he assures me, it is just a turn and he is very tired.

When Caroline has finished, Mike gives me a signal that he would like to have another go. I turn the request down, a decision which angers Mike. I can understand the problem, but I am afraid that if he tries again and once more has a turn, then both his confidence in the public speaking element and the effect of the evening on the audience will be spoiled. My decision is not popular but I believe it to be the right one and stick to it. It is easy to make the popular decision but more important to make the right one.

After the dinner Mary is invited by Peter Balin to take a trip first thing next morning in a Cessna 173 and see the sunrise over Table Mountain. She is bursting to accept, but realises that there is a very heavy day ahead and being up in the sky was no place to be should there be any last-minute changes to the programme. In any case, everyone is very tired and will need to have a lie in.

So she puts duty first and declines the offer.

DAY
Forty

Friday
11 October 2002
Paarl to Cape Town

We ride Harleys into Cape Town and Mary gets an unexpected presentation

Bearing in mind the very heavy schedule for the day, Mary has organised a late start, with an 11am rendezvous with Ad Keukelaar and the Harley Davidson Club for this is the grand day of our entrance to Cape Town in a convoy of Harley Davidson cycles.

But first there is a challenge. Caroline tells Mary that the team are exhausted and asks if they could skip the social visits in the afternoon. This is a problem as the visits have been arranged by Linda and Aldo Girola, who have personally set up the entire programme and we would be letting them down. It was why Mary had scheduled a late start, so the team could have a lie in and recover their strength. Mary tells Caroline she will think about it.

Caroline then reveals that rather than take advantage of the late start and have a lie in, she had been up at the crack of dawn in Peter's Cessna – the flight that Mary had turned down to ensure she was fresh for the Cape Town grand entrance and for the rest of the day.

We all decide that the social programme must be completed.

We head off to the local petrol station and there they are – massive numbers of Harley Davidson motorcycles, all with their riders in position. We meet Jana Forrester,who is one of the Rotarians who has worked so hard to make it all happen for us. Jana tells us if we are ever going to do anything similar again, she would like to be involved.

Mike goes first on Ad Keukelaar's bike, being hauled up onto the pillion and told to grip with his arms around Ad's neck. I am on the next bike, followed by Caroline and Miles and then all the other Harleys that have turned up to take part. We are guided by a police escort.

Amongst the riders is a wonderful enthusiast aged 88. For 60 years he had yearned to own a Harley Davidson, but it had not happened for him. Then, when talking about his dream to a friend, he was told that at the age of 86 he was now too old to fulfil it. That was all he needed. A visit to Ad Keukelaar soon kitted him out with a gleaming model and he is here with us today to ride it with all the pride he can muster.

With their gloriously throaty roar, the Harleys burst into life and we process beside Table Mountain into Cape Town. We again wave at the crowds as we pass, bathed in sunshine. As we enter Cape Town, we spot the banners strung to the lampposts that welcome our arrival. We drive to the City Hall where the Mayor has arranged a reception.

He makes a speech and then calls Mary forward to accept a presentation which she does with a wink at me. We have both realised that with her title of Project Director the Mayor has assumed that she is the leader of the entire project. I feel she deserves the glory and in any case we do not want to embarrass the mayor by pointing out his mistake.

I am worried about Mike. When we arrive at the Town Hall, he is pale in the face and is gasping for water. I ask if he is all right.

Mike explains:

If I thought the camel trip was frightening, riding on the back of a Harley Davidson into Cape Town was absolutely terrifying. This time it should have been no worry because there was a low backrest and sides to hold me. I told myself I would be safe. However because these supports are below where I can feel, my brain was saying you may think you are safe but the failure of the brain to get this message means it tells you that you are going to fall. It has the effect that I felt totally insecure despite having my arms locked around the unfortunate driver's neck and shoulders. About halfway along the trip to Cape Town I felt an almost irresistible urge to stop and get off into the following cars. Again I had a parched mouth and was almost hyperventilating but I had a determination to complete this method of transport. So determination overcame the terror and we made it to the end. It took some time to be able to speak other than pleading for water, which Robin immediately provided.

It is time for the social visits that were in question in the morning. Caroline and Miles go to the Athlone School for children where they are charmed by the singing of the choir. Mike and Jon visit a rehabilitation centre for people with spinal injuries. Mike is intensely moved by the experience, and he sets a burning beacon of hope for the injured. If he can go around the world doing what he is doing, then so can they.

In the evening, we dine on lasagne at a fund-raising dinner attended by members from the fifteen Rotary Clubs who have put together the programme. I learn that it is the first time they have combined to work on one project. They applaud our adventure but it is they who should be applauded.

DAY
Forty-one

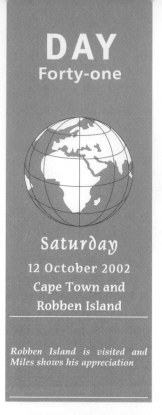

Saturday
12 October 2002
Cape Town and
Robben Island

Robben Island is visited and Miles shows his appreciation

Miles wants to look his best, and asks if he can get a haircut. Our host arranges for a stylist to come to our digs and she trims Miles' hair as he sits outside on a balcony overlooking the sea. Carbonara has a massively swollen ankle but an x-ray reveals no break and he is given pain killers to enable him to continue filming.

Once more the sun shines, and we are all up early bound for Robben Island. Not strictly a progression on our journey around the world, it is still a 'must' for us and we are deeply moved by the experience. We travel out by the ferry and I take the chance to talk individually to Jon and to Caroline. They are both aware that there is a natural danger for a split between those who are on the adventure and those who have worked so hard to make it possible and we discuss ways in which any problems can be overcome.

Back from Robben Island, the team reflect on what they have seen – and pack in another means of transport

A helicopter arrives to pick us up from Robben Island. Miles approaches Mary. 'We have done a helicopter before, Mary, so this trip will not count. Why don't I stand down and you fly back to Cape Town on the helicopter?'

It is a wonderful gesture. Mary has masterminded the whole organisation and Miles appreciates this and wants to show his appreciation.

So we take off into the sunshine, head for Table Mountain and see Miles disappearing into the distance as he waits to be driven to the ferry and brought back to Cape Town. But he does not have to do this. There is enough fuel in the helicopter for it to fly back to Robben Island and rescue him.

In the afternoon, we have our social programme to perform. This time it is the South African branch of Riding for the Disabled. Mike presents a stunning picture as he sits in the sun, taking tea and talking to recent amputees. Sadly we learn that the riding facility is under the threat of closure as the land they are renting is wanted by the government for housing. Some 25 million rand is needed to enable them to stay.

In the evening we dine at the Hildebrand Restaurant owned by Linda Girola. Right on the Waterfront, it is one of Cape Town's most popular restaurants and we eat copious quantities of food. Linda has done a wonderful job for us in South Africa, blending forms of travel with a superb social and welfare programme.

It is a heady mix and one that becomes a full part of our future programme.

DAY
Forty-one and Forty-two

Saturday—Sunday
12–13 October 2002
Cape Town, S. Africa
to Mumbai, India

Indian memories flood back, and the adventurers prepare to cross India

Welcome to India, a land of stark contrasts, a land of vast diversity and a land full of surprises. A country that proudly proclaims through screaming headlines and heart-warming pictures the birth of her billionth baby.

Welcome to Bombay, now known as Mumbai, the great commercial capital of India where affluent apartments overlook abject slums. The City has the dubious distinction of having the single largest slum in the world, with a population of 700,000, and this is just one of a number of slums in the City.

India was very special to Phileas Fogg. It was there he met his Indian Princess, who became his life partner, it was there he rode his first elephant, it was there he overcame one of the most difficult sectors of his journey.

India was very special to Caroline for it was there that she had her previous great adventure of riding an elephant across 1000 km and becoming a trained Mahout, an adventure later covered in a one hour television documentary *Elephant Girl* and in the July 2001 UK edition of *Marie Claire* magazine.

India was also very special to me. On my first visit, I had fallen in love with the apparent chaos of Mumbai, with the smells, the sounds, the massive wave of people as they pour out of Victoria Station, the colours, the festivals, the noise and bustle.

So we were always going to journey through India and I contacted Bobby Sista for help.

I had first met Bobby in Brussels where we were both attending the AGM of the Worldcom Public Relations Group, one of the world's leading consortiums of independent public relations consultancies. I had decided to have an early breakfast, and seeing him sitting alone, chose to join him, even though I had never met him before. I found him to be a delightful business colleague who became a good friend. Warm, cheerful, dignified, intelligent, he ran a major advertising and public relations business in Mumbai.

We developed a friendship and mutual respect for each other, first as business partners as we worked together on a business awards scheme, World Young Business Achiever and then as friends, as our knowledge of each other grew. So when my own business took me to India, my first call was with Bobby, who invited me to dinner.

He and his wife Sheila lived in a magnificent apartment, high in a tall block, with a panorama window overlooking the Arabian Sea. His guests ranged from the father of the Indian high tech industry to a man flown in from Bangalore just to meet me. A finalist of World Young Business Achiever in Belfast, he claimed that the fame he received from his participation had been fundamental to his marketing. As I had organised the Belfast World Final, I felt proud to see him again.

We ate a home-made Indian meal and talked long into the night. One guest outlined that India's problem was illiteracy and that he was developing a new scheme to make people literate in five weeks, a scheme which would transform the economy. The government had just completed the first experiment in its implementation and were ecstatic with the results. Another felt the problem was overpopulation, that sufficient contraception was available and the real problem was that the men would not have the operation nor would they allow their wives to take precautions.

This gave Sheila Sista the chance to outline her view that one of the greatest problems faced by India was the suppression of women and only when women were given their rightful equality with men, could India hope to progress.

It was a delightful evening and I thanked Bobby profusely as he drove me back to the Taj.

I also remember a visit to Crawford Market, a concoction of smells, dead birds, sweating humanity, fruits, spices, trinkets, beggars and peddlers, secretly pulling fingers under the cloth to complete a confidential deal.

It was natural then that when we decided that Around the World would go through India, Bobby should be the first person contacted.

I found that he had retired but he introduced me to Shyam Grover, a friend of his who worked in public relations in Delhi and who was also a member of the Worldcom Public Relations Group.

Shyam took to the idea immediately, outlining proposals to Mary which caught the spirit of Around the World admirably – some fund-raising, some challenging means of transport and some 'hoop-la' as he delightfully named the fun events.

But we had a problem and it was all about Mike.

I had been warned that a mosquito bite could kill him. He has no immune system, is very vulnerable to illness and changes in diet are to be avoided. India has its problems, as any visitor will know – Bombay Belly is well documented and can be more than serious, even for someone who is fully fit. I remembered that Claire-Louise, our ever willing Girl Friday, had spent some time on her own in India and had been totally devastated by an upset stomach. What chance would Mike have, I wondered.

Maybe we should not chance our luck, maybe we should bypass India.

Mike would have none of it – he was sure he could get through India without any problems. My problem was that if he did not make it, the whole adventure would be off and we would let down everyone still to be visited, who were working their butts off for our arrival.

The arguments were long and hard, but in the end we reached a compromise.

Caroline contacted Neeraj, who had organised her elephant adventure, and he came up with a deal which could work. The adventurers would cross India as quickly as possible, staying in top quality hotels. The programme would be easy, with no fund raising and no inspirational visits to clubs, disabled organisations or societies. Furthermore, we would simply pay for the whole thing and not worry about finding donated accommodation.

Mary and I felt very uneasy, for we were breaching everything that was to do with the spirit of Around the World – there was no way we could feel comfortable about simply paying for an organised trip that included sightseeing for the adventurers but no on the ground activity that was inspirational for others. We also felt that buying all our food and accommodation, without doing any fund-raising, was a cop-out and against the spirit of the adventure.

However, we also knew that if we were going to cross India, it was very important to all the volunteers that lay ahead of us, that we did so successfully and that all the adventurers came through fit and well, so buying ourselves out of trouble became acceptable.

With significant reluctance we turned down the very exciting and challenging programme devised for us by Shyam and took the Neeraj option.

But we were still worried. Caroline told us that Mike was finding the South African programme difficult, and at one point, she suggested he skipped one of the most important welfare visits because he was so tired. Mary and I spent some time with him discussing the possibility of his staying on in South Africa to carry out hospital visits to meet young people who had been paralysed through rugby injuries and then rejoin the team in Bangkok, but in the end we all agreed that this would still have breached the spirit of Around the World.

So the final decision was made to follow Neeraj's programme and pay for it and for Mike to stay with the team as they travelled through India.

Ironically, the visit across India did produce an illness that meant sending home one of the team – but thankfully it was not Mike, nor Miles or Caroline!

Neither Miles nor Mike had visited India, so they looked forward to the sector with considerable enthusiasm. For Caroline it was quite different. Every since her elephant adventure, India had become a second spiritual home. Her diary records her excitement.

I am back. My heart thumped as our plane reached the final descent. Getting through the very special formalities of immigration into India and going through customs seemed endless but as we emerged into the arrivals section I heard that familiar shout 'Casey Boy'. It was Neeraj. I cannot find the words to capture how emotional it is to return to India to the place where my life changed, where I met, loved and was challenged by my elephant Bhadra when I carried out a lifetime dream. The smells, the sounds, the curious faces, the heat, the grit, the unpredictability, the coloured lights, the music, the dust, the smell of chai, the shaking heads. Seeing Neeraj's face and looking into those eyes that so often gave wise counsel, the smile, the mad English he speaks, our common language.

Monday
14 October 2002
Mumbai, India

Caroline introduces India to Miles and Mike and meets an old friend

I clutched my Ganesh, I felt back in my second home, it was as if I had never left.

Neeraj has arranged transport and soon the adventurers settle down for their first Indian meal, some Old Monk Rum and Kingfisher beer. There is a listlessness about them, and it is not long before they settle down in the luxury of the hotel bedrooms.

DAY
Forty-four

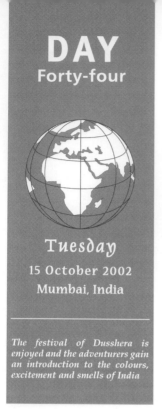

Tuesday
15 October 2002
Mumbai, India

The festival of Dusshera is enjoyed and the adventurers gain an introduction to the colours, excitement and smells of India

It is morning and the sun is rising and it is one of India's many festival days – Dusshera, a festival which celebrates the victory of good over evil and is described in the Hindu book of Ramayana. The festival day is traditionally proceeded by a nine-day fast and at sunset on the final day Hindus burn the effigy of the King of Sri Lanka, who kidnapped the wife of Ram.

The adventurers decide to join in the fun on Juhu, one of Mumbai's beaches. Mike, Miles and Caroline mingle with the teeming crowds who are exploding with excitement. It is a wonderful phantasmagoria of colour, beating drums, dancing, flowers, incense, tikka, colourful saris, wide-eyed children, trance-like beating, luminous pink candy floss, coconuts, balloons, kites.

Dolls of Durga and Shiva are immersed into the sea as the crowds become frenetic.

Hey, where did we leave Mike?

Festival of Dasara
(short guide)

Vijaya Dashami (also known as Dasara, Dashahara, Navaratri, Dusshera, Durgotdsav) is one of the very important festivals in India. Celebrated in the lunar month of Ashwin from the Shukla Paksha Pratipada (the next of the New moon day of Bhadrapada) to the Dashami or the tenth day of Ashwin, Dasara is Nepal's national festival. The word DASARA is derived from Sanskrit words 'Dasha' and 'hara' meaning removing the ten (10). In Sanskrit, 'Vijaya' means Victory and 'Dashami' means 10th day. 'Thus Vijaya Dashami' means victory on the 10th day.

Dasara is also known as Navaratri, as in the first nine days the Divine Mother Goddess Durga is worshipped and invoked in different manifestations of her Shakti. The 10th day is in honor of Durga Devi. The basic purpose behind this festival is to worship feminine principle of the Universe in the form of the divine mother to remind the teachings of the Taitareeya Upanishad, 'Matru Devo Bhava'.

Dasara coincides with the period of rest & leisure of the farmers after their strenuous hard work in their farms & fields, hence they invoke blessings of Durga in order to have a rich harvest in the next coming season. In India harvest season begins at this time and as mother earth is the source of all food the Mother Goddess is invoked to start afresh the new harvest season and to reactivate the vigor and fertility of the soil by doing religious performances and rituals which invoke cosmic forces for the rejuvenation of the soil.

On the day of Dasara, statues of the Goddess Durga are submerged in the river waters. These statues are made with the clay & the pooja is performed with turmeric and other pooja items, which are powerful disinfectants and are mixed in the river waters. This makes the water useful for the farmers & yields better crops.

Vehicles and huge machines in factories are all decorated and worshipped as Dasara is also treated as Vishwakarma Divas – National Labor Day of India.

Dasara is the festival of Victory of Good over Bad, God over Devil.

Mike is aghast as, sitting on the sand in his wheelchair, eye to belly-button with the activity, he is surrounded by dancers and beating drums. He takes it all in, fascinated as he drinks in the cocktail of cacophony of senses that India offers. Miles displays yet again his fine sense of rhythm by joining in with the other dancers, as always apparently totally untroubled by his lack of vision. Caroline is simply a self-detonating explosion of sheer joy. It is India, her India, and she has brought the adventurers to live it and love it with her.

Day creeps in to night, the sun sinks down into the Arabian Sea, and the adventurers sip fresh coconut milk.

Then they notice that in the excitement, Mike's wheelchair has sunk into the sand and his wheels are half covered. A few tugs, wiggles and pushes rectify the situation and they take him to dry land to try to get the sand off his spokes. They discover that half of it is dog shit.

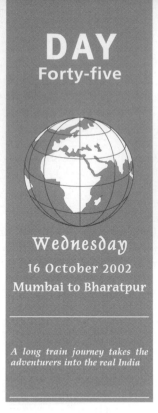

DAY
Forty-five

Wednesday

16 October 2002
Mumbai to Bharatpur

A long train journey takes the adventurers into the real India

It is train time again.

I remember my first experience of being at Mumbai's Victoria Station. As I entered, a train arrived. With the train still moving, the doors burst open and a seething brown mass of humanity ejected onto the platform. Then, like a demented tidal wave with its edges bouncing off walls and being whipped into a fury by the railings, the mass thundered towards me engulfing and carrying me to the street outside, where my feet finally found some meaningful traction with the pavement and control was restored. It was an astonishing experience that reminded me of how, as a child, I used to dive into the breakers at the Long Strand in Portrush, Northern Ireland, and let them hurl me helter-skelter onto the beach. My mother had chastised me for my recklessness but I came to no harm and learned the excitement of trying to stay in control when the forces of nature are hurling you along in a direction where they, and not you, wish to go.

Getting on an Indian train with a wheelchair is an awful lot easier than getting on a train in Monte Carlo. Amongst the maze of cardboard boxes, bundles of cloth, traffic jams of people, 24 degree heat and 90 per cent humidity, the adventurers board the train in total and utter calm. They set off for Bharatpur, a journey of 15 hours on the Paschim Express – 2AC sleeper train.

It is a day for talking. As the train rolls through the Indian countryside, Mike talks of his incident that robbed him of many of his faculties, and of how he never imagined that he would now be travelling around the world. We have always made it a rule that where Caroline and Miles went, Mike would also go and that opened his horizons and made him try things he would not normally try – like riding an ostrich. It also made him persevere when he felt that he could not do something, like the moment when, in Cape Town and on the pillion of a Harley Davidson motorcycle, he was overcome by fear and wanted to stop but refused. Now Around the Word is opening up new vistas for him and he is keen to get home and pass on the message.

Miles talks of his home in Duffield, England and his wife Stephanie. He reflects how hard it was to leave her for the time it is taking to complete Around the World, and he worries about his parents in law who have

Our luggage boards the train to Bharatpur

moved in with them to share their home. Miles and Stephanie have agreed to build an extension for them, but he is worried about progress, about the fact that Stephanie is having to cope on her own and about the cost of the extension and being able to pay for it. He also is concerned for his job at the Royal National Institute for the Blind, for once again he is away from his normal duties and is trying to keep things moving through the use of his laptop.

He tells of the time his son asked him if his sight could be restored by an operation, would he take it, and he genuinely had to say he was not sure.

Caroline reminisces – in her mind she is back travelling with Neeraj, barefoot, dusty and dirty, on top of her elephant. She thinks about her next journey and wonders what it will be. Possibilities, potential projects and adventures pass through her mind.

> I find that when I travel, it seems to open up my mind in a way it doesn't when I am stationary for too long

she writes in her diary:

> That sense of movement makes my mind move and I find ideas flowing through my brain and even better my sense of conviction that I can achieve them. I get that feeling that anything is possible, you just have to want to do it.

A long day passes as the train trundles on. It ends for Caroline and Neeraj when, after talking 'immense amounts of drivel' as she puts it, they find themselves locked out of their compartment and have to find an abandoned bunk where they spend a sleepless night due to an overactive air-conditioning unit.

DAY
Forty-six

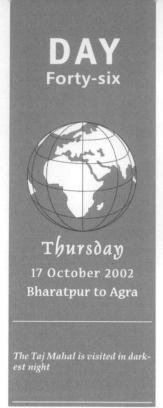

Thursday

17 October 2002
Bharatpur to Agra

The Taj Mahal is visited in darkest night

The train pulls into Bharatpur.

It is dawn. The sky is framed with a thin silvery veil hiding a blushing rising sun. Everything is stirring slowly, the smell of chai and bleary-eyed cows hangs in the air. There is the sound of morning prayer, a shuffle of tired feet. The Indian dawn offers an enticing promise of a wonderful day of travel and experience.

The team set off for their next target, the Taj Mahal at Agra. The plan is to use Ambassador taxis, ox-drawn carts, cycle rickshaws and auto rickshaws.

Neeraj has a saying 'Let it be'. It is a warning not to get too upset when things go wrong. The adventurers are forced to learn very quickly that certain things only happen in India and by leaving western minds behind the mishaps can actually be enjoyed ... An early chance to put the saying into practice is presented.

The group battle towards Agra taking a kamikaze detour through rural India, coping with ox, cows, hairy oversized pigs, camels, bicycles, rickshaws and other bizarre vehicles. Finally, the Taj Mahal is reached but it has taken much longer than planned and it is deep into the night. Nothing can be seen.

Ox drawn carts provide another way of getting there

The dejection is removed by Miles.

'I don't know what you are complaining about, you are seeing it now exactly as I see it.'

He punctures the mood of doom and replaces it with laughter.

'Let it be.'

Time to leave the Taj Mahal and get to the hotel. The mosquitoes are attacking and they pose a major threat to Mike. After negotiating the steps with Mike and his wheelchair the group approach the exit. It is not the one used to enter. Whilst the entry door had been ten foot wide, this one was only three feet wide.

Lifting a 4ft 7inch man and his wheelchair through a three foot door is not easy. In fact, it is impossible – but let it be. Nothing is impossible to the Around the World team. Jon and Caroline have successfully managed lifts onto camels, into tipper trucks, helicopters and cardboard boats, this should be easy. In any case there is no choice as if Mike cannot be pushed through the eye of that needle, he will have to stay overnight, a tasty meal for the mosquitoes.

In a series of circus-like contortions, Mike is mauled like a piece of plasticine and eased through the gap. It is so tight he flashes his bottom as his trousers are pulled off him!

Let it be, let it be.

The adventurers go for a ride in an extraordinary vehicle, Miles teaches them the meaning of the cry TIGER and Caroline returns in triumph to Delhi riding an elephant

This is the day of the triumphal entrance to Delhi. Miles, Mike and Caroline and team manager Jon get up early and prepare to board the means of transport. I am heading for Bangkok to prepare for our arrival there and get some pre-publicity.

A unique vehicle draws up at the hotel. Unlicensed for road use, but in a delightfully Indian way, it comes with a police escort. It is made up of a generator, four wheels, a large wooden chicken coop and a sort of steering wheel. Route Director Stuart Nussey will have no problem passing this as a unique means of transport. Memories go back to the wonderful Eric and his belching steam machine in Northern Ireland.

Mike is lifted on board. The travelling coop is decorated profusely, with garlands of marigolds, and for comfort there is a sheet-covered mattress with pillows. The drivers are outstandingly proud of their vehicle which they have built especially for us.

The machine sets off for the 22 km drive towards Delhi. Miles throws flowers at the endless crowds who cheer, and at the mad cyclists who seem to be trying to commit suicide as they shout out their welcomes. There is a police car somewhere but it is not to be seen. Traffic scuttles out of the way as we shriek and blow our horn. Miles adds his vocal talents by shouting out his family call TIGER every time some poor unfortunate gets in the way. The Indians are so thrilled with this that they take up the call and whoop out TIGER every few seconds. It is exciting, magical, unique.

Three kilometers from Delhi the vehicle rattles and sneezes to a dusty stop.

There we meet the elephant which is to take the adventurers to the Irish Ambassador's residence.

It is a moment of enormous poignancy for Caroline who captures it in her diary.

We meet Bull Bull, a 15 year old cow elephant. Mortifyingly I found myself crying, it is amazing how emotional it can be to return to India and be near an elephant. God, the urge to be back on my journey was total. Bull Bull's mahout saw me cry and told Neeraj to explain that he still misses and cries over his first elephant. That was after he picked his jaw up from the ground on learning that I was a trained Mahout!

Caroline checks out her elephant driving skills as we near Delhi

Mike and Miles are loaded onto the elephant, Mike delighted because people told him he would never ride an elephant, Miles gushing about the gait of Bull Bull.

I ache to touch Bull Bull's head and neck as I had ridden Bhadra. As if the mahout read my thoughts he got off the neck and offered me his seat on her shoulders. Within a second I had my legs around her neck and felt that familiar feeling I love so much – seeing the world from the back of an elephant, feeling it underneath you, smelling its breath.

Bull Bull sets off with her precious load, loping her way through the streets of Delhi. She pulls up in front of Philip McDonagh, the Irish Ambassador and the team dismount.

Riding an elephant is recorded into the log book.

But the madness is not over. Disappointed at only seeing a pitch-black version of the Taj Mahal, a taxi is commandeered at midnight – no sleep that night for the team – and after four hours, the adventurers stand in front of the Taj Mahal, mausoleum of the mughal Empress Mumtaz Mahal, and see it at sunrise. It is a symptom of the bonding that has taken place that Miles goes along too. After all, daylight makes no difference to him.

Taj Mahal, mausoleum of the mughal Empress Mumtaz Mahal

But sitting in the gentle warm redness of a soft sunrise in the world's most romantic building, Mike is devastated to get some very unromantic news, texted to him on his mobile phone. His girlfriend Sue, who was to fly out to Hong Kong for a midway reunion with Mike, has decided to break off their relationship. It is a great irony that in the presence of something so lovely, the moment should be destroyed by something so heartbreaking.

We are 47 days into our adventure, have still not reached the halfway point and all the main players are still physically and mentally fit.

But Aoife is not well. She has suffered bouts of poor health on the journey and in India the problem becomes serious. Jon talks with her and decides not to risk her health any more. She must return to the UK at once for specialist medical attention.

Aoife has made an enormous contribution to our adventure. With her magical Irish sense of humour and her undoubted talent for writing shown in their daily diary on the web site, she has brought her own dimension to the project and there is no doubt that she will be missed. India has, after all, claimed its victim and whilst I am sorry that we are to lose Aoife, I am thankful it is not one of the three adventurers.

So Aoife goes home and to skilled medical care. Let it be.

Last day in India. After returning from the morning visit to the Taj Mahal, the adventurers have one more means of transport to complete before heading off for Bangkok.

Mike goes camel riding and finds it more difficult than an ostrich

The phrase 'shaken and stirred' comes to mind when thinking about riding a camel. After his camel adventure in South Africa, Mike does not think another camel ride can be as bad.

Mike is wrong, totally wrong. He is scared stiff, so to make things more acceptable, it has been agreed that whilst Miles and Caroline should ride the camel au natural as it were, Mike could have the luxury of a cart attached to its rear.

Mike is not enthusiastic. He sits down low in his cart, unable to move, and with a direct view of the camel's backside. He wonders what it has had for lunch and seeks an umbrella. Alas no one has one to hand so Mike trusts to luck.

Perched precariously on the back of his cart, Mike is bounced about as the camel reaches full gallop. It is a wobbling, throbbing mass of muscle, and Mike's cart has no suspension, no gear change and no brakes. Rock and roll takes on a new meaning. The camel, with no sense of occasion, pulls the cart over boulders which has the effect on Mike of sitting on a pneumatic drill.

He worries about his back spasm attacks. After the cobbles of Rome, he had them constantly for two days. What is a fifteen minute ride on a camel going to do to him?

The camel reaches its destination and Mike disembarks, another means of travel safely negotiated.

It is time to leave India. Adventures there have been plenty. But Mike has coped with them all and is leaving fully fit and able to continue with the rest of the adventure. Mike, Miles, Caroline and Jon hug each other, knowing that one of the most worrying sectors has turned into sheer magic.

I breathe a sigh of very great relief.

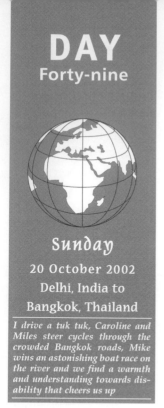

DAY
Forty-nine

Sunday
20 October 2002
Delhi, India to
Bangkok, Thailand

I drive a tuk tuk, Caroline and Miles steer cycles through the crowded Bangkok roads, Mike wins an astonishing boat race on the river and we find a warmth and understanding towards disability that cheers us up

It is early – very early – but I am determined to be at the airport to meet the adventurers as they come in from India. As usual, I have come to Bangkok a day before them to check out arrangements, attend to publicity and get my briefing from Henk, Addie and Tom.

Getting the Bangkok sector established had proved to be quite a challenge.

One of the first steps we had taken when we started it all was to find the friendly services of a good travel organiser, one who knew the ropes and how to get under them, one who could charm upgrades for us and one who knew how to find the lowest fares. My quest took me to Bales Travel in Dorking where Mandy Nickerson, Lydia Boyd and her team fell in love with our adventure and offered their help.

We booked all our major airline tickets through them and they never let us down once, despite the many changes we made. But they did more than that. When they were at the Travel Trade Show in London, they invited us to be guests of honour at a dinner they were holding for their ground handlers and others around the world. We were invited to tell them about our adventure and seek their help.

Caroline and I spoke whilst Mary worked the room, collecting cards from anyone she felt might be a useful contact for us. One of them was Addie Samerton of Destination Travel in Bangkok.

Addie was magnificent. A fund of knowledge, nothing was too much trouble for her. She became our first helper in Bangkok.

A chance chat with Sir Tom Farmer brought Henk Kiks into our Bangkok team. Sir Tom had recently returned from visiting Henk, who ran a firm called B-Quick which fitted tyres and exhausts. And it was Sir Tom who told Henk about us. He immediately volunteered to project manage our visit.

Finally the team was completed with the addition of Tom Van Blaircom, of TQPR, a leading public relations firm in Bangkok. Like me, Tom was a member of The Worldcom Public Relations Group and once more, on learning of our adventure, he offered the services of his firm free of charge.

Between them Addie, Henk and Tom make a formidable team.

When I told them of my plan to meet Miles, Mike and Caroline on arrival at the airport, Addie immediately sprang into action.

So on the morning of 20 October Addie's driver picks me up from the hotel at 4 a.m. and takes me to the airport, where I am delighted and honoured to be given the full VIP treatment and invited to wait in a special lounge. Then I am fetched and taken to the gate where Caroline, Miles, Mike and Jon arrive. I am just in time to be there to greet them. It is a wonderfully warm welcome, Mike having gone through India without a hint of medical trouble, though after getting him through the gate at the Taj Mahal we are certain he is a bit more bendy. Caroline is still flushed with the adrenalin of being back with her beloved elephants and Miles smitten with the smells of India. It is Miles – ever the philosopher – who realises that I could have met them at the hotel, but had got up especially early to be at the airport to greet them.

'Robin, thank you for being there for us,' he says in that quiet voice of his and I know he means it. Miles can be very lovable at times and I feel a great warmth for him. I recall his thoughtfulness in giving up his seat on the helicopter from Robben Island so that Mary could enjoy the thrill.

We check in to our hotel. It is before check in time, which means that Mike's adapted room is not ready. It is a major blow to him for after two nights without sleep, and added to the upset caused by the bad news from Sue, he is out on his wheels. He is offered a temporary alternative which turns out to have a loo and bathroom that are inaccessible to him. He tries to wash and change only to get stuck in the bathroom door with his front wheels just down a step and the back wheels stuck fast in the narrow room.

'There was no way I could extricate myself' he tells me. 'So Jon had to come to my rescue. After a considerable lack of sleep, the unexpected news from Sue and the need to freshen up quickly before our start of the 'ways' in Bangkok, it seemed like the last straw and resulted in a few tears.'

Soon, Mike's adapted room is ready and there is an accessible shower with room for his Seatcase, a fold-up mini chair.

It is action time again, the television cameras are there, as are the reporters and photographers. Henk points to a tuk tuk – a motorised three-wheeler with room for four, and tells us we have to find our way to the Grand Palace in it.

'Who is driving?' I ask.

'One of you,' smiles Henk. He has a lovely mischievous grin.

There is no debate about who is driving for Miles has taken the - driver's seat.

'I used to ride a motor-bike before I went blind,' he says. 'I can do this.'

We all get up on board, Miles starts the engine and heads off into the Bangkok traffic. Wild shouting from the three of us fails to stop him running into the back of a stationary police car. Sometimes I think Miles forgets he is blind. I rethink the proposition. The traffic in Bangkok is chaos

Robin driving Tuk Tuk with Police motorcyclist (*inset*) and Caroline behind

gone mad. Miles and Caroline cannot see, Mike cannot reach the pedals. There is only one person left and that is me.

'Come on Robin, no time to show fear. You can do this,' I whisper to myself.

We set off again, with Miles, Mike and Caroline hanging on at the back. I sense they had more confidence when Miles was driving. He is waving his white stick around the tuk tuk, shouting warnings out to the watching crowds.

I am having a battle driving the thing. I am terrified of stalling it in front of all the cameras, so I decide to stay in one gear, and use a combination of frantic revving and furious use of the clutch.

But where am I going?

'Follow that police motorcycle' Henk had shouted at me. The snag is that as we make our jerky progress into the cyclone of traffic, the local paparazzi are not going to let a small thing like a police motorcycle get in the way of their good story. Our tuk tuk is engulfed with a tidal wave of reporters, photographers, television cameramen, in their own tuk tuks, cycles, and running along beside us. In the middle of it all, the normal Bangkok traffic surges and flows around us. Some Kamikaze cameramen come up along side me and shout 'Smile'. I do so, but a fine flow of Anglo Saxon words fill my brain.

We are still amazed at the reaction to us, and as Mike said later:

In Bangkok I had never seen so many camera lenses pointing at us as we went through the streets. It was an insight into how celebrities must feel and I am not used to it. I am not sure I ever would be. There have been other times like this, such as the ride into Carlow when I feel that too much attention is being paid to me. I don't feel it is justified and I find it strange what I have done to deserve it. I am uncomfortable when people say I am amazing about how I cope. After all I am merely living my life. Despite this, it has become apparent that our 'message' of living life to the full has been well accepted and the reactions we have had have been wonderful. When someone says we have changed their attitude to life it is a very humbling experience and something I will never forget.

Back on the tuk tuk, we continue to make our erratic progress.

'Are you sure you can drive this thing?' asks Mike. Once again, I realise just how much he trusts us. If I am about to crash, Miles and Caroline can jump off, as can I – but not Mike.

'Mike, can you see a police motor-bike?' I cry out in desperation.

It is Miles who answers.

'I can' shouts Miles, 'It is just up in front.'

At times I could murder him. He often catches us out by pretending he can see.

Suddenly the traffic swarm parts. I see a roundabout of sorts, with a policeman on it. He waves me to the right, so I turn – and there up ahead of me stands The Grand Palace.

Flushed with confidence, I twist the accelerator and open up the tuk tuk. No formula racing car ever went faster, as we storm to the Palace. Crowds cheer, and there are the faithful Henk, Addie and Tom, tears of laughter streaming down their cheeks.

Thoughtfully, they are ready for us. It is hot hot hot, and we are dripping with sweat. Henk plies us with water and cold towels. The cameras records it all, even the wiping off of the sweat. What a television shot that will make, I think.

Time to move on, and this time we climb on board rickshaw cycles. We decide that Miles and Caroline should do the driving, Mike and I would navigate. We are to get as far as the river.

Caroline sets off at a furious pace and in the panic to keep up, she causes a wonderful aura of mayhem. We later learn that the need for speed was dictated by her knowledge that she is pouring with sweat, her Around the World outfit is crumpled, squashed and travel-worn, and Mike keeps telling her that the television cameras are about to catch up! Her efforts are in vain, for the next day, the papers are full of a very puffy and sweaty Caroline panting to get her bike moving.

Meanwhile Miles, with me in the passenger seat, is riding as though he is sighted. He really is uncanny, having developed acute senses through which he seems to feel obstacles that lie ahead. I give him commentated instructions, and he thanks me for them, but I realise how inadequate I am at it. Go a bit right is hardly a good instruction to a blind man riding a bike – how far right and for how long? Why are you telling me to go right? What is in the way? Is there any danger or is it nothing to worry about?

We reach the river. Now our task is to take one of the long boats downstream to our hotel. But first, Henk has organised a reception for us. A tent is set up on the lawn, there is tea and sandwiches, and many people, all of whom want to meet us. Vunsadej Thavarasukha, The Director of Tourism of Thailand, makes a speech. We learn that Thailand is making a special effort to increase the quality of the facilities it provides for disabled tourists and we congratulate him for this. But we also tell him that it is not so much the facilities but the way disabled people are treated that counts. Retaining dignity is of paramount importance. We remember the handlers at Luton Airport who treated Mike like a load of potatoes, in front of all the other passengers and did it so badly that they split open his skin. We remember the complete gentleness, affection, understanding of the people in Thailand. The analogy is complete when a small girl comes to Mike in his

The media get set to film Mike boarding the long boat, clearly I have seen it all before!

wheelchair, offers him a cup of tea and, with Jon standing next to him, asks him, 'Do you take sugar?'

Only we understand the irony.

We board the long boat. Fascinating things, they originated when some bright spark put a massive lorry engine onto a boat, fixed a long propeller shaft to it and the whole thing worked by lifting the engine in and out of the water.

As I have driven the tuk tuk, Caroline and Miles have pedalled the cycles, we decide it is time for Mike to have a go.

We strap him to a box next to the engine and off we go.

Of course, Caroline, Miles, Jon and I know what is about to happen. Mike simply opens the throttle full blast and with a bellow of surprised rage, the motor roars into top revs and off we hurtle, leaving a startled and outmanoeuvred media boat in our wake.

The race is exciting, exhilarating and probably very dangerous. Mike keeps the engine flat out, the media try to catch us, and small boats using the river flee. Once again Miles goes into emergency mode by standing at the bow and waving his white stick at everyone. Cries of TIGER ring out.

We reach our dock. We are wet, but deliriously happy. Henk has been in the boat with us and I later learn that he told Sir Tom Farmer, who invited him to help, that he was overcome with admiration.

It is Caroline's birthday and two of the staff who work for her have ordered a magnificent chocolate cake of sinful proportions. The team present her with a stuffed elephant and she swears to take it with her for the rest of the adventure.

A good day, with tuk tuks, rickshaw cycles and a long boat added to our growing list. We send details off to Route Director Stuart Nussey, confident that he will approve them all. We have used cycles before, but never of the kind presented to us in Bangkok and certainly never in such traffic.

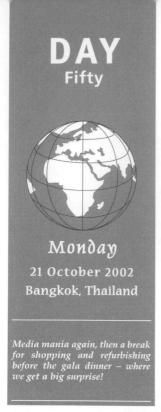

Media mania again, then a break for shopping and refurbishing before the gala dinner – where we get a big surprise!

Live TV is always a fun challenge. We start this morning with an appearance live on breakfast television. Our driver, complete with Henk in tow, picks us up early from our hotel and we head off into the early morning rush hour. Traffic jams hold us up and then there is an explosion of rage as our driver realises he has missed a vital turning to the television studio.

We arrive just in time, are rushed through make up and take our positions on a large sofa. The interview is in English, a translator tells the viewers what is going on. We find we are becoming quite famous. Film footage of the previous day's travels are shown and it brings home to us what an amazing adventure we are on. We all watch and are unable to appreciate that we are watching ourselves. Television is funny like that. It makes you larger than you really are. We all realise how easy it would be for us to be deceived by the messages put out about us and make the mistake of believing them.

Morning television gives us an early start to another day in Bangkok

When the broadcast is over, we go back to our hotel. We have the rest of the morning and early afternoon to prepare ourselves for the gala dinner in the evening. It is a time for shopping, for cleaning, catching up on e-mails and resting. The problem with shopping is that anything we buy has to take a trip with us for the rest of the adventure or be posted home at once. There are great bargains in laptops, but we are already baggaged up with techno stuff and adding to the pile of luggage is not a good plan. But it is fun to look and to sample new foods.

In the evening, we are taken by luxurious limousine to the Sheraton Hotel where the Rotary Club have organised a dinner to raise funds for the Prosthesis Foundation of Thailand. By now we have attended many of these functions but still I am concerned about the right speaking order. Technically my best speaker is Miles, for impulsiveness and establishing rapport with the audience it is Caroline, whilst emotionally it is Mike. I decide once again to use Miles to open and win them to us, Mike to get them really plugged in emotionally and Caroline to deliver the big finish.

As usual, there is the pre-dinner drinks reception to attend. Henk Addie and Tom tell me how astounded they are with the adventure. They had all wondered if we would live up to the reputation we had established on our web site, as they read details of our approach to Thailand, and all three agreed that we were as good as our reputation! This is an enormous relief to us, it is very hard knowing that there are crowds of people who have turned out to meet what they see as 'heroes' and to realise that it is you they are talking about.

We move into dinner and there is a bedlam of chatter around the room. The first course is served, and whilst this is happening, the Master of Ceremonies invites me to talk. I am horrified to discover that instead of waiting for silence at the end of the meal, we are going to have to battle our way through the eating and serving of the courses. To make matters worse, many of the diners simply ignore us, and go on chattering away loudly and animatedly to each other. We do our best but it in our view it is a disaster. Little do we know at the time that about half of the audience – the ones that were making a noise – cannot speak English and we have no translator. We feel better when other speakers talk, regardless of the fact that no one is listening.

Steve Miller, Regional Director for Rolls-Royce in Thailand, presents us with ornate glass tuk tuks to commemorate our visit and the main feature of the auction, slotted in between more speeches, is four model tuk tuks and a copy of *Around the World in 80 Days* signed by all of us. There are two lady auctioneers and their double act is lively, entertaining and brings in the bids.

At the end of the evening, our hosts from Rotary and Henk tell us that it has been a great success. They assure us that the speaking arrangements over the serving of food is quite normal, and that the guests who did not speak English were fully briefed on our adventure and were there to show their support.

It does us all good. We have become accustomed to total silence and full attention when we speak and it is quite difficult for us to move into another culture of speaking.

Any reservations we have vanish after the dinner. We are all surrounded by guests eager to congratulate us, to encourage us, and to thank us for coming to Thailand. We later learn that enough money has been raised to buy 500 rudimentary artificial legs.

Today we say thank you to the wonderful Amari Hotel and take our leave of Thailand

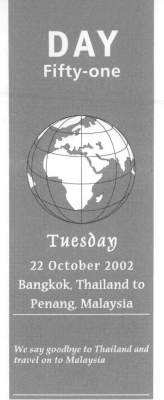

The trouble with our adventure is that we have so little time to develop friendships. Henk, Addie and Tom have been wonderful to us during our time. Nothing has been too much trouble and when the cameras have been focused on us, they have stood quietly out of the way and made no attempt to get publicity for themselves. They are truly great people and we have fallen in love with them.

We have lunch with Pierre-Andre Pelletier, General Manager of the Amari Hotel, who has most generously donated our accommodation. It is genuine Thai food of the highest quality. What a feast! The courses just keep coming with everything beautifully presented and decorated with flowers. The drama of the meal is emphasised by the fact that outside a tropical storm is bending the palm trees almost down to the ground, water is showering off buildings and black clouds are hiding the sky.

It was Mary who had worked out that by now, the team would need a break. South Africa had been heavy with speaking duties and visits, whilst the travel across India had posed some major challenges. Ahead lay the very busy schedule for Singapore, before the frightening schedule for Hong Kong.

So she had decided to make the journey down the Malaysian Peninsula as stimulating, but as easy and relaxing, as possible, with a break of thee days in the sunshine, away from the crowds.

Guy Chaplin was the man who worked the miracle. Another member of the Worldcom Public Relations Group, he ran the Malaysian office of TQPR. Whilst I did not know him well, I had known one of his senior staff Angela Tan, for some time through our mutual Worldcom membership. Some six months before the 'off' I wrote to Guy telling him of the adventure and he invited me to visit him to discuss what might be possible.

I found him to be wonderfully enthusiastic and supportive of our adventure. He would attempt to find sponsorship for us, and he talked about many exciting means of transport that could be used. However, when I told him that an ambition was to have a sector by car with the blind adventurers driving, his eyes lit up.

The Malaysian Grand Prix Circuit was one of his clients.

'Why not get them to drive high powered rally cars in their own race on the track?' he suggested.

At first it seemed impossible. Miles is completely blind whilst although Caroline can see a bit, she has never even driven a car. Then I remembered that what we were doing was all about not accepting things are impossible.

'OK Guy. If you can fix it, you have got a deal.'

Guy is as good as his word. By the time we have reached Bangkok, he has a complete programme in place – some wonderful means of transport, a break at a luxury seaside resort, and a unique five lap race on the Malaysian Grand Prix circuit between Miles and Caroline.

I was later to learn that Guy had not been able to line up a major sponsor to take up all the costs, but nevertheless, he went ahead and set it all up, bearing any expenses himself. Whilst it is our job to inspire, it is people like Guy who inspire us.

I think about my own positioning. There is a massive welcome and social programme waiting for us in Hong Kong and Mary is going out there early to oversee its organisation and help prepare everything for our arrival. But there is a similar programme being set up in Singapore by the International Foundation and it is clear that as we approach them, they too would welcome one of the team to be there in advance so that things could be checked out and pre-publicity obtained.

I decide that Jon can be in charge for the Malaysian sector and I should get to Singapore to help there. I regret this decision when I ask Guy where he has arranged for the team on their first night in Penang.

'The Eastern and Orient Hotel.'

'Is that a 3, 4 or 5 star hotel?' I ask.

'They like to think it is a 6 star hotel,' is the reply.

I travel to the airport and check in. Only then do I discover that I am not wearing my topper. I have left it in one of Destination Asia's car which Addie Samerton had so kindly provided. A frantic phone call reveals that the top hat is now on its way, with new passengers, to a holiday resort outside of Bangkok. It is tragic and I wonder if I will see it again.

As I am about to board the plane, my mobile rings and it is Henk.

'Robin, we have found the topper, and will get it to your hotel in Singapore.'

Henk is a wonderful, marvellous man.

On arrival at their hotel in Malaysia, the team are allocated a butler to look after them. Nothing is too much trouble. They are given the current exchange rate in Euros, UK Dollars and Sterling to three decimal places, and the hotel receptionist has phoned in advance for a cocktail order which is ready on arrival.

Mike is delighted with his room. Because of the layout and thought gone into special facilities needed for disabled travellers, he is able to enjoy almost complete independence. The room also allows him to take a shower unaided, only the third time this has happened since the start of the adventure.

Hotel shower rooms have been a particular problem to me

he writes in his diary:

> And after staying in innumerable hotels I have found only two that are equipped for me to have a shower independently. The Oberoi in Mumbai and the P and O in Penang were both superb but the latter lacked an emergency call and the shower seat could have been more substantial and padded. The small folding wheelchair I have called the SEAT proved to be an invaluable piece of equipment and has allowed me to take showers on it in three other hotels albeit with someone to propel me. One of the most frequent difficulties is the basin which more often than not is placed in a way that prevents getting closer than arm's length because in the chair one's knees are against it.

Miles, however, has an unusual problem. Because of the size, layout, and the stylish but different furniture it takes him quite a time to find his way around.

'Most hotel bedrooms are alike in their layout so I usually know where things are' he explains.

Caroline adopts her normal means of exploration by believing she can see everything and walking around confidently until she bumps into things.

The team meet on the cocktail terrace. It is now evening, and they agree that they are once again staying in one of the great hotels of the world.

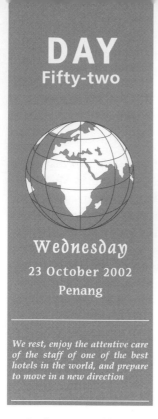

We rest, enjoy the attentive care of the staff of one of the best hotels in the world, and prepare to move in a new direction

The P and O in Penang is a wonderful hotel. The staff are attentive to the special needs of the team and have an instinctive understanding how to deal with people who have special physical challenges. It is so easy to help too much, so easy to patronise, so easy to speak to the enabler and not to the person direct. The staff make none of these common mistakes.

Now over fifty days into the adventure, the team reviews progress. On setting out they believed that the major challenge was to undertake over eighty ways of travelling and indeed the title of our adventure emphasises this point. However, in South Africa it became clear that there was a more important thing for us to accomplish. It was clear that in visiting people who were facing up to some kind of physical or mental challenge and talking to them about our adventure, we were opening up new doors for them, and shining some light into dark places.

And so, engulfed in the luxury of the hotel and the love of its attentive staff, the team rest, recover and talk about how they are going to fulfil the real message of our adventure – to encourage and enable others to live their lives to their full potential, no matter what physical and mental challenges are to be faced.

Originally, Around the World in 80 Ways was intended to be a one-off adventure. However, it is now clear to me that we are making a mistake if we do not continue to support what we have started. It is unfair to light a torch and not help to keep it burning. So many times I have listened to motivational speakers light up an audience and know that without support the fires lit will soon burn out. I decide that when we are all home safe and sound, I will look at how the messages we are putting out can be supported by an ongoing Around the World Foundation.

Jon is talking about guiding a blind person. He and Miles have been through many adventures together and although Jon has never trained as an enabler, he has learned much from the association.

The team ride trishaws, cross the Penang Bridge in a Lagonda, use a funicular railway and argue about costs

'Let's suppose that I give the warning '*Careful*' to Miles. What does that mean – duck? Stop? Slow down? Move right? Or what? I often say '*steps ahead*', but I don't say whether they go up, down or around a corner, when we are going to get there, how steep they are or why we are bothering to go up and down them in the first place.'

Miles readily says that Jon has saved his life on at least two occasions and it is chastening for the rest to learn that, although Miles trusts Jon totally, Jon himself is still learning how to guide Miles.

Then there is Mike. By now the team know that there is nothing that upsets Mike more than being left out of anything the others are asked to do, because of his own challenges. How about a swim? Why not jump over this gap? If you hear me blow a whistle, run for the nearest exit? Let's go and buy a pair of shoes? Paddle this canoe? Ride this bicycle? Let's have a shower? Mike is utterly extraordinary in the way he refuses to accept that he cannot do things – but the reality is that there are some things that are just not on and we have made it a rule that unless we can all do it then none of us will do it.

In addition Mike has to meet that very strange challenge that people like him must face. He is handsome, intelligent, eloquent, and able to do most things. Yet people automatically assume that he is stupid, unable to talk, has no need to be fashionable, and must be spoon-fed. How stupid, how insulting.

Caroline is holding up to the pressure well. Her main characteristic is being stubborn. She simply will not give in. On her Indian journey by elephant, she cried herself to sleep many times, with pain, with the difficulty of what she was trying to do, with loneliness and with coping with being the only girl in an all-male expedition. Yet not once did the thought of giving up and going home even enter her head. She was there to do a job and she would do it whatever the odds. On Around the World, she is working like a horse. Even with her partial sight, so many problems fall to be solved by Jon and Caroline. Whilst she is playing the role of a heroine adventurer, she has no qualms about lugging the luggage around, pushing and pulling trolleys, begging for upgrades on flights for Mike, not herself, and generally getting things put right that in her view are wrong. Her charisma and stubbornness often mean that she gets her own way, even when another way might be the right way to go.

Whilst their stay in Malaysia was planned by Mary as a relaxing break, the team need the adrenalin rush of undertaking some means of travel each day, so after the usual media conference, they mount trishaws that Guy Chaplin has found and head off for Penang, a journey that takes them 40 minutes. Douglas Fox is waiting for them in a wonderful 1934 open-topped Lagonda and he takes them over the very spectacular Penang Bridge. Many other drivers hoot and cheer as the adventurers pass, but they realise it is the car, and not they, that is the subject of admiration.

Then it is up Penang Hill by vernacular railway and another means of transport.

Appearances are deceptive. Mike is highly impressed with the funicular railway as he wheels towards the train, for the doors are wide enough for wheelchair access and there is only one step. Halfway up, however, he has to change trains and it is another story, for the wonderful access facilities available at the bottom have disappeared. However, having manoeuvred Mike on trains in Monte Carlo and exited the Taj Mahal through a 3 ft hole, in and out of a helicopter, a cardboard boat and a tipper truck, the present challenge presents no problems and Mike reaches the top – only to find that between him and the most magnificent view of Penang Island there lurks a wall which exceeds the height of someone in a wheelchair.

The evening is spent with Adrian Brown, Manager of the O and E Hotel, who hosts the adventurer to a marvellous dinner and they are at a loss how to thank him.

But a problem arises.

Knowing of my great concern about running out of cash, Jon decides to have a team talk and see where cutbacks might be made.

Miles has a massive telephone bill and at hotel rates, this has become a major expenditure item. Jon mentions this to Miles and asks him if he could cut down. His reaction gives all of us an insight into how much Miles relies on his laptop to communicate and keep in touch with the world. For Miles, regular e-mail contact is important for his laptop has special voice activated software and he does not have the facility that others do of going into an internet café. He points out that we try to get travel upgrades for Mike to help deal with his pressure sores and we should show the same consideration towards him.

It is very unusual for Miles to talk about the downside of being blind and we all realise that, like the rest of us, the pressures of what we are doing are beginning to tell.

Fifty-three days on the road with hardly a break can take its toll. Mary has so successfully foreseen this and now comes the masterpiece, arranged at her request by the wonderful Guy Chaplin.

But first there is a cramped twelve hour journey by van from Penang to Dungun. The spectacular jungle scenery helps to make the journey pass quite quickly, with stops only for toilets, a puncture and a roadside coffee.

On arrival at the Tanjong Jara Resort, Miles, Caroline and Mike find that Mary and Guy have arranged a magnificent surprise for them. They are not in an hotel, but an exclusive resort with all the luxury amenities. Four nights accommodation and food are offered to them, thanks to sponsorship owners YTL. Stunningly designed to offer a wholesome lifestyle experience, the resort is magical. The rooms overlook the beach, the food is fantastic, the weather perfect and the staff brilliant. They have even built Mike a ramp to allow access to

Luxury lazing on the beach, Mike resumes his relationship with lying on the sand, and the team prepare to go motor racing

the shower and the loo! Phileas Fogg never had it so good on his adventure!

In her diary Caroline writes:

Waking up to the sound of the sea only minutes walk away is wonderful. This place is beautiful, it is built into a tropical jungle with each room hidden amongst trees throbbing with the sound of beetles and birds and all with a view of the empty beach. Every attention has been paid to make this place utterly relaxing, all the buildings are made out of wood, are low and hidden by thick vegetation.

At breakfast the team decide what to do – go relax on the beach, by the pool, have a complimentary massage.

Imagine not having been on a beach in nine years, especially when you love sun, sea, sand and swimming. Since his incident Mike has avoided beaches because of the safety factor of getting stuck in sandy ground.

The team determine that if they are going for a swim, then so is Mike. The day before, Mike has watched the rest jumping around and playing in the sea whilst he sat in his chair on the grass, not even on the sand because it was too soft for his chair. Though everyone had a great time, Jon kept looking at him looking at them, and wishing he could join in.

And so you shall Mike, for now it is time for your swim. Jon and Caroline chair-lift Mike out of his wheelchair and carry him down to the water. Unknown to us, before she left Ireland, Caroline had asked her fitness trainer to strengthen her muscles for lifting Mike on and off things. How thoughtful and caring is that! Caroline supports him with her legs and lets the sea crash over him. Like the time he discovered he could scuba dive, Mike develops an inner explosion of delight. He could not feel the sand between his toes, but once again he felt the sea on his back.

For Caroline there is a special task. The Malaysian Grand Prix race between her and Miles is soon to take part, she will be driving a Lotus Elise and not only is she not allowed to drive, she does not know how to drive, having never driven a car in her life.

Lessons are hastily organised, first in a van and then in a Peugeot Saloon. Caroline drives 200 yards forwards, attempting to get into fourth gear, and then reverses back. Having done this a couple of times, she declares herself fit for the grand prix. Always the optimist, is our Caroline.

The Sepang Malaysian Formula One Grand Prix circuit outside of Kuala Lumpur has been the scene of many dramatic races. But never in the history of motor racing has anything taken place to rival the extraordinary race held on Wednesday, 30 October 2002.

The day of the great Grand Prix when two blind people race each other in a Proton Formula Once Pace Car and a Lotus Elise

Caroline is nervous and is shaking at times. Miles is smiling the smile that tells the rest that he is nervous. Mike is still suave, but he too is looking uncomfortable. Jon is rather more white than normal.

Of course they are nervous for the Around the World Challenge that Guy Chaplin has arranged for them is for Miles and Caroline to have a five lap race on the track driving high-powered cars, with only Jon and Mike in the passenger seats to tell them where to go and when to brake. And whilst Miles used to drive when he was sighted, Caroline has never driven a car before, except a couple of practices lasting five minutes on a beach in Malaysia. It is like stepping up from walking along a beach to running in the Olympics in one go.

Guy has stuck his neck out in a big way. He has invited a coachload of media, including four television stations, at least ten newspapers and a host of specialist racing magazine representatives, to witness the event. They refuse to believe it is not a hoax.

The day starts hot and humid with two media conferences, one in Kuala Lumpur and the other from the hallowed Ferrari pits on the track. The second is addressed by Edward Tan, the Malaysian Lotus representative, who is also nervous for he has agreed to allow a blind man he had never met get into his brand-new race tuned metallic-silver Lotus straight off the showroom floor. For Caroline, there is a highly souped-up Proton car, used as a safety car in the Grands Prix.

The media are sceptical, they suggest either that the two are not blind, or that they will go very slowly. It is true that on a good day Caroline can see a few metres in front of her, the rest is a blur, but Miles is totally blind and neither of them have any intention of going slowly.

First, the team are driven around the circuit by Admire Shahrul, the Sepang Circuit professional Principal Instructor, to give them a feel for corners, straights and chicanes.

Then it is time for the race. Guy has arranged for the full circuit Grand Prix team of marshals, safety, first aid to be in attendance. The Chief

Marshall gives his briefing, explaining the meaning of different coloured flags. He and his team are stunned into quizzical, unbelieving silence to be told that the flags would be superfluous as both the drivers are blind and would not see them!

Miles has a final chat with Edward Tan and then heads for his Lotus, using his white stick to find it. One of the track officials hands him a helmet and Mike passes him his white stick for safekeeping. At that point the whole impossibility of what is happening strikes the official, who now realises that he has just put a totally blind man in the driving seat of a very powerful car and that very man is about to drive off and race another blind person. He shakes his head is disbelief. It is a moment of great absurdity.

Miles lowers himself into the driving position, puts on his helmet and then puts his hand out the door and onto the tarmac. He is so close he can flatten his palm on it.

Caroline is still surrounded by a crowd of media who continually probe her. She confirms that she is registered blind, has never driven a car before and yes, she is about to race another blind driver in a Lotus Elise whilst she would drive a Proton Grand Prix safety car.

Mike is lifted out of his wheelchair and placed next to Caroline. Jon takes up position with Miles and very gently they set off on their practice lap.

Jon and Miles spend it furiously trying to establish a working communications system for explaining when to accelerate, brake and how much to steer/understeer in and out of the corners that hit them with bewildering rapidity. Soon they get into a rhythm, with Miles yelling at Jon to shout directions more loudly to be heard over the Lotus race-customised engine capable of 9,000 rpm in each gear. There are so many factors to keep in mind and accurate split-second timing is essential, highlighted by the car drifting at times, accompanied by the pungent acrid smell of burning rubber being sucked into the Lotus cockpit. Mike simply tells Caroline what to do, but she has an instinctive feel for it.

For Caroline and Mike, the experience is different. Unlike Miles, Caroline has never driven a car before. Unlike Miles, the wellbeing of engines and their vital statistics are not of importance. Unlike Miles, she does not have to worry about when to change gear, for the Proton is automatic. So she and Mike use their practice laps to rehearse their communications code – faster, slower, left, right. Not Einstein stuff, but hopefully it will work.

But high noon has arrived. It is time for the race to start.

There is media bedlam on the start line. Television cameras, recorders, notebooks, cameras, and screamed out questions fill the air. Highly nervous track officials wonder when they will wake up from the nightmare, but realise it is all too real. Edward Tan wonders in what condition he will get his Lotus back. Guy Chaplin wonders if he has done the right thing.

Caroline positions herself in pole position on the grid, right where world-champion Michael Schumacher had positioned his Ferrari recently at the start of the Malaysian Grand Prix.

Miles draws up next to her.

Then the media withdraw, the flag drops, Caroline floors her accelerator, the automatic gear copes with the outrageous abuse and keeps the engine roaring, the tyres scream out in startled agony, a strip of rubber carpets the track and Caroline and Mike hurtle off into the distance.

Jon and Miles do absolutely nothing for two seconds as Jon has not been looking in the right direction and has missed the dropping flag. His first inkling that the race has begun is seeing Caroline and Mike roar off in a cloud of high-powered dust.

A frantic yell from Jon results in Miles flooring the accelerator, dropping the clutch, and accompanied by a ferocious roar from the engine, they head off in hot pursuit as Miles cannot bear the thought of being beaten by an Irish lady with just two driving lessons under her belt. Blindness has nothing to do with it, competition is the adrenalin-pumping reason for his misery.

Back at the start, there is chaos. The television camera teams, expecting the two to head off at around 20 kph, have been completely outfoxed as both cars hit over 100 kph within seconds. Camera air shots abound. There is extreme and immediate consternation amongst the onlookers, and in particular Edward Tan who has just seen his gorgeous Lotus hurtle off being driven by a man who is completely blind. The whole closed-circuit television monitoring around the track is fully operational, with officials and race instructors checking out progress on all screens. Their body language shows signs of extreme mental agony.

Carbonara wants to get some good camera shots of the action on the circuit and so Guy, who is no slouch when it comes to driving high-powered cars, takes him out on circuit. He hits the straight, has his car flat out at 170 kph, but cannot catch up.

Caroline takes one trip off the track, but manages to keep her engine running and is soon guided back on route by a calm-voiced Mike. But it is enough to let Miles take the lead. Caroline rejoins the race with a focused calm.

'Please let me pass Miles' her heart thumps, as a steely determination replaces her pre-race nerves. Mike makes the calls, and Caroline catches up with Miles. But it is not enough, for although Miles makes one hair-raising skid, caught in full gory details on his tape recorder, he stays ahead and crosses the finishing line first, receiving the chequered flag.

Both cars are back in one piece. Both drivers are back in one piece. Both navigators are back in one piece.

Miles climbs out and immediately and in all innocence, asks for his white stick. The media go bananas, now they know it is not a dream, now they know that a blind man has just driven a car at 200 kph and that a woman, who is registered blind and has never driven a car before, has been tracked at over 140 kph.

Caroline pulls up after Miles. She runs and screams like a banshee on Benzedrine, jumps onto Miles and shouts, I was driving, me myself and I was driving. She is on a high, a very high high, and so is Miles. So too are Jon and Mike, who have shown enormous bravery and have guided their charges safely around the circuit.

Now it is time for the podium. Someone yells out that Mike will not be able to get to the top of his podium. How daft, if two blind people can drive cars at over 150 kph, getting Mike onto a podium is easy peasy. Of course, moments later everyone is on the podium, drivers and navigators in a state of pure euphoria.

It is over. The impossible challenge has been achieved. Now on my own, I pour myself a large gin and tonic and savour its relaxing balm.

For the Around the Word challenge, the events on the circuit were not about motor racing, they were about trust. For Miles to drive his car at 200 kph, he had to have complete trust in Jon. For Caroline to drive her car at over 140 kph she had to have complete trust in Mike. And for Mike and Jon to be in the cars at those speeds with blind drivers, they had to have complete trust in Caroline and Miles.

I know that the event had been set up to showcase the fact that by building up confidence and trust between people, the impossible is totally possible.

Thank you Guy, and thank you Miles, Mike, Caroline and Jon. You were brilliant.

Remember the date. 30 October 2002 – the day when trust between people won the day.

We are in Singapore.
Problems! For some time, Caroline has felt pain under her arm. She is one of those people who will not call a doctor until she is convinced that the end is nigh – anything else is treated by a stiff upper lip and a good talking to the affected part.

Caroline gets gory, we add the duck song to the fish song, our charity status is questioned Mike gets a touch of the nerves and Mary dances on the stage

She lifts up her arm and Mike, not the most squeamish of people, lets out a yelp. Her armpit is alive – red blisters, yellow liquid, rancid poison oozing, the poor girl must be in agony. But with her eyesight, under her arms is not an easy place for her to see in any case, and she has missed the infestation that has been spreading. Miles insists on having the gory scene described to him in detail for in his previous adventures he has acquired excellent amateur knowledge of bumps and bruises and is sure he can offer a diagnosis and treatment. On learning the gory details even he quickly decides that more skilled assistance is appropriate.

We bundle Caroline to the doctor, who gives her an almighty telling off for not coming earlier. A brief check also reveals an extensive sore on her leg. Ointment is applied in vast quantities, and we make her promise never to leave it so late again to seek medical aid.

My topper has been delivered to the hotel, none the worse for its short holiday by the seaside in Thailand and I am glad to be reunited with it. It has become an emotional part of me and as soon as I put it on I become Phileas Fogg.

Our first means of travel is by amphibious vehicle, otherwise known as a DUKW, pronounced Duck. As we are boarding, Mary calls me on my mobile phone from our hotel, where she is checking out the arrangements for the gala dinner. There is a major emergency.

Dawn Wee's dinner is to be held that night to raise funds for local charities to be distributed through the Singapore International Foundation, we are also to receive some of the proceeds to keep us on the road. With only eight hours to go before the dinner, Mary has been advised that the Singapore government has decided that we are not a proper charity and that the function cannot take place – this despite the fact that we had sent our charity number and trust deed in advance.

I am asked to contact the Scottish Charities Commission at once and get them to confirm that we are a legitimate charity. I point out that it is midnight in Scotland and there would be no one at the Scottish Charities

Commission and by the time their office was open, the dinner in Singapore time would be over. In addition, our solicitor who arranged the charitable status – Gavin McEwan of Turcan Connell in Edinburgh – could be reached at home, but he could not do anything until the charity commission opened.

No confirmation, no dinner, I am told.

I do some quick thinking – I call it that, Mary calls it slow pondering, probably somewhere in the middle is about right. We have been invited to have tea with the President of Singapore that very afternoon and I decide to seek his aid. I tell a Director of the Singapore International Foundation about this. I am told to calm down, it is simply the Government showing us who is in charge, I must stay out of it, they will handle it. The dinner will be reinstated as long as I leave it in their hands and do not interfere.

I take their advice and board the garishly yellow DUKW, a left-over amphibious vehicle from World War Two that is to take us downtown. The team are tired from their journeys and Mary and I are deeply depressed at the latest challenge to be thrown at us.

A guide on the DUKW starts to chatter bonhomie – probably right for happy tourists but very wrong for our mood at the moment. She has misjudged her audience and babbles on incessantly, pouring out statistics about Singapore. Who cares? At that moment, certainly not us.

All set for a watery trip and to learn the Duck song

If she would but stop for a second and study the party, she would realise that something is amiss. But she is in autoguide mode and we are fed up.

Mike is still deeply upset about the text message he received in India from Sue breaking off their relationship. He had been looking forward to meeting her at the next sector in Hong Kong. He woke up depressed and as the day grows on, everything seems negative and he is struggling to hold back the tears.

Caroline, Miles and Jon are deeply infected by Mike's unhappiness but there is nothing they can do about it other than offer their love. I am concerned about Mike, but am beside myself with anxiety over the possible cancellation of the dinner, which is to generate some very badly needed funds to enable us to continue our adventure.

But incredibly, despite all of us being in the blackest of moods, professionalism comes to our aid. Slowly we rediscover our normally bright spirits. We have all been given little plastic ducks, and now a quite insane duck song is blasting out over the loudspeaker. Caroline joins in somewhat hysterically, the others take her lead. Miles finds out that by blowing into their beaks, the ducks can be made to quack and in no time we are all quacking in time to the music, as the DUKW churns itself downriver to our next destination.

Suddenly we are in good form. My mobile rings. It is Haris from the Singapore International Foundation. We have been cleared as a proper charity and the dinner is to go ahead. More hysteria breaks out. We now sing and dance the duck song, quacking vigorously like children, arms flapping like wings, as the adrenalin pumps relief into our bodies. Yes, we can go to the party, but we are having one right now.

Well, almost, for with a cough and a splutter our worthy floating Duck breaks down right in the middle of the river! We have overheated, cries the captain, and must wait for the engine to cool down. A crewman goes aft and pours some more water into a tank. Mike suggests we sing *For Those in Peril on the Sea*, but he is outvoted. So too is Jon's suggestion that he give another rendition of The Fish Song. We do the only thing possible and all go into yet another furious chorus of the duck song. Just as we reach a climax of quacking, there is a bang, a cloud of smoke and once again we are moving. The engine has been restored to good health, possibly by our singing suggests Miles, and we move to the pier.

After a spot of canoeing we are far enough down river and is time to meet the President and his wife.

The Palace is grand and we are announced. The room is hushed and we decide to remain in a dignified silence which is hard for by now we are all in a giggly mood. Miles and Caroline are the worst, when they get the giggles nothing can stop it. Then he appears – the President of Singapore and his wife. It is another of those crazy around the world moments.

The team about to enjoy afternoon tea with the President of Singapore and his wife

I expect Jon to break into the Fish Song or Miles to blow his quacking machine but decorum prevails.

Tea and sandwiches are served. The President moves amongst us, chatting the way Presidents do. He speaks about our courage and of the example we are setting. His wife retires to a table and the women present are invited to join her for tea. The President, having spoken to all present, having consumed his tea and finished his sandwich, decides it is time to retire. His assistant crosses over to his wife and announces that the President wishes to depart.

'Well he will just have to wait,' announces his wife. 'I have not yet finished talking to these ladies, and will be about another five minutes.'

The terrified servant passes the message on to the President. There was a time when it would be 'off with the messenger's head' but no longer. Women are in charge and the wise man will recognise this. The President resumes his chats until his wife is finished and then they withdraw.

But there is a problem. There is a gala dinner to attend and Caroline's outfit, a shimmering black number, has no sleeves so her rash will be exposed to everyone. She and Mary decide to go shopping to find something new.

Mary writes:

Perhaps the guiding hand that Phileas Fogg talks about is with us as Caroline and I go shopping. Caroline is desperate for a new outfit with sleeves to hide her rash at the gala dinner tonight. Also, we are both badly in need of some girly time together.

So we hit the shops. I find shopping with someone who is visually impaired is a challenge. I look, see something I like and head for it. Caroline has to inspect each rail closely, taking everything in garment by garment, rail by rail, until she sees something she likes. Then she has to negotiate the changing room, hopefully not knocking over a display. Caroline does not act or look as if she has a serious sight disability and this can be quite disarming as she charges ahead whether it is at an airport terminal, shopping mall or heading for an underground.

We are inside the curtained-off area, a possible outfit in her hand. Caroline is tearful. It is the first time for weeks she has seen herself in her underwear in a room full of mirrors.

'I look awful' she cries, standing close to a mirror and inspecting her arms. 'I will never find anything nice that will cover me up and will let you all down tonight.'

'Caroline' I say as I back away from seeing myself in the mirrors, 'You are beautiful and WILL find something.' Then I start to giggle.

Caroline faces me. 'What's so funny?'

'It is ridiculous. Here we are concerned about what we will look like tonight and yet we have just had afternoon tea with the President of Singapore and his charming wife and what were we wearing? Sweatshirts, khaki trousers and trainers!'

We both giggle together and the stress of the outing disappears, we become two women together having fun. And yes, we do find something for Caroline to wear at the ball.

Can a guiding hand help you shopping? I believe it can.

Now it is evening and we are all at the Grand Ball. Dawn Wee has done a magnificent job and the cream of Singapore are in attendance. It is a bright, happy, glittering, dazzling occasion and Dawn and her husband, who founded Stamford Tyres, one of the largest suppliers of motor tyres in Singapore and Malaysia, are in charge.

The guests take their dinner and it is time for us to perform. Mary goes first, but all is not well. It is a large room, there are too many lights on, and in a corner a very noisy party of guests are telling jokes and paying little attention to the stage.

During her talk, I get a message from Mike. Already upset about the text message from Sue, he finds the noise in the room during the speeches unnerving and tells me that he does not want to speak. I ask Caroline to do his spot instead.

Caroline has passion. When she is roused by anger she has a double helping. She rips into her speech by saying how hard it is at times to be a superstar – yet that is what everyone present is expecting her to be. She says it is even more difficult when the lights are on and when some people – and at this point she looks at the noisy revellers – are proving competition.

The room goes quiet, caught up in the unexpected drama that is unfolding.

Caroline then tells the guests that tonight one of our team is depressed and not in top form. Mike has taken stage fright and has asked if he can be excused from speaking.

'Sometimes we too need a bit of a break. We are not superhuman and tonight it has caught up with Mike.'

But Caroline goes on to tell Mike's story, of how he got his injuries, of the enormous courage he is showing in undertaking Around the World in 80 Ways, more than the rest of us. She asks them to show support for Mike by welcoming him on stage and helping him to get over this nerves.

Mike takes the stage to warm and sustained applause. He talks in that quiet but dramatic way that we have got to know so well. The audience is spellbound as they experience the same love that we have all developed for Mike and his example.

The ovation is spontaneous and generous, and the evening bursts out into a dazzling bubble of love and warmth. Guests give generously to charity and the night finishes in spectacular fashion when Mary explodes in an outburst of sheer high spirits and she and Caroline go on stage to dance to the band.

Alas, Jon does not get a chance to sing the Fish Song. Well no, it is not alas at all!

Mike later recalls the incident.

On the morning of our big dinner in Singapore, I thought about the speaking and felt that I simply could not do it. It was most peculiar and there was no reason for feeling like this. I was very down, worried and confused. Everything seemed awful. Caroline picked this up and was very helpful to me. I hoped that a busy day would take my mind off the fear to some extent but I saw everything in a negative light.

Caroline arranged to sit next to me at dinner and we talked about things unrelated to the adventure. My mood lifted until it was the team's turn. Again I felt unable to go on stage to speak and Caroline arranged to talk before me, allowing me time to relax. She spoke brilliantly telling the audience that everyone has a bad day and that I was having one and did not feel up to speaking but would do so because as a team we all rose to a challenge. She was right of course, I found myself on stage and able to talk as well as ever.

Dinner is over, money is raised and I thank the wonderful Dawn Wee profoundly. She has organised a tremendous night for us and I begin to realise the power of the women who have helped us – Brigetta Forsius in Nice, Mary Munley in the Red Sea, Linda Genola in South Africa, Addie Samerton in Bangkok, Dawn Wee in Singapore, and shortly to come, Doris Ho in Hong Kong.

And of course, there is our own Mary who has done such an enormous job in making the whole adventure work.

There is also Caroline. Since Aoife left through illness, she has been the only woman on the journey and has become 'mum' to Mike and Miles. Caroline may seem tough, but underneath I now know she is a wonderfully warm, caring and often insecure woman. Her long talk with Mary whilst shopping in Singapore gave her the chance to open out with another woman and reveal her soft spot and just how deeply she felt the responsibility for the welfare of the men on the adventure, and of seeing it through to success. What can seem a tough nut has a very soft underbelly.

If there is a glass ceiling it is time they smashed it into smithereens.

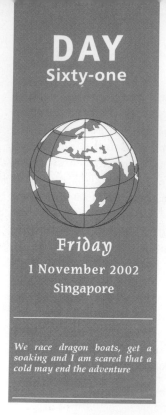

We race dragon boats, get a soaking and I am scared that a cold may end the adventure

Once more to the river and this time we climb on board dragon boats. They take them very seriously in Singapore. Mike is loaded into his with love and great care and once again, he finds himself in a nautical situation where gripping the sides, rather than the paddle, is required of him. He has come a long way since his experience on the Liffey in Dublin on the cardboard boat, but he is still not able to balance and paddle, but whilst then he looked terrified, now he looks as though he is Admiral Nelson.

But none of us are allowed to paddle here. Dragon boat racing is a very serious business, and there is no room for us to paddle, let alone sing our duck song. We are told quite firmly that we must sit still, upright and straight, stay quiet and not interfere with the working of either the boat or the crew. Yes, Captain!

I am placed right at the bow of my dragon boat, the only thing in front of me being a large drum and a man to beat out the time. I hang on to the sides of the boat but am told off – keep your hands in the boat, is the command and I obey.

Then it starts – a rhythmic beating of the drum and with every beat, muscles are called into play and the boat glides forward – boom ... boom ... boom – just like in the film *Ben Hur* – and with every boom a shudder of power makes the boat surge forward.

Now we are in open water. There is a change of rhythm. The booms become urgently threatening. The boat shoots faster. I grip the sides and then remember that I have been ordered not to do this. I think I will get a dozen lashes if I am not careful. But without anything to hold on to, I fear I will fall. I wonder how Mike is getting on, but am hanging on myself and dare not turn round. Still faster beats the drum, still faster goes the beat and now we are up to full speed. It is wonderful, exciting, stimulating, joyous and for us, frightening.

I notice it is raining – really raining. It is a major downpour but the rain is warm and we do not mind. Beating our way through the rain is all part of the excitement. I am still wearing my top hat and Mike shouts that the dye is running down my face and I am beginning to look more Dracula than Phileas Fogg. I thank him for his courtesy.

We want to go on, forging our way through the rain, but our destination lies immediately ahead.

Dragon boat racing is exciting but highly disciplined

Crowds have gathered at Stadium Cove where the Life without Limits extravaganza has been organised to link up with our adventure. It consists of an exciting programme of sports for young people and there are many charity stalls selling local crafts. The crowd see us and they rush down to the pier to bid us welcome. It is still pouring down in buckets, but the welcome is massive and warm. We are all soaked but do not care. I have black streaks of dye from my top hat all down my face, but still manage to smile. The seat of Mike's wheelchair is impregnated with rain, we dry it as best we can, but there is little to be done.

It continues to pour down as we visit the stalls, take part in the sports and enjoy our luncheon. I am worried about the health of my team. I am told that because the rain is warm, there is no danger of chest infection. I am unconvinced. With his paralysis, when Mike wants to cough, he often has to ask for an assisted cough. Hopefully he will not get a cough or cold. In any case, we are still not yet at the halfway mark in our adventure, and taking a needless health risk today when there is still so much to do is foolhardy and selfish.

I decide we must withdraw and order taxis. It is not a popular decision with the team. They reason that if the crowd can put up with the conditions, so too can they. But the crowd are not going on around the rest of the world, they have time to stay at home and nurse a cold. In any case, I feel it is irresponsible to take risks when there are so many people who have worked so hard to set up their programmes and are now keenly waiting for our arrival. I stick to my guns, the taxis are ordered and we return to our hotel to dry out. I am deeply concerned. A cold will not stop Caroline or Miles, but a cold could kill Mike.

I have a sleepless night and only recover when Miles, Mike and Caroline appear the next day none the worse for their soaking.

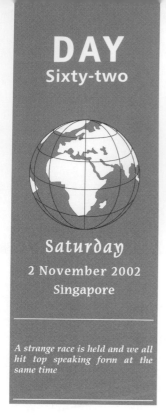

A strange race is held and we all hit top speaking form at the same time

We are a bit unnerved by our means of transport today. The Singapore Polytechnic has been set a challenge – to invent and make three vehicles suitable for disabled people to use. For one full month there has been hammering, banging and welding and now the machines are there for us to inspect.

For Mike there is what is called a 'four by four' wheelchair – hand driven, its purpose is to be all-terrain. Its inventor had often noticed how wheelchair users get into some difficulties covering bumpy ground, but no longer, for this contraption is highly sprung, highly geared and remembering that Mike has no legs and cannot pedal, it is driven by hand power alone.

'Interesting,' muses Mike with more than a touch of suspicion as he leaves the safety of his own tried and tested steed and lowers himself into this new vehicle.

Caroline is also puzzled. She is told she has to stand upright in her vehicle. 'It is for people who have injuries and cannot sit down' the inventor explains. We try to figure out what such an injury might be but are stumped. We are told it is for hemiplegics. A small electric motor provides the power.

For Miles and myself, there is a very unusual cycle for blind people. It comes in two pieces, one piece is like a conventional cycle, with all the necessary apparatus such as pedals and handlebars, the other piece is a sidecar with pedals, so I can help with the horsepower.

I cannot see how the extra power is related to Miles' disablement and ask what special feature there is in the machine to help with blindness.

'You are it,' explains the inventor, 'for you can shout out directions and you have pedals to compensate for your extra weight.'

Of course, how silly of me.

Roland Tan, Director of Student and Alumni Affairs, talks to us and explains what it is all about.

'For many years, our students have been developing innovative products for rehabilitation for the needy. We want to offer you the use of these vehicles, we hope to encourage more people to contribute their skills and talents to benefit the disabled and help them better fit into society.'

His talk again reminds us of the extraordinary enthusiasm our adventure has inspired and we must continue to devote ourselves to its fulfilment in inspiring others to live their lives to the full.

We have been instructed to race along a route on the public roads to arrive at a hall where the students and their friends will be present to learn how their inventions had coped.

The flag is dropped, once again giving Mike and I, being fully sighted, an advantage. We set off, surrounded as usual by media and the curious. We are joined by Chan Soo Sen, Minister of State and by the Singapore Polytechnic's Principal, Low Song Fook. Each of us has been assigned a cyclist from the Polytechnics cycle club to ride outside us and keep us safe.

Mike is the first to show. His arm strength means that he has no trouble propelling his machine at some speed and very soon he moves into a healthy lead, with Miles and I having co-ordination difficulties and Caroline's electric motor going rather too slowly for her liking.

But soon Mike is in trouble as one of his pedals falls off. Frantic mechanics bang it back on, but it is a botched job and the machine refuses to move smoothly any more. Mike perseveres, his massive arm strength keeping things in motion, sweat pouring off his brow.

Meanwhile Miles and I are having our troubles. We are surrounded by excited students on cycles who forget that Miles is blind. Sadly so do I and we miss a turning. Wild screams come from my guide cyclist but it is not a good time to discover he speaks no English. Frantic waving sorts out the problems but we have lost a lot of distance and Caroline, though still crawling along at a snail pace, is in the lead and Mike is ahead of us.

But not for long. His right wheel has decided to go in a different direction to his left wheel and now Mike is furiously trying to pedal a sideways walking crab along a public road. Again he stops for repairs, I urge Miles on and in a spurt of excitement we overtake the luckless Mike and the furious Caroline who has still not found out how to get any more speed out of her motor, having discovered that Irish swear words have no effect at all. She knows that shouting at it does not make it go faster but it helps her.

We are all spread out and the police decide to stop the race and collect us again into one bunch – rather like the safety car in a grand prix. So just as we have gone into the lead Miles and I have to wait for the others to catch up. Caroline is with us in a flash, then Mike, with both his wheels now pointing roughly in a suggestion of the same direction, puffs up alongside.

'All right Mike?' I cry.

'Sure thing Captain,' he replies.

The policeman shouts out 'Go' – at least we think that is what he says – and off we hurtle. Mike again shows his arm power by going straight into the lead, but it is short-lived as, once more his wheel drops off and he crashes. He does not come to harm, but we all stop to be sure.

By this time, Jon, sensing trouble, has doubled back into the start point and has picked up Mike's own wheelchair. A substitution is made and we race off with Mike at his accustomed speed, Caroline urging her one speed stand-up vehicle to do something spectacular and Miles and I puffing and pulling along in our own awkward contraption.

The finish line is ahead, and Miles and I are in the lead. But once more we are to be frustrated in our endeavour to get a podium finish, for I have noticed that the bar between his cycle and my sidecar has cracked and urgent action of some sort is needed as we are about to part company. I grab Miles' cycle and hold it with all my strength against my sidecar, closing down the crack but now the geometry is out of kilter and progress becomes more difficult.

We close in on the line, but our machine is about to split into two. Mike, now in his usual wheelchair, hurtles past us all and wins. Caroline, still unable to get any more speed out of her contraption, comes in second whilst Miles and I slew in a poor last, Miles pedalling furiously and wondering what is amiss, me holding the two pieces of our machine together for long enough to finish the race.

Mike's comment to the media sums it up for all of us. Asked what he thought of his machine, he suavely remarks that a road test would have been a good idea.

It has been wonderful fun, and we are full of admiration for the students, who have done so much to help in the rehabilitation of disabled people. Theirs is an example to the rest of the world and we determine to see what we can do to help spread their message.

Now we have to speak to the students. They have been assembled by the Polytechnic and the National Youth Achievement Award Council, with the support of the Singapore International Foundation and as we peer into the theatre, we realise that there are a very large number of them. They

Caroline and her escorts out in front on the special vehicle chase

applaud our entrance and then sit in silence, waiting for the magic to infect them.

We strike gold. Something inspirational has happened and we are all on sparkling form at the same time. I go first and even cameraman Carbonara is moved to say he has never heard me so good. I know I have set the room on fire, but Mike, Miles and Caroline keep the room blazing. We all have our different styles, sometimes they clash, most times they blend but today they produce a miracle of motivation. There is power, there is passion, there is magic and the students roar their praise. Mary is our strongest critic, remaining professional at all times and not being deceived by the public relations tricks or the noise – but her eyes are ablaze with pride for the team, and her praise is spontaneous, sincere and total.

'You were all just brilliant,' she says.

But there is not time for us to enjoy the hero-worship for we must get on with our journey, this time to the airport.

Oh no, not bicycles again.

Yes, but to our relief we have to do no pedalling nor any steering. A driver rides the cycle and we just sit in the sidecar waving regally to the crowds. Miles does this particularly well, though one of us has to whisper to him where they are!

'There is a group of children waving at you at seven o'clock, Miles,' whispers Mike and Miles turns in the required direction and returns their greetings.

Unlike my machine in the race, the cycles stay attached to the sidecars and we make a dignified exit from Singapore, with only one incident.

It happens going downhill. We are supposed to be in formation, but I notice that my cycle is swiftly catching up with Jon in front. I glance at the driver and see there is panic in his eyes. I realise that the brakes have failed.

I ponder. I am sitting in a sidecar, dressed in top hat, frock-coat, cravat, white shirt, black trousers, spats and immaculately shined shoes, the very personification of Phileas Fogg. What do I do? What would he do? Leap off to save my life? Stay on board, confident that my driver has the situation under control? And what if the driver suddenly leaps off the machine, should I take over the controls and save everyone, as is done in the films?

Don't be daft, there is only me to save.

My pondering is interrupted by the sound of crashing metal as we hurtle into the back of Jon's machine. Fortunately a dented hat is the only casualty. My machine is damaged beyond recovery as is my driver, who is physically all right but has lost face and is inconsolable. Jon, his driver and his machine are still roadworthy and they decide to continue. I hail a passing cycle taxi, catch up with the rest and complete the journey with some loss of dignity and, as I discover later, a sore finger.

Farewell, Singapore, you have served us well.

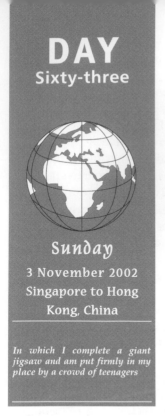

In which I complete a giant jigsaw and am put firmly in my place by a crowd of teenagers

Help!

It is a warm afternoon. I am in Hong Kong and I am sitting up on a stage specially built at the old airport. Beside me there are other top brass but no one has told me who they are, whilst in front of me a crowd of thousands of young people stretches out into the distance. A man is making a speech, but it is in Cantonese and I do not understand a word of it. Every so often I hear the words Robin Dunseath, but have no idea what he is saying. I wonder if I am going to have to make a speech, and knowing no Cantonese I swiftly improvise a short Phileas Fogg type entertainment that needs no language.

But I do not have to make a speech. Suddenly everyone leaves the stage. Not having a clue what is going on, I follow them in my top hat and fixed smile, wondering where we are going. Mary, realising that I am totally out of my depth, rescues me and takes me to the front.

A large piece of jigsaw is put into my hands and I am taken to the old runway, where I discover a massive jigsaw. I realise I am to put one of the last pieces in place. A television helicopter hovers overhead as I perform the necessary duty. I discover it is hard to smile upwards at a camera in a helicopter whilst looking down to see where I am putting my piece of - jigsaw.

Then it happens. The man with the microphone says something in Cantonese. At once, thousands of children standing at the far side of the jigsaw point at me and then, letting out a cry, sprint towards me, screaming their adulation. I wave at the advancing horde and prepare to sign autographs, but they run right past me. A pop star has appeared behind me and it is he who is the centre of their attention. Feeling remarkably foolish, I withdraw.

Mary asks me for my autograph. We both laugh.

That is my entry to Hong Kong.

Two years before, I had told Mary that cold letters are useless.

'Writing a cold letter to people is a waste of time. We must only seek help from people we know, or who know people we need to know' I said pompously and guru-like for I am supposed to be a guru in such matters.

'Of course' she said in the way women have of agreeing with you when they have every intention of disagreeing with you.

And so her daughter Claire-Louise did her research, identified the Hong Kong Jockey Club as a possible partner in Hong Kong and told us to tackle them with the project.

'Only write to them when we have found someone we know who is connected with their committee and will open the door for us, we only have one shot at it. Write a cold letter and you will blow it!' I again warned.

Needless to say, Mary ignored my advice and wrote a cold letter to Lawrence Wong, the Chief Executive of the club, who replied asking us to come out and talk to William Yiu, his Director of Charities, about the project.

We met William, Doris Ho, Head of Charities and Grace Yeung, Manager of Charity Projects. Like the man from Delmonte, they said Yes – so much for my advice on cold calling. To Mary's eternal credit, she never once rubbed it in. After the meeting I bought her a cocktail called Around the World in the Marriott Hotel Hong Kong and she smiled sweetly at me.

Getting the Hong Kong Jockey Club on board was a massive breakthrough. Until then, all we had was the idea, now we had reality. We were to be hosted in Hong Kong by one of the most powerful clubs in the region. It was the example we needed to bring in the others.

The Hong Kong Jockey Club were amazing. They devised a three month 'Yes Can Do' campaign to climax with our arrival when they planned a week of related activity. All the time we were working our way across the globe to them, they were running activities related to our core message of inspiring people to live their lives to the full. The biggest jigsaw in the world, I learned, was one of these projects, featuring our logo in the piece.

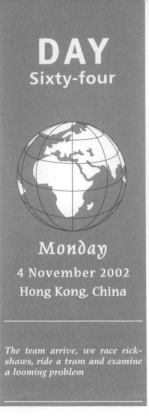

The team arrive, we race rickshaws, ride a tram and examine a looming problem

I had put in the final piece in the jigsaw ... To do so and to coincide with the Jockey Club timetable, I had left the rest of the adventurers behind in Singapore. Now I am at the airport to meet them.

The Jockey Club has power and I discover that they have arranged for Cathay Pacific to take me airside right to the door of the aircraft so I can greet them as they arrive.

As usual, it is Caroline who leads the way, followed by Miles, then Mike and Jon. At first they are stunned to see Phileas Fogg standing there to greet them, but soon surprise gives way to pleasure as we are once again reunited.

We move into the arrivals hall where Mary is with the Hong Kong Jockey Club team and the inevitable mass of media. A large banner welcoming us to Hong Kong is held high by volunteers. A furious media scramble takes place as reporters and photographers grapple to get their stories and pictures. Doris Ho from the Jockey Club, who has since become a good friend, takes command and moves us to the transit train, our first means of transport in Hong Kong. A special carriage has been reserved for us and the

We make it to Hong Kong, the halfway step on our adventure

media and we spend the trip in energetic interviews, persistent photography and learning the Chinese for Yes Can Do, their motto for the programme.

We pile out in Central Station where we find rickshaws, our next means of transport, ready for us. I get into one pulled by Miles, Mike takes a ride on the Caroline-powered vehicle.

Once again the intense rivalry between Miles and Caroline takes over. Although both are registered blind, they hurtle their rickshaws through crowded streets of Hong Kong, with Mike and I screaming encouragement and a breathless Hong Kong Jockey Club staff, and an even more breathless Hong Kong media, running along beside us. Eventually we reach the City Hall and dismount. We hand the rickshaws back to their very relieved owners, who had feared for the welfare of their livelihoods as we thundered our way through the crowed streets of Hong Kong in our respective rickshaws.

Once again Caroline has won the race with Miles, and he is stage furious, accusing her of cheating. We know it is all in fun, the others – including the usual scrum of media – are not so sure! They simply do not realise that we are now so closely bonded that we know each other's acts.

We decide we cannot visit Hong Kong without taking a trip on a tram and a very special one is produced for us, magnificently decorated with coloured lights which make it look as it if has come from fairyland.

But first there is a surprise. Mary and Doris Ho have arranged for Miles' wife Stephanie to be flown to Hong Kong; they have met her at the airport and smuggled her into Central Hong Kong. Suddenly, as far as Miles is concerned, Stephanie walks out of nowhere when he is boarding the tram. It is a very exciting and happy reunion.

We climb on board and off we clank, with the ever-present media filming our progress and the people of Hong Kong, who now realise who we are, cheering us on and wishing us luck.

But immediately we hit a problem. The tram is open-topped and the only way to ride upstairs is up the narrow and twisting staircase. There is no way we can get Mike's wheelchair up it, indeed getting it on to the tram was quite a task, so we leave him downstairs as we go upstairs.

No sooner are we upside when we decide we cannot do this, and go down again to join Mike. Mary and Caroline set to work. They take Mike to the twisting staircase. Mary kicks off her shoes, puts on her 'I can do this' face, and makes Mike put one arm around her, with Caroline taking the other arm.

They set off up the stairs, Mary going first but backwards, Caroline going last shouting out instructions to Mary, and Mike grabbing the handrail for dear life and shouting encouragement. I am reminded of that film of Laurel and Hardy trying to get a piano up a flight of stairs. I want to help, but the two are trained lifters and I have a bad back that would spasm if I tried to do what they are doing.

'Frankly, I rather enjoyed the experience' said Mike later. 'Being squeezed between two such lovely girls was well worth the effort.' Always the charmer.

The television cameras whir as this strange caterpillar made up of Mary, Caroline and Mike creeps up the stairs. By now the onlookers have realised what is happening, and almost unable to believe their eyes, they begin to cheer. Mary, Caroline and Mike reach the top of Everest and our party is reunited – on the open-decked top of a Hong Kong tram.

We proceed in a stately fashion, waving at the cheering crowds, until we reach our destination – our hotel. It is the end of our first day in Hong Kong and we have used an airport express train, rickshaws and a Hong Kong tram.

In planning the adventure, Mary had decided that as the halfway point, partners could join the team for the duration of the visit. Miles' delightful and long suffering wife Stephanie has made her surprise entrance. Caroline's husband Fergal had felt that seeing her for a few days and then leaving would be too hard to do and they had decided he should stay at home. Mike's girlfriend Sue had broken up the relationship whilst he was in India, whilst Jon's wife was unable to travel.

It is not going to be the weekend reunion that we had planned. But Mary and I have a bigger worry. It is now clear to me that Jon has done a terrific job with the team – but I am uneasy. I feel he has become a member of the team himself. Instead of the travelling group being made up of Phileas Fogg, three adventurers and a team manager, there are now four adventurers, no Phileas Fogg and my original concept of a manager has disappeared.

To make matters worse, both Mary and I feel we are now treated as outsiders and not insiders. In our tasks, it is not possible to be with the team all the time, and now when we join, the four have bonded so tightly that they do not welcome us as one of them.

'When you arrive, it is rather like the visit of the headmaster,' Mike tells me. In a way it is true. I notice that when I attempt to impose my will, there is dissent, and they look to Jon for guidance. Mary and I decide that we cannot leave Hong Kong with the problem unresolved. She also tells me that my management and leadership technique went out of date years ago, now it was all about empowerment.

'Leaders have to lead and that means making decisions and sticking with them' I pontificate.

'Quite' she says and I know she is just humouring me. I decide to reflect on the situation but it is difficult at the age of sixty-six to change one's style.

We have other reasons for worry. We have run out of money. It is clear to me that there is no finance to pay for the team to cross America. The adventure could be at an end. I sit down to work out a crisis plan.

I count up the means of transport that we have used, consult with Stuart as to how many he will accept as being different and realise that when we reach San Francisco we would have used more than the target of eighty entirely different means of transport. Crucially we would still have just enough money to fly the team home 'stand by' from San Francisco.

So I decide on the rescue plan in which we would fly as cheaply as we could direct from San Francisco to London. This would complete our mission successfully and we would not have to meet the costs of tracking all the way by land across America and then flying home from the East Coast.

With this knowledge as a background, Mary and I plan a crunch meeting with the team towards the end of our stay in Hong Kong. Good business sense calls for the San Francisco short cut and would also stop the present split from developing into something more damaging. Mary and I determine that unless we can heal the rift and in some way solve the financial crisis, then we must move to the rescue plan and arrive home early, but with perceived success.

'We can still say we went around the world in 80 ways' I argue, 'All we will change is we will get home earlier.'

That decision is for another time, right now we must get on with the adventure and with some more means of transport. We all share the same feeling but it is Miles who puts it into words when he says that having run an amazing three-month programme building up to our arrival, they must be very concerned whether our band of merry adventurers could match their expectations, let alone exceed them.

'I hope we don't let Hong Kong down' he says and we all agree. We had not meant to be heroes, but that is the role Hong Kong expects of us.

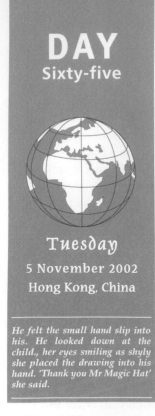

He felt the small hand slip into his. He looked down at the child., her eyes smiling as shyly she placed the drawing into his hand. 'Thank you Mr Magic Hat' she said.

It is our second day in Hong Kong and we now realise that the purpose of our adventure has changed. Suddenly the means of transport are no longer that important to us, their importance has been taken over by the inspiration we can give to people who are facing challenges. Of course we had been aware of this as a concept many times before on our adventure, for who can forget moments like the children from Phab at Kilkeel in Ireland or the Jack and Jill babies in Galway? For Mike, riding into Carlow on horseback with the Carlow Hunt had made a very large impression about the inspirational qualities of our adventure… and there was the whole of the South African sector.

Our first task is to pay a visit to the Ebenezer School and Home for visually and mentally impaired children. It is to be another rollercoaster ride for us, for it is clear when we arrive that the build-up has given the perception that we were some kind of superstars.

The children applaud loudly as we enter and I speak first, remembering that their understanding of English is very poor. I speak very slowly so that those with a grasp of English can learn, and then wait for the translator to interpret my words to those who have no English.

My top hat causes a sensation. I tell them the story of our adventure and hand over to Miles. When on form he is one of the UK's top motivational speakers and gives the interpreter real problems in trying to convey his passion – but it is still a formidable experience. It is Mary, with her ability to communicate with children, who wins their hearts.

Questions are invited after we have finished and the children are asked if they can suggest some means of transport for us to use. Their responses are charming, unusual and challenging, I love the way children are free to use their imagination and wish that as adults we could retain some of this magic, rather than being dulled down by conventional thinking and behaviour.

Now, a small group of them stand up to entertain us to music which they play on recorders and drums. It is utterly delightful. When they have finished we move amongst them and once again feel the love and excitement that only children can give when you bring a little magic to them.

Too soon it is over and I feel a tug on my frock-coat. I look down and a very small girl pushes a piece of paper into my hand and, too shy to talk, scuttles off. It is a coloured drawing of me in my top hat that she had done whilst I was talking, and it was titled Mr Magic Hat.

Mary wrote:

> He felt the small hand slip into his. He looked down at the child, her eyes smiling as shyly she placed the drawing into his hand. 'Thank you Mr Magic Hat' she said.

Farewell Phileas, you have served me well – but to these children, I will for ever remain Mr Magic Hat, and I will wear that name proudly. It is funny the effect that hat has on people. In the UK people tended to ignore it, even when boarding planes, but in the Far East, it is a centre of attraction and people come up to me and ask about it. I wonder which of my grandchildren would one day demand it should they ever retrace my journey around the world.

But soon we discover the morning is but a test for the afternoon for we are taken to the magnificent Hong Kong convention centre where we find we are to address the largest audience of our entire adventure. Over 4,000 young people are there, waiting to hear what we have to say.

When asked to speak to 4,000 schoolchildren you can almost hear your stomach turn. To discover you are to do it through a translator as the audience's first language is Cantonese is a quite terrifying experience.

But it gets worse as the moment approaches. Normally we speak off the cuff, finding the dynamics of the event or the occasion turns the adrenalin flow into a torrent of eloquence. But we are totally banjaxed by being asked by our translators to tell them in advance what we are going to say, so that they are prepared! No way, we cannot do that.

Once again, I go first and make a hash of it. My translator has difficulty in understanding me and what is normally a spontaneous and passionate flow of colourful words becomes a dirge interspersed with a stumbling translation. Miles goes next, and makes a better job of it. Next is Mike who performs in his usual quiet way, and he captures the magic, as they listen intently to his story of how he overcame his massive and potentially life-destroying injuries, which they can all see.

By this time Caroline, who normally speaks with the speed of a machinegun, has worked out she will have to try something different. To our complete astonishment, she gets them all to do a Mexican wave!

' I was not sure that it was culturally the thing to do, and I was a bit nervous to try it out' she said to me later, 'but if I were a school kid who had been sitting all that time without being able to make a noise I would be fed up.'

And they make a holy racket of sound as they leap to their feet and do their wave, accompanied by lusty cheering. It is quite a frightening sensation when 4,000 children yell at the tops of their voices. For Miles and

The dramatic Hong Kong skyline, taken from our Junk

Caroline too it is a moment of magic. It is an 'audio' Mexican wave, accompanied with cheering, enabling Miles and Caroline to watch and follow the audio wave, despite their sight limitation, as it rolls from one side of the auditorium to the other. From that moment, Caroline and therefore we too have them in our pockets, as they begin to laugh at our jokes and applaud our stories.

There are few audience situations that pose such a challenge and the team's answer, led by Caroline, is bizarre but it works and shows yet again that we are up to any challenge.

After the meeting, it is back to the hotel, a quick change into our posh outfits, and then we are off to the races, guests of the Hong Kong Jockey Club. We hardly recognise ourselves. Miles scubs up particularly well, and cuts a fine figure of a stylish gentleman at leisure. His lack of eyesight is not physically apparent, but his eyes give his face a look of quizzical distinction that makes him particularly attractive.

The race course is a surprise. Originally built on the only piece of land that was flat enough to take a race course, it is now surrounded by sky-scrapers which, in the evening, provide a million light sparkling background to the races. Whilst the buildings look magnificent, they hide a tragic story, for many people bought them as property prices rocketed, knowing that whatever they cost, they would be worth almost double in under four years. Sadly since Hong Kong was returned to China, both the economy and property prices have crashed and many of the flat owners are now hopelessly trapped in a desperate negative equity situation with little chance of recovery.

We dine sumptuously in the corporate suite of the club and then lose a lot of money backing a horse called Around the World. Mike takes over as tipster and we lose even more money.

Mary greets me with a purposeful look. She tells me that she has noticed I have been a bit breathless at times and in cahoots with Doris Ho, a medical examination of my heart has been arranged for later on this morning.

The inspection is thorough and intensive. Mary comes with me to make sure I do not lie to the doctor. He asks me if I get breathless climbing stairs. I say a firm 'no' which gets me into serious trouble later with Mary, who knows it is not true. But I have come too far to be sent home now.

In any case, his machines tell him that my heart, though still going at its own erratic and eccentric pace, is strong and healthy and he passes me to continue.

The morning is taken up with media interviews and having been given a good bill of health, I rejoin them. The journalist, listening to Mike, Miles and Caroline telling their stories, breaks down in tears and needs to leave the room to compose herself – another first for Around the World in 80 Ways!

We attend a magnificent luncheon, then a seminar and in the evening we meet to sort out our differnces.

Then we go to luncheon at the Hong Kong Jockey Club clubhouse, where a large number of top executives have been assembled to meet us. Remembering our means of transport, we travel very grandly in the Rolls-Royce provided for the former governor and now used by British Consul General, Sir James Hodge KCVO CMG.

It is a splendid luncheon and we perform our usual inspirational speeches. It is very unusual for us all to be on top form at the same time. Sometimes, I make the top speech, other times it is Mike, or Miles or Caroline. But this time, because she has hunted out Hong Kong and managed the project so brilliantly, I invite Mary to make the keynote speech – and she stuns everyone in the room, outshining the three of us.

She says that she wants to thank you, Mr Wong (The Chairman of the Jockey Club) for not putting her original letter in the waste paper bin, but for reading it, taking an interest in it and giving his approval to participate. She explains to the hushed guests that until his decision, Around the World was just an idea, and it needed some organisation of the prestige of the Jockey Club to break the barrier and come in, setting the example for others to follow.

'You just do not know what you started' says Mary.

And with that, she leaves the speaker's podium, crosses the room, flings her arms around the surprised Mr Wong and gives him a massive hug.

He is reduced to tears.

It was Mary who first wrote to the Jockey Club, helped me sell the concept to them, and then working closely with Doris Ho and the club's own staff, helped them to mastermind a full three months' support programme of activity, leading up to our arrival. It was the most spectacular sector of the entire adventure, Mary hunted it out and made it happen and yet I feel she is not getting enough appreciation for her work from the adventurers.

I decide that this is another aspect that must be discussed at our crunch meeting.

The evening produces yet another challenge. After the luncheon, we lead a management seminar for the Hong Kong Jockey Club. At very short notice, Jon has put together a slide show of our adventure so far and even we are reduced to silence as we are reminded of the people we have met and the adventures we have enjoyed over the past 65 days. It seems unreal, as though it all happened to someone else.

Now we are to face Hong Kong Jockey Club scholars and talk to them. For us, it seems we have made the same speeches nine hundred and ninety-nine times, but we must remember that it is the first time each audience has heard us. But by the evening we are tired, numb, bored with listening to ourselves and it takes a major effort to capture the sort of live dynamic that is typical of our show. But once again, the magic returns as our audience responds and whilst we are not at our best, we leave knowing that we have made our mark. We have lived up to expectations and we know the students went away thinking differently from when they entered the room.

We are tired, but I am determined to get some thoughts off my mind so I call a meeting of the whole team. I put my view to them simply – that we are in deep financial trouble, and that the four – Miles, Mike, Caroline and Jon – have locked so much into each other that I feel they are drifting from the plot. They are no longer three Phileas Fogg adventurers fulfilling a bet, instead they are Mike, Miles, Caroline and Jon, travelling around the world. Instead of welcoming other members of the team, without whose efforts they would not be taking part, they were beginning to believe that they were the story and that no one else was playing a major role. I told them that this was grossly unfair to others who had given so much of their time, and produced such brilliant results without any funding, and on a volunteer basis.

I also outlined that as we were out of money, we had no choice other than to bring the team home from San Francisco, having completed eighty totally different means of transport.

The reply is vigorous, the rebuttal firm. The team refuse to think of returning from San Francisco and say they will find their own way across America and home without the help of myself and Mary, if need be. They will not contemplate failure to complete our original mission.

They see our point about the split and apologise, but say it is in the nature of the adventure that this would happen. Mary and I should not be offended, but accept the reality of the situation. Of course they appreciated all the help and support, but they were the ones that were actually doing the adventure and it was natural for them to concentrate on that.

I decide to adjourn the meeting and I retire to reflect on what to do next.

I have used many of my worldwide contacts to help in the adventure, some are business colleagues and some are friends. I realise that I am particularly sensitive that each should be acknowledged by the adventurers for the amazing contributions that they have made in getting sponsored accommodation, food, travel and entertainment and making up the social and educational programme. I am upset that in their diaries, carried on the web site, so few of these people are being acknowledged for the roles that they have played.

But I also realise that I am jealous. The whole thing was originally my idea to give me a wonderful time travelling around the world using all the means of travel and then going on the speaker's circuit later to make a fortune telling of my experiences. By bringing in Miles, Mike and Caroline, and the support team, I had completely changed my vision and it was no longer my personal dream. Furthermore, because of my management role, it was no longer possible for me to do all the travel. I realise I am particularly jealous of Jon, who is doing the job that I planned to do, once I had made the decision to include others in the party. I had pulled out of this because I accepted that, at sixty-six, I was probably not the one to be the day-to-day carer and enabler for two blind people and one paralysed man. Am I letting this jealousy, which I have tried to hide, influence my decisions?

Probably.

I share my thoughts with Mary who tells me that I am over-reacting but I am not so sure. I know she is usually right, but I feel very strongly that due praise and acknowledgement must be given to everyone who helps us, and that this is not happening.

There is a knock on the door and it is Mike. He wheels in and it is clear that after we left, the team also had a meeting to discuss what to do next.

Mike makes it clear that they fully appreciate what has happened and assures us that there is no question of not accepting our position and acknowledging what we and all the others have done. He says that the team is unable to contemplate going on without us. Whatever it costs, we must find a way out of our difficulties. He also assures us that they fully appreciate the voluntary effort that so many people have put into the adventure, and will from now on try to ensure that they receive due thanks from the adventurers.

I thank Mike and decide to sleep on it.

But sleep does not come easily. I wonder if they know how hard it is for me to spend so much time in organisation and worry, when in my original dream I would have copied Phileas Fogg and set off without burdens.

We enjoy lunch at a nunnery, make a wish at a tree and are bowled over by the Felix Wong Children

We are exhausted, but the Hong Kong Jockey Club has given us a break and the day is to be spent sightseeing. In the morning, we travel by bus to the Lok Ma Chau lookout over China. As usual the media record everything we do, their interest in us is insatiable. The bus journey has been long and Mike takes himself off to a quiet corner to empty his urine bag. As he is so doing, he looks up to discover a television crew are recording his every act. Normally we welcome the media, but when Mary notices that one has taken up a seat in our own private bus, she decides that enough is enough and asks her to get off. It is done politely but firmly and we are thankful.

But another scene, of crucial importance to our continued adventure, is played out. First Miles, then Caroline and then Jon speak to me on their own – Mike had already done so the previous night – and assure me of their complete loyalty and appreciation to both myself, to Mary and to all the others around the world who have, are and will be helping.

Miles puts it best.

'Robin, we do not really know you and that is the trouble. You say we do not treat you as one of us, but then you always keep your distance. We need you to drop your guard a bit, share some beers with us, and we will respond with gladness.'

He makes me think. I have always felt that those leading others should keep a distance but maybe I am wrong in this instance.

I decide to take a new approach with them in San Francisco.

I talk to Mary. She has been doing her sums and is confident that the Hong Kong programme will bring in a substantial sum for the Around the World Foundation – maybe more than we thought. She shows me how this money can be used – very sparingly – to get across America. We decide that with the air cleared, we will stick to the original plan. Secretly I realise that we will know roughly how much has been raised in Hong Kong by the time we leave, and if it is not enough, we can still pull out and fly home directly from San Francisco.

Lunch is spent at the wonderfully peaceful Chi Lin Nunnery and then we visit the Banyan wishing tree at Lam Tsuen. The tree is very old with roots gripping the ground to try to retain its hold on life. The idea is that you write a wish on a piece of manuscript, which has an orange tied to it.

You then fling your wish as high as you can into the tree and if it is caught in the branches your wish will come true.

I fling up my wish, and television cameras record that it gets caught in one of the highest branches. Miles, unable to see where he is throwing his, once again proves his astonishing powers by landing his wish. Caroline, as usual, ignores all the rules and keeps throwing up more messages and oranges until one sticks.

'It says nothing about the wish coming true only if it is your first orange that sticks' she explains.

Mike, somewhat hampered by his lower trajectory from his wheelchair, cheers us all up by landing his wish as well.

We look at this ancient tree and see a thing of beauty. Its old skeletal bones are covered with oranges in various stages of decay, with their brightly coloured wishes all flapping in the wind. That tree has the dreams and wishes from people from all parts of the world, all ages and walks of life, hanging from its silent and gnarled branches.

Evening time means more work, this time with the winners of the Felix Wong Awards. Felix Wong died young, and to mark his memory, his parents had introduced the award to encourage young people to meet adversity in their lives and to recognise those young people who have demonstrated courage and made real improvements in their lives despite their difficulties.

By this time, my heart problem is causing excess tiredness and I ask Mary to stand in for me at the event. She does so and returns deeply moved.

The children had told their stories, and of the incredible hardships with which they battle. Each of our adventurers felt inadequate in front of the courage of these people. The message was that there is no point in running away from ghosts for they will follow you, you have to stand up and confront them, face up to the problems and deal with them.

The team were later to tell me that rather than inspire the children, they were the ones who had been inspired. Both Mike and Caroline, affected by the children telling their stories, spoke much more personally about themselves than before. Because of this, a journalist present got a scoop story, but Mary asked that it be not used, a request the journalist agreed to in tribute to what we are doing.

DAY
Sixty-eight

Friday
8 November 2002
Hong Kong to
Kau Sai Chau

It is back to business for today we are to get on our way by canoe from Hong Kong central to the island of Kau Sai Chau where we are to travel further by playing golf

I am unsure whether Stuart will allow playing a hole of golf travelling from tee to green as a genuine means of travel, but I decide to accept the challenge anyway as we are also here to inspire and two blind people and a third in a wheelchair-playing golf surely fits that bill.

The morning is perfect, the sky an intense blue. We have travelled to the New Territories and are reminded just how beautiful Hong Kong can be. Most people think only of visiting the skyscraper factory that is in the Central District, completely unaware that on the other side of the island, and in the New Territories, there are vast tracts of wild and most beautiful country with views that make your hair curl.

We board our canoes, and are surrounded by hundreds of other canoes, full of shouting teenagers who have gathered from all over the territory to accompany us. We meet Rosanna who organised the canoe extravaganza and we

The canoes line up for the start of the paddle to play golf

find her a delightful addition to all the wonderfully enthusiastic, crazy and creative folk who have made Around the World such an exciting adventure. We paddle out into the green water, covered with twinkling jewels of bright light as the sun beams down upon our progress. Word is out that I have a heart condition and my paddler keeps trying to get me to slow down. Mike does his Kate Winslett impersonation, staring out over the bow as he is paddled along by Jon, whilst Miles and Caroline ignore everyone else as they indulge yet again in their own personal race. We are surrounded by yellow canoes, crewed by brightly dressed youngsters shouting encouragement to us, and by a boisterous media, determined to capture the historic moment without falling in. I am reminded of the frantic scenes as I drove a tuk tuk through Bangkok, surrounded by the media and other interested parties, all buzzing around us in their own variety of vehicles. For tuk tuks, substitute canoes, the scene is the same.

It is a 100 canoe scramble to the finishing post and in the excitement no one records who got there first. Caroline, Jon and Miles leap into the water for a cooling down swim. I go ashore to be met by Mary who tells me that a sailing junk nearby has come specially to take us for a sail – and another means of transport – but due to the unauthorised swim, there is now not enough time, and that trip has been abandoned. The Captain, who has been looking forward to the sail, is not amused, but these things happen. We make our apologies and move on to our next means of transport.

We are to travel from the jetty to the clubhouse of the Kau Sai Chau Golf Course by golf buggy. I know what is coming and sure enough, we are soon to be in it, driven by Miles with Jon shouting out instructions and waving a white stick out in front of him!

On arrival we are joined by Benny Liu, a Paralympics medallist and a former member of the Hong Kong Fire Service, who had lost his leg saving the life of a lady in a fire. Each of us is allocated to a team and given a colour. Each team is also allocated to one of the professional golfers at the course, led by Club professional Mark Reeves.

Once again, the media surround us as we set out, determined to capture the full story of the hole of golf played by two blind people, one man in a wheelchair and one man with a bad heart … Miles is lined up behind his ball, takes a swing and to everyone's amazement strikes the ball with the sweet spot and sends it soaring exactly in the right - direction. Because he is blind he has to rely on our reaction to know if he has been successful, and our astonished yells and cheers give him the good news.

Mike has balance problems, and with one hand holding firmly on to his wheelchair, he does a one arm swing towards the ball, and like Miles, catches it cleanly and off it soars towards the pin. The spectators yell, not able to believe what they are seeing.

Mike lines up what turns out to be a superb shot

My turn and, totally put off by the success of Miles and Mike, I scuff my ball a few yards along the fairway. It never takes off, but at least it is in the right direction. The crowd are relieved that at least one of us finds golf a challenge.

Caroline follows and sends a goodly piece of Hong Kong flying off in the direction of the hole. We know the ball is in there somewhere, but it takes some time to locate it.

Now we are on the green. I have to make the first putt, which I do with some relief and élan. Miles asks his caddy to click his thumb and finger over the hole and promptly holes his putt. Mike and Caroline follow.

By this time Miles, who is a fitness freak, has become tired of the slowness of golf, and blind though he may be, sets off on a run in the general direction of the clubhouse. Caroline, who can see a bit, sets off after him and the pair are seen arm in arm heading for a very large bunker. Caroline spots it at the last moment and they arrive safely at the clubhouse, where Mary has made good friends with the General Manager Kevin Yeung and he is there to take us to lunch.

In the afternoon, the Hong Kong Jockey Club has arranged a fund-raising carnival on the racetrack and thousands of children and their parents have turned out. We make a dramatic entrance. Mike is dressed as an Emperor and is carried into the arena on a splendid sedan chair. Caroline and Miles are dressed out in brilliantly coloured robes and are on horseback. Mary and I share a two-person cycle. We move into the arena,

Ready for our carnival
at the Hong Kong
racetrack

take our places next to Lawrence Wong and other officials from the Jockey Club and open the carnival by letting off a thousand coloured balloons, all in a chain. The sun is shining, the crowds are cheering and applauding, everyone is laughing and smiling. It is yet another wonderful, moving, warm moment in our adventure.

We disappear into the crowds. Mike is shooting arrows into the target at the archery stall, surrounded by hordes of admiring children. His upper body strength means he can shoot a good arrow, but the usual balance problems cause him some difficulty. Miles, meanwhile is still on his horse and is trying to get permission to ride it round the racetrack – this time with no avail. Caroline is chasing up volunteers to place coins around the race-track with the aim of getting enough to go right around it. Mary and I have found a wonderful children's choir and we sit on the grass in front of them with Jon and let them sing to us. We applaud wildly and I doff my top hat to them, a gesture that is greeted with shrieks of delight.

It is a wonderful afternoon, and we ponder at how much these people have entered into the spirit of our adventure with their magnificent Yes Can Do campaign. We are humbled by their enthusiasm, efficiency, and hard work.

Now it is evening and once again we are off-duty. Doris and William from the Jockey Club have hired space in the Peking Garden Restaurant and we are enjoying a completely informal party – and there are no media present! We use it to thank the team from the Hong Kong Jockey Club, who have been outstanding. William and Doris, who headed the team, Grace, Esther, Christine, Patricia and Mark, all of whom have tended and nursed us throughout a very busy programme, who have watched out for our needs, put up with our whims, and been a joy to be with. We know we are deeply indebted to them.

Benny is there with his two children, and I talk to them about the importance of making the most of their lives. It is a friendly off the record event and it lets us drop our guard and get to know the Jockey Club people as friends.

We board the junk and find it is full of disabled children. Like the *Tenacious* which we sailed from Nice to Monaco, the craft has been specially adapted to let disabled people experience the joys of sailing. We are to join them as crew.

Our first task is to haul up the sails. What I assume to be a simple task proves to be backbreaking. We all take hold of a rope and pull to the rhythmic beat shouted out by our captain. It is not long before I am exhausted. I look around and see Mary, Jon, Mike, Miles and Caroline are doing their bit with energy and vim, with Carbonara filming the scene. All around us, significantly disabled children are all attacking their own tasks with the same degree of excitement, as we drift out into the apparent chaos that is Victoria Harbour.

Slowly order takes over as the sails are fully hoisted and the wind catches them. We sail triumphantly past Kowloon and towards Hong Kong central, the end of our journey. And dur-

Our last day in Hong Kong and it is back to our means of transport. This time we have to sail in a junk back to central Hong Kong and then return to the airport to move on to San Fransisco

ing the sail, we sit and listen as each of the children on board does a party piece. Some are so disabled they can hardly sit upright, some can hardly speak, but all are encouraged by the other children to do something and all their performances are met with the same enthusiasm they would greet a pop star. Yet again, we find ourselves trying not to cry.

One little child in particular captivates us. He is very small, disabled, can hardly sit up, can hardly speak and at first is unwilling to even try ... but the other children encourage him with love and support and eventually he sits in front of us. It is quiet. He opens his mouth and at first nothing comes out – then a fumbled word ... he stops, hurt by his failure but they urge him to go on ... he tries again ... and again ... and again until he manages to stumble through his one line verse. Joy explodes on his face, tears rush to our eyes. We have so very much to learn about love from these children.

We pull into the pier where a crowd have gathered. The media have not been allowed on the junk but they are there in full flight as we arrive. We jump off and give them our impressions of Hong Kong.

To all of us, it has been an astonishing and humbling experience and we are the better for it. The hospitality, efficiency and friendship of the Hong Kong Jockey Club team has dramatically demonstrated that our team are nothing without back-up support. It is the Hong Kong Jockey Club team that has made Hong Kong such a success, we have simply filled the roles

Hurry up Mike, you will miss the plane! We were all so sad to leave Hong Kong

we promised to fill. We have not let them down, but they, not we, are the stars and we all know it.

For me, this reminder could not have come at a better time. And I am happy for another reason, for as a result of our stay in Hong Kong, my money worries are over and there is just enough in the kitty to complete the original programme. We do not have to come home from San Francisco after all!

DAY
Seventy

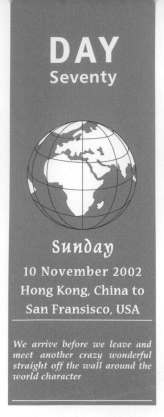

Sunday

10 November 2002
Hong Kong, China to
San Fransisco, USA

We arrive before we leave and meet another crazy wonderful straight off the wall around the world character

Richard Dupell is a one-off. San Francisco is where Phileas Fogg landed when he hit America, so it was essential that we made the same landmark. But we knew no one in San Francisco to set up our programme. Once again, Sir Tom Farmer came to the rescue. He had lived there for some time and still has a sister in the area – but he introduced me first to a friend of his, John Moorehouse, who had just returned from the Golden Gate City.

He listened to my story and than said, 'You need Richard Dupell.'

He e-mailed Richard, saying, 'Here is a job for Fratelli Bologna.' He outlined our task and Richard got in touch with me.

'I am your man in San. Look no more.'

And so another crazy characterful colourful wonderful lively and unorthodox character joined the Around the World in 80 Ways team.

In the late seventies, San Francisco was prime film making territory and Richard had the bright idea of getting a zany group of actor characters around him and offering them as a team to casting directors for crowd scenes. He called them Fratelli Bologna because he liked the sound of it. Italian and a bit crazy.

Their first assignment was as a bunch of paparazzi style reporters. When the script called for the press to be there, creating atmosphere by camera flashbulbs and screamed questions from frenetic reporters determined to get their stories and pictures, Richard's gang turned up en masse and gave a spanking professional performance.

Thus Fratelli Bologna became the casting director's dream. Whenever a group of up to ten was needed, as press reporters, waiters, hecklers, demonstrators, a gang of crooks, they went straight to Fratelli Bologna. Cleverly Richard kept the group in character even off-screen. They became a daily feature in the streets and drinking establishments of San Francisco as they hung around together – always dressed in character outfits, always half acting, always making an impression. Film after film featured them in the background. They even took themselves to Disneyland in Orlando where they were employed to mingle with the crowds and improvise on anything that happened to create atmosphere and entertainment. On one occasion, when all the 'stars' of the Disney general parade suddenly went on strike, it was Fratelli Bologna who held the crowd spellbound with their act for five hours, improvising with the audience and getting them to join in. Richard's own personal highlight was to appear as one of the cop car drivers in a James Bond film car chase, when he ended up with his car rolled and upside down.

Sadly the film industry moved on from the streets of San Francisco and without it, there was no future for Fratelli Bologna in its present form. Most of the characters found other things to do but Richard kept the formula alive, though in a different market.

He developed his concept of spontaneity into a corporate training technique. At senior management training sessions, he and his team would act out scenes from real situations confronting management and get them to join in so the story moved in the direction of the consensus of opinion in the training room.

Like everything to do with Richard, it was unusual, spontaneous and deserving of rich reward.

We arrive in San Francisco three hours before we left Hong Kong! Our flight tickets had been very generously donated to us by Cathay Pacific, the only airline in the entire adventure to show any genuine interest and support for what we are trying to achieve and we are grateful to them. Richard and his gang are at the airport to meet us. I am wearing my Phileas Fogg top hat so that Richard can quickly establish who I am, but I need not have bothered. Apart from the fact that a party of two blind people and a third in a wheelchair is fairly conspicuous anyway, Richard and his friends are holding up a very large Welcome to San Francisco banner. They take us to our hotel, The Ramada Plaza in Market Street. There is a Starbucks in the lobby and we gulp down hot chocolates before going to our rooms to unpack for the umpteenth time. Apart from having a team dinner in the evening, the rest of the time is spent recovering from our journey.

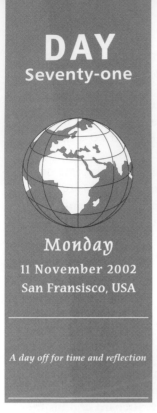

DAY
Seventy-one

Monday
11 November 2002
San Fransisco, USA

A day off for time and reflection

Today Richard meets us in the hotel and briefs us about the programme for the next few days. Then it is time off to recover from the long journey from Hong Kong. For me the flight to Hong Kong gives time to reflect on our remarkable journey, for we are now past the halfway mark and are on our way home.

On the flight Mike is lying down next to me, across two seats. Why on earth did I take the decision to bring him along? In his own words, most of his doctors and certainly his friends expected him to be flown back to hospital from some far-flung corner of the world in a bad state. I had been told he had no immune system and an insect bite could kill him. I had been told that changes in diet were very dangerous for him, yet the journey involved almost daily changes in diet. I was told he had to take his pills regularly, yet the time changes involved would make this almost impossible. The previous year he had spent 214 days in hospital undergoing routine maintenance, I needed him to be fully fit for 100 days to go around the world and tackle all sorts of challenging means of transport. Legally, I was warned that in taking him despite all these warnings, I could personally be held responsible if anything untoward happened to him and I could be sued by his family.

At the time of the decision, I knew someone else who could take Mike's place, for through my World Young Business Achiever programme, I had met an adventurous paraplegic who presented a television programme, who loved the idea and who begged me to take him. Yet, despite all of this, I had stuck with taking Mike along. There was no logic to my decision. By all the facts in front of me before we set out it was the wrong one, yet Mike is sleeping soundly next to me on the plane, he is as fit as he has been for ages, and I am glad I made the decision that I did. Mike has added so much to the project. Everywhere he goes, a crowd assembles around him, he attracts media attention, he is an inspiration to all of us, attending to his special needs binds us closer together and in his own way he is a powerful speaker.

Caroline sits behind Mike. I once asked Caroline if, having planned to fulfil her dream of riding an elephant across India, she would ever have passed on her berth to let someone else do it, and take a back seat.

'Absolutely no way' she said. I knew then that she was the only one of the three who really understood the sacrifice I had made to step aside from doing it myself on my own, and let her, Mike and Miles undertake it.

Caroline has been a tower of strength on the adventure, turning her hand to any jobs that needed doing, be they helping Mike to shifting luggage. She has also been our 'chatter upper' showing an amazing talent for getting anything from upgrades on flights to free champagne in bars. She has massive determination, and anyone watching her speak will assume she is a girl who knows exactly what she wants, where she is going and how she is going to get there.

But at times we have seen a different Caroline, and I know that she is a girl who needs very strong support. She can fly to the stars, but there has to be someone standing behind her to pick up the pieces when she misses, dust her down and put her back up again.

Jon has rebuilt the job I gave him in a way he wants to do it, and the adventurers have accepted this. I remember something that Mike wrote about him.

> Jon has proved his great ability as an enabler time after time for all of us, but especially for me. He has a great instinct for knowing what is needed and what I can do for myself. This has caught me out a number of times when I have been lazy and his response has been, 'You can do that yourself'. He has been suitably protective and has resisted offers of help from enthusiastic helpers. The important thing is that disabled or not, one is able to achieve more of anything by working with others. In the area of disability a carer can easily restrict a person by being over-protective, but Jon has a natural ability to know when to help and when to let me sort it out on my own.

Jon has a brilliant career ahead of him as a leader of young people.

Miles sits in front of me, to the right. As usual, he becomes the centre of attraction and gets VIP attention from a young stewardess, who is enraptured by his accomplishments.

Miles has an incredible ability to focus totally on the adventure he is undertaking at the moment, then when it is over, to put it in the past and move on. At the moment, it is scuba diving with Around the World that has caught his attention, but I know that on his return he will focus on microlighting, for he wants to undertake an adventure with his friend and microlight pilot Storm Smith.

Miles is our deepest thinker, our philosopher, and when on form, our top speaker. Despite being unable to see an audience, he has an uncanny knack of making them forget this. His eye contact with individual members of the audience is remarkable and his animation is that of a seeing man. He is also the one who frequently tells me how much he appreciates the fact that I have included him in my dream.

Throughout the adventure, he has understood that Mike is the one who needs most help and on many occasions has stood aside patiently to let Jon and Caroline attend to some of Mike's more complicated needs. He is the one who has understood how hard it is for Mary to have put so much into setting up the organisation and yet not take part in all the means of travel and visit all the countries on the route.

I hope that on his return, Miles will free himself of the burden of working for someone else and will set up as a freelance motivational speaker. He is a stunning speaker and being his own boss will be the right thing for him.

On this flight my mind also turns to others who have helped, and in particular Mike Thomson our ever-patient volunteer bookkeeper. I had found him through Cramond Kirk, where I sing in the choir. Throughout the entire adventure, he has battled with different currencies, difficult banks, absence of proper paperwork, lack of communication, inexplicable expenses, shortage of funds. Throughout, he has remained calm and in control. It is no wonder he has become a friend.

Now I am in the Ramada Plaza in San Francisco and on day 71 of the project. How am I feeling? The management task of setting it all up, finding the money, being responsible for the welfare of the adventurers, has taken a toll. I try hard to convince myself that my choice to bring in others rather than do it on my own was the right one, but I am not sure. Right now, I wonder why I took on the additional heavyweight burden when it would have been so easy just to live out my dream the way I wanted to, without heavy costs, without responsibility, without all the publicity, social visits and so on.

I ask myself what would I do if I could turn the clock back? Right now, Monday, 11 November, the jury is out on that one.

I have another problem that needs my urgent attention. Alas, my topper is beginning to feel the strain. The material around the featured 'spring brim' has worn through and the wire around the brim is poking out. I am not sure where I can find anyone to fix top hats in San Francisco but I head off downtown. The answer lies in an unusual destination – a hardware store. There, the matt black insulating tape looks highly promising. I buy a roll, tape it round the brim and the job is done. Topper is restored, if not to full glory, at least a passable imitation.

It is our first official engagement. Richard has explained to us that San Francisco, being such a colourful and off the wall place, has shown little interest in our party, accepting us as being entirely normal and not doing anything unusual. What is unusual about two blind people, another in a wheelchair, a fourth with a wobbly heart, going around the world in 80 ways, being filmed by a one-eyed cameraman and managed by a guy who has a hearing disability? They see them every day in San Francisco.

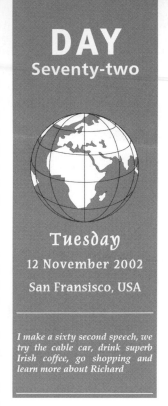
I make a sixty second speech, we try the cable car, drink superb Irish coffee, go shopping and learn more about Richard

So, there would be no big television interviews, no cheering crowds, no parades, no glittering gala lunches or dinners to raise funds. Just an immersion into the wonderful world of San Francisco.

Today is my son Ashley's birthday. I decide against phoning as it is the 'wee hours' back home, so I text him instead.

We are guests for lunch at the St Francis Yacht Club. It reminds me of the many hours spent as a child at the Royal Ulster Yacht Club in Bangor, Northern Ireland – top echelon, pictures on the wall of yachts crewed by bearded aristocrats in uniform and white caps, tradition and ancestry oozing out of the very bricks and a strict code of behaviour being the order of the day.

We are not the guests of honour, but the Captain invites me to speak for two minutes. During the lunch, I try to make out what to say and at one point, I decide to ask Caroline to take the spot as in two minutes I feel she could make a bigger impression that I would. Caroline, however, feels it would best be done by me.

I stand up, open fire, give a very powerful and telling ninety seconds worth and sit down. The speech has electric impact and apart from opening up some donations to help with our costs, it brings in Peter Stoneberg and a trip in a hot-air balloon – more later.

The lunchtime speaker is The British Consul General to San Francisco Roger Thomas and he tells of the time he spent in Iraq. In the light of future events, his stories of the development of Iraq's nuclear chemical and biological weapons programmes and the lengths they went to fool the UN are very revealing.

After lunch we remind ourselves of the need to pack in some more modes of travel, so we head off to ride the famous cable car. We feel like

We add a San Francisco tram to our records

tourists as we clamber on board, Mike next to the driver, Miles, Caroline and I hanging on to the side bars. It is a thrilling experience, Carbonara is in his car and does a reasonable impersonation of Steve McQueen as we hit the bumps, and once again I am struck by the magic of our journey as a one-eyed cameraman tries to drive a car and film us going over the notorious San Francisco bumps.

We end up at Canary Wharf and head for the Bueno Vista Bar, famous for introducing Irish coffee to America.

'Irish coffees all round' I order, and the gang of myself, Jon, Mike, Miles, Caroline, Ed Gallagher, a blind San Franciscan who is taking us sailing tomorrow, Carbonara and two film students he has acquired to help, plus the indomitable Richard Dupell, sit down to enjoy them.

They are great and I try to pay.

'They are on us' says the owner and I discover that Caroline has told him all about us and what we are trying to do.

'In that case, I still want to buy my round, so bring us another set.'

We drink them and I ask for the bill.

'They are on us again.'

Determined to pay for my round, I order yet one more for each of us and ask for the bill.

'Listen friend, people like you will not pay for a drink in my bar. There is another round on its way for you.'

We drink up and pull out.

'Now you are all like me, legless' says Mike and we all collapse in laughter.

That place must sell thousands of Irish coffees every day and I determine to tell an Irish friend of mine, Bernard Walsh, who has developed a product called Hot Irishman, a concoction in a bottle that makes the production of a true Irish coffee easy and quick. There must be a sales opening there for him.

We head off for the shops. Boots, hats and jeans are tried and Mike asks to look at some spurs. The attendant misses the joke, brings him some and only realises he is being wound up when he tries to fit them on Mike. It is like the time Mike handed over a pair of shoes to a street shoeshine man and asked him to clean them.

Two and a half hours later, the team emerge. We have kept Richard waiting and I can see he is getting impatient but the rest of the team have not noticed. It is another of those moments when I feel that the adventurers do not always appreciate what is being done for them by others.

Shopping with the men is quite an experience and we leave with jeans all over the place. Thankfully the shop assistants enjoy meeting us and nothing is too much trouble. Miles spends more than twenty minutes trying to decide between two different boots with a marginal colour difference and the shop assistant learns more about how to be with people who are blind. Just because he cannot see, how dare we question his right, just like the rest of us, to get the colour he wants. The shop assistant understands this. Wonderful.

But for Mike the highlight of the day has already happened. Wheeling himself along the street, he finds a magical tailor who measures his leg length on the side of the street to appear five minutes later as Mike is having a beer in a nearby pub, holding a pair of perfectly adjusted trousers for his inside leg measurements of 15 inches. The alteration only costs $7. Maybe I should have asked him to fix the brim of my topper.

Richard returns us to our hotel but is back later to take us to dinner. We walk round the corner to the local restaurant and there Richard tells us more about himself.

A fifty-two year old actor, he has packed so much into his mad and crazy life and we squirm in our seats with inadequacy as he runs through some of his adventures which range from the Vietnam war, his modelling and acting and the work he does now with his unique business theatre. We eat the most divine fish and sip Manhattans, Richard's favourite, iced teas which make Miles fall comatose, and wine. We fall in love with Richard – a soft crazy talented out there thespian whose life is like a soufflé of a cult book or psychadelic movie.

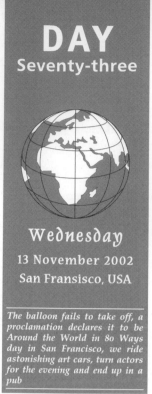

The balloon fails to take off, a proclamation declares it to be Around the World in 80 Ways day in San Francisco, we ride astonishing art cars, turn actors for the evening and end up in a pub

We have a false start. As a result of my 90 second speech at the yacht club, Peter Stoneberg has invited the team to go hot-air ballooning at the crack of dawn. So we are picked up at 4 a.m. for a 6:30 a.m. flight.

We head off in a people carrier, seats removed so we can all fit in and pass an hour singing every ridiculous song we can think of from Jingle Bells to Yellow Submarine, via our famous duck song from Singapore. Sadly when we get to the take-off area, we are surrounded by fog – Filthiest Fog, as one of the team calls it. We all groan and hope there are no more like that. Phileas Fogg would have sent the perpetrator home.

To make up for the disappointment Peter takes us to see his incredible collection of race cars and Miles is in heaven when his Formula 1 car is started so he can hear and record the mighty roar of the exhaust note.

We return to San Francisco and are rewarded by a fabulous dawn view as we cross The Golden Gate and stare out towards Alcatraz. It is worth the trip for the race cars and for that view.

But we have to prepare ourselves for one of the greatest challenges in our entire adventure. Richard has booked a theatre and an audience have bought tickets. I assume he wants us to do our usual speech show, but oh no, I am so wrong. He wants us to play the Life Game, the special technique he has devised for corporate training in San Francisco. In short, the evening will consist of Richard interviewing us, but with four improvising actors present, and as a point comes out in our discussions that is particularly poignant, they are to take over and act out the scene, either as it happened, or how it might have happened, had a different decision been made at the time.

We are very nervous and confused and not sure we have the hang of it, but decide to go along with Richard.

Before curtain up, there is a surprise. In planning the programme with Richard and helping him through a very difficult patch, Mary has discovered that in San Francisco there are a number of special art vehicles that have been used to travel to the desert Burning Man Festival. She asks Richard and needless to say he knows all about them and how to contact the owners to see if they would be willing to use them to transport us to the theatre. This he does and of course, he charms them into joining in with us and providing another amazing means of transport.

Art Car, San Fransisco

So we travel to the theatre in what was originally a car but is now a work of art.

Mine is stunning – a welded two story high metal fish with a swishy tail, Miles rides a tactile Devolution car which is totally covered in 3-dimesioal knick-knacks including music boxes, chandeliers, and so on, whilst Mike is in a submarine complete with periscope, fins, propeller tail and a fantastic 'ping' sound. Caroline is in another fish car, with scales made of broken CD discs.

Richard Dupell tells the story:

My excitement began to build as I approached the parking area behind Plaza San Francisco. The hotel had generously agreed to allow the cars and their crews to assemble there for our mini-parade to the performance venue. After a lot of thought and planning, there the vehicles were; the imposing 'Fish Van' for Robin, Devolution for Miles, Edith, Objet d'art for Caroline and Ping for Mike. I met the team in the hotel lobby and brought them around to meet the transportation and the team that had created them.

A short twenty minutes later we drove the Adventurers in their Art Cars through a roll-up door in the SomArts Cultural Centre. As we positioned each vehicle in the viewing gallery, I knew the event was going as planned and the satisfaction I felt was incredible. The actors were arriving and last-minute light and sound adjustments were being made. The audience had arrived and the excitement in the theatre was palpable.

At 8:00 p.m., after a brief introduction to the Life Game format, I bring on the actors and the four adventurers. In the Life Game, guest interviews are watched by the actors who are asked to spontaneously create improvised scenes. The combination of interviews and improvisation creates a truly unique, and in this case dramatic, evening of theatre.

I present the adventurers with a proclamation from William Lewis Brown, Mayor of San Francisco, declaring 13 November 2002 Around the World in 80 Ways Day. Then I interview the four adventurers. It is truly inspiring. After the show, my professional actors tell me how difficult it was to 'get off the bench' to improvise scenes as they were so fascinated by the stories told by the adventurers.

In many ways the show is traumatic. I ask Mike how he felt when scuba diving and he tells the story of how he could shake the hand of the person who had caused his disability, as had it not been for him, he would never have scuba dived, let alone do Around the World in 80 Ways. At once improvisation actor Reed Kirk Rahiman, in wheelchair with his feet tucked under his bottom, takes up the story and with another of the actors improvises their version of a future meeting between Mike and the person who caused his injuries. He, recognising Mike, tries to flee assuming Mike would want to hurt him – Mike, however pursues him to try to tell him it is all right, he is living a new life and has no desire for revenge.

And at that point there are tears, and not least from Mike, in the theatre.

Other highlights of the evening include the re-creation of the race car driving in Malaysia, Miles, Caroline and Jon dancing the 'Ostrich Dance' and the singing of the 'Jon Song' a tribute to team manager Jon Cook who is in the audience.

The evening is an enormous success. The four of us have appeared on stage, with a paying audience, in a highly challenging format of blending with improvisation actors and we have all come through with flying colours.

We retire to a nearby bar with Richard and some of the actors where we celebrate a marvellous evening, held to raise funds for the Bay Area Association for Disabled Sailors, an organisation run by another magic Around the World Character to take central stage tomorrow ... Ed Gallagher.

Today we are driven in a vehicle supplied by the Recreation Centre for the Handicapped to the Saint Frances Yacht Club where we are to sail in two sloops specially rigged for people with disabilities, provided by the Bay Area Association for Disabled Sailors, with Ed Gallagher in charge.

We sail in sloops and hay barges, and are presented with a certificate of congratulation by the Executive Director of the Port of Oakland

Ed is totally blind, but sees that as no hindrance. He discovered the joy of sailing even though blind and has since taught hundreds of blind people to sail. His job today is to take us on our first sector, from central San Francisco to the hay barge *Alma*, moored about an hour's sail away at the Hyde Street Dock.

I am to sail with Ed and Miles, the others are in the second sloop. We start to climb on board. Ed warns about the slippery deck and advises us to take care. Miles starts to climb on board and heeding Ed's warning, I guide him as carefully as I can, from the dock onto the deck. In doing it, I slip and crack my leg against a hawser. Both Ed and Miles being blind, do not see the mishap and I keep my silence.

We sail out into the river and I am in agony. A massive lump careers up in my lower shin and I wonder if I have sustained a fracture – but decide to hold my silence, whilst Miles and Ed drink in the enjoyment of the sail. Ed has a helper with him to make sure he is going in the right direction and he sees my pain but I motion him to keep quiet and he obeys. We sail close to the other sloop and I see Mike and Caroline once more drinking in the excitement and exhilaration of travelling in Around the World in 80 Ways

We approach the *Alma* and at once I see that I will be rumbled. I can now hardly move my leg and there is no way I can get on board without help. I let Miles go first and I then shout out my problem. Two sturdy crewmen from the *Alma* carry me on board, I am plonked on deck, a bucket is lowered into the sea, filled and I am told to submerge my leg in it. The *Alma* sets sail for Oakland, our destination and every so often the ice-cold water in my bucket is replaced. The swelling goes down, and I pull out my leg. It is a wonderful mixture of blues, reds and yellows and is many times the right size – but the ship's Captain who doubles up as doctor has felt it and decided there are no breaks of any significance and I should just grin and bear it, which I decide to do.

The *Alma* is a converted hay barge and is operated by the National Park Service with a full time Captain and a volunteer crew. *Alma* often takes

disabled parties out sailing and the Skipper has devised an interesting but not too comfortable rig for winching disabled guests on board. Mike uses it and manages all right.

The sail on the *Alma* gives me a chance to check on the team. Caroline comes to me and talks at length about her family back home and her upbringing. She also tells me just how much Around the World means and has meant to her and thanks me for thinking up the adventure. After a while the pain in my leg subsides and I find I can move and spend time with Mike. He talks with confidence of achieving the rest of the journey ahead and I feel an enormous affection for him. Mike can be suave, arrogant, pestering, but he has to put up with so many challenges and of all of us, he is the one that has shown most courage in undertaking Around the World.

As always, Miles is at the bow of the *Alma*, interviewing the crew, handing out his cards, talking into his recorder. We all now understand how Miles uses his tape recorder as a camera. He cannot see images, but he can record them – the sounds of what is happening, the commentary from those involved, the descriptions of the action. He has a stunning recording of the massive loss of control he suffered when racing Caroline during the Malaysian Grand Prix Circuit and Murray Walker could not have caught the atmosphere more succinctly – a massive screech, cries of delight from Miles as he gets an adrenaline rush with the slide and then Jon's calm and quiet voice; 'Drive Miles, anywhere, Caroline is thundering down on top of us.'

We reach Oakland. By now a crew member has found a 'camper's cold compress' and I am able to limp along. I walk down the gangplank and am greeted by Tay Yoshitani, Executive Director of the Port of Oakland Authority, who presents us with a certificate of congratulation and takes us to tea.

We drink Long Island Iced Tea with Tay who tells us the history of the docks and the area. We realise just how miniscule is our knowledge of the world.

Back in the hotel, Jon and Caroline come to my room and we talk long into the night. With most of our adventure over, and urged on by Miles, I have decided to change from being the leader into simply being a colleague and they notice and appreciate the difference. Instead of being one step away from them, I become one of them. It is a warm and affectionate meeting and I feel the better for it. Leading the group and the responsibilities involved have weighed heavily on me, and being able to let go for a while is wonderful. I learn that Jon and Caroline, Miles and Mike, have realised my difficulties more than I had thought and in coming to be with me, they are showing their love and appreciation.

DAY
Seventy-five

Friday
15 November 2002
San Fransisco, USA

Mary and I have an enormous decision to make

At the very first bonding weekend, held at Caroline's dad's place at Cross in Ireland, we had decided that our journey would have added spice through the introduction of three adventure sections. In these, nothing would be planned, I would leave the team for Jon to lead, he would be given a date and place to start, a date and place where I would meet him at the end, a budget to keep to and some tasks to accomplish. Nothing would be organised in advance and the team would have to use their initiative to get through.

It was an idea that was greeted with enormous enthusiasm and the sectors were set for Monaco to Rome, Bangkok to Singapore, and the big one, San Francisco to New York.

However, the previous two had not worked out as planned. Instead of spending four days travelling from Monaco to Rome, the team had gone straight to Rome to sort out the Indian visas which Caroline and Aoife had not obtained before leaving Ireland, and the adventurers had ended up spending the time in a holiday villa in Tuscany and a hostel in Rome. Whilst they had worked hard and had achieved all the tasks set for them, it was not the programme that had been planned.

For the Malaysian sector, Mary overruled the plan, for she realised that having just completed exhausting sectors in South Africa and India, and with two more exhausting sectors coming up in Singapore and Hong Kong, a better plan would be to arrange for the disabled adventurers to have a rest and relaxation break, so she and Guy Chaplin ended up by producing a highly organised sector with a luxury three-day break.

That left getting across America as our only chance to be true to our original idea of adventure sectors – but once again, we have hit a major snag.

Caroline is the cause, but for wonderful reasons. She has learned she has been voted a winner of the highly prestigious Irish Person of the Year Awards and has been invited to attend a presentation in Dublin on 16 November – right after the start of the adventure sector!

And there is more of the same kind of news to come. The Junior Chamber of Commerce tell her she has been voted one of their prestigious awards in the Top Ten Young People of the World, and can she be in Las Vegas to receive it on November 25 once again right in the middle of the sector.

Mary , Stuart and I have a conference. It is clear that either Caroline must decline attending the two awards ceremonies, or we will have to park the rest of the team whilst she travels to Ireland to receive the award and then returns, to go with the team to Las Vegas, and the second award ceremony.

But the situation has been further complicated by a call from Jimmy Spankie, who interviewed the team on 4 September in Cramond Kirk in Scotland. Formerly one of Scotland's top television presenters, Jimmy had a contract to fly each year to visit a firm called Logisticare in Washington DC and coach their people in presentation skills. He had told them about Around the World in 80 Ways and they asked if Jimmy could arrange for the team to visit on their way through the USA. The day they suggest is right after Caroline's visit to Ireland and before her award in Las Vegas. So the timetable now became crazy.

Stuart outlines to us how it can be done. The team would stay in San Francisco and wait for Caroline to return from Ireland, then they could all fly east to Washington DC for the Logisticare event, then fly back west to Las Vegas for Caroline's second award, and then head east again across the USA for home.

So the three of us reach a decision.

I will return home as planned and start work on the return of the adventurers and the triumphant celebration luncheon. This was to have been organised by the Leonard Cheshire Foundation to raise money for their funds but had fallen through. A subsequent offer by Rolls-Royce had just been withdrawn so a new sponsor had to be found, otherwise precious Around the World Funds would have to be used. Sorting this out becomes a priority for me.

Mary will fly out to join the adventurers for the Washington DC programme, which she organised in conjunction with Jimmy Spankie and Robin Wrinn of Logisticare. Our first idea was for Mary to then stay with the team until they got home. However, for Caroline to attend her awards ceremony in Las Vegas, it would be necessary after Washington DC to return the team to California, backtracking for the first time in the entire project. Because of this, Mary decides to head for home and help find a sponsor for the celebration luncheon and undertake its organisation.

Stuart, Mary and I finish our conference with the realisation that we now have something of a dog's dinner for the USA instead of a triumphant adventure sector – Caroline is going home for twenty-four hours, the team will be parked in San Francisco doing nothing for three days, then after travelling east to fulfil the engagement in Washington, they would have to go back west again to California and to Las Vegas for another awards ceremony, before heading for home.

It was not what had been planned but the honours awarded to Caroline were a matter of great pride to us all, and we decide to turn a blind eye to the break in our adventure and to celebrate instead Caroline's wonderful achievements.

I sit down with Jon and we talk the adventure sector through. I tell him that the programme is set between San Francisco through to the award ceremony in Las Vegas, but then he is finally free to undertake the intent of the adventure sectors and use his and the adventurers' initiative to get the team to New York in time for their flight to London on 1 December using as many means of transport as he can find, spending as little money as possible and raising some funds to cover costs and to donate to charity.

And so on 16 November, I fly home London to prepare for the return, Mary starts packing for Washington DC, Caroline flies back to Dublin to collect her award, Miles, Mike and Jon settle down to enjoy an unplanned break in San Francisco.

DAY
Seventy-six

Saturday
16 November 2002
San Fransisco

We all manoeuvre into our places for the rest of the journey home

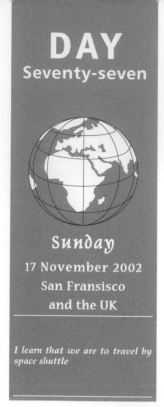

For Miles, Mike and Jon, it is a day for sightseeing in San Francisco. Carbonara decides to spend the day getting some more background filming of San Francisco.

Back in the UK I grab a few moments with Mary before she heads off for Washington and she tells me of her plans for the return to London. They are stunning. She has been dealing with the Smurfit people who provided us with the cardboard boat on the Liffey and they have come up with a spectacular idea for the last means of transport to the Reform Club.

They want to produce a cardboard space shuttle and two of their people have designed one in their spare time. Can they go ahead and make it?

It is a wonderful idea and it makes me immensely cheerful.

I see her to the airport and then turn my attention to the arrangements for the return. Unknown to the team, but not to Mary, I have to undergo some further medical tests as there are concerns about my health.

I am home to sort out the return to London event, Mary is on her way to Washington DC to be with the team on their courtesy visit there, the team are on their way from San Francisco to Washington DC via Charlotte, North Carolina.

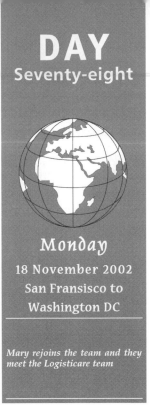

DAY
Seventy-eight

Monday
18 November 2002
San Fransisco to
Washington DC

Mary rejoins the team and they meet the Logisticare team

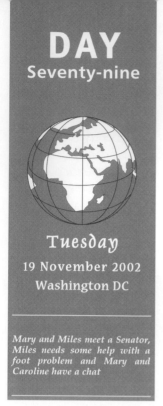

DAY
Seventy-nine

Tuesday
19 November 2002
Washington DC

Mary and Miles meet a Senator, Miles needs some help with a foot problem and Mary and Caroline have a chat

Mary takes up the story.

Halfway across the Atlantic I remember that I hadn't cancelled a meeting, the trip to Washington came up very quickly whilst we were in Hong Kong. A decision was made that Robin would travel with the team to San Francisco, I would return to the UK and join the team in Washington. I still had just enough holiday days to cover the trip. Jimmy Spankie our friend from Cramond had arranged with Logisticare, a company dealing with transportation for people with disabilities, to host a dinner in Washington DC, a meeting with a Senator and an opportunity to see the very best of facilities for the disabled. In return we would meet disabled people, Miles would do a 10 minute motivational video for training purposes and we would have some unusual means of transport.

Arriving at Dulles Airport there was a message on my mobile. Carole Gray my administrator had gone through my diary and assured me that she had dealt with changes. Carole is one of our ATW angels and so often ensured that I was at the right place at the right time with the right stuff.

Sitting in my hotel room I wondered how on earth I had managed to get to The Watergate Hotel – THE Watergate Hotel, although the taxi driver at the airport informed me he didn't know where it was!! Then perhaps I wasn't the kind of fare he expected coming off the London flight. Tired, shoeless – yes shoeless, on arrival at security we were asked to place our shoes in order for them to go through the security screen – only with the excitement I had forgotten to pick mine up and hadn't realised until I was sitting inside the taxi! He had the grace to wait for me while I went to pick them up.

Jon, Miles, Caroline and Mike arrived the next day – I was shocked to see how tired they all were; the next couple of days weren't particularly strenuous, but I knew that it took every ounce of determination for the team to stay cheerful and inspiring, which of course is inspiring in itself.

I met Miles for the first time at the bonding weekend at Cross, now I am sitting with him in a clinic whilst his foot is being examined – he picked up an infection and now it needs medical attention. We were to meet the rest of the team and go to Congress to meet Senator Johnny Isakson, Member of Congress, Sixth District Georgia – there was a mix up in timing and it ended up just me and Miles at the Senator's office. It was a good meeting and Senator Isakson wanted a picture of himself with Miles for his website – Miles insisted that I was in the photograph as well – 'Mary is our Project Director' he said.

Miles and I joined the rest of the team in the hotel, we were all going to go out to dinner together but decided that we would rather have a picnic in Mike's room – so Caroline and I headed off for the local deli.

All day long I felt that Caroline needed to talk to me. A couple of times I asked her if she was all right. She always replied 'I'm fine' but I knew something was badly wrong. At last over deciding what beer to chose she finally asked if she could see me later.

'Yes of course' I replied and gave her a hug.

What a fun night we had, we all needed to let our hair down, I was able to update everyone of the return event and let the team know that the last means of transport would be a space shuttle vehicle, designed by a team at Smurfit UK. Also that Tim Haddock, the young man we met in Northern Ireland would sing his 'Around the World' song at the return luncheon.

I had two visits to my room later that night – one was Mike and later Caroline. It was good to see Mike alone – we talked about what it would be like for him on his return, the things he wanted to get involved in and how grateful he was for the opportunity to be on such an adventure.

Then a very miserable Caroline arrived, barely waiting for the door to close before she was sobbing loud heart-rending sobs. We sat on the sofa together and I hugged her until the crying stopped.

Caroline was emotionally and physically exhausted and it was a good twenty minutes before she could speak. Then slowly I began to realize what was wrong. She had been home to Dublin to collect her award and in doing so she has spent time with Fergal her husband whom she missed so much. She had also seen family and friends. Within 24 hours of being in Dublin she flew back to Las Vegas then almost immediately she had to catch a flight to Washington. It was no wonder she just wanted to curl up in a corner. She had given all she had, there was nothing left to give.

We began to talk, ranging from childhood memories, the feelings we both shared about the 'boys' and the times in our lives that perhaps we should have said 'No'.

Caroline cared so deeply for the adventurers and now being the only woman after Aoife's departure, she had to cope with the strain of being mother, sister and nurse to Mike, Miles and Jon and it was beginning to tell. She had also kept a daughterly eye on Robin when he was with the team, it upset her so much that she had not realized how ill he was in the Red Sea.

'The boys can be so annoying' she said. 'They forget I am a girl and I get so lonely and I want to go home.'

Scrambling for some words that would help her I thought of Claire-Louise, my daughter, who whilst travelling through India became ill. It had been an ambition of hers to travel to India alone and when she phoned me, she had had enough.

'Okay' I said, 'There are these choices. Get to an airport, any airport and I will arrange for a ticket home, you can be in your own bed within 36 hours. Or I can get on a plane and bring you home. Or you can take a deep breath, reach deep inside yourself, rest and get well and continue on the journey. In making your decision think how you will feel if you give in and come home.' I told her I loved her and put down the phone. I felt awful but I knew my daughter. She continued with her adventure.

'Thank you Mum' she said.

Turning to Caroline I said, 'You have these choices. You can be on a plane tomorrow and back in Dublin within 36 hours or you can dig deep within yourself and continue. But, Caroline, start letting go of the 'boys', for when the adventure ends, they are going to have to manage without you and you are going to have to manage without them and move on with your life.'

The silence between us was tangible. She took a deep breath, looked me straight in the eye and said, 'Thank you Mum. I so wanted to be a part of this adventure, I would certainly never forgive myself for not seeing it through.'

Even later that night I thought of Claire-Louise and Caroline, both of whom have brought so much to other lives and into mine.

Caroline and I sat together for a couple of hours, laughing and crying together. When she left, I wish I had made a decision that I regret I didn't, I wanted to stay with the team and see them home. Claire-Louise was working on the return event with Sharon of Smurfit, Coman was helping with the PR for the return and Robin was ensuring that all those who should be there would be, and Carole was keeping tabs on everything. But, I had a job to do, and my holiday days had all been used up.

When I waved goodbye to the adventurers, I knew it took a tremendous amount of courage for them to return to Las Vegas and get organised to get across the USA. Next time I would see them would be at Heathrow – our conversations together had all been about getting home, they still had to get across America – dear God keep everyone safe.

It was with a feeling of great pride that I set on my journey home, back to Phileas Fogg our dangerous dreamer – his idea had challenged all of us, so many people's lives had been affected and changed for ever ... My mobile rang as I got off at Heathrow, it was Carole, checking I was okay, going through my diary ...

With Mary and Robin back in London, Jon is now in charge of the first real adventure sector and in his diary he writes:

Having crossed the USA from San Francisco to Washington DC, we crossed back to Las Vegas so we could restart our journey. Washington had been cold and as we flew over we could see all the fresh snow which had allowed the ski season to begin in earnest. But as we approached Las Vegas, crossing the Grand Canyon and the Hoover Dam, we saw the wonders of the Nevada desert and knew we were heading back into the sunshine. By the time we arrived the sun was strong and we were in our shirtsleeves. We headed for the Strip for some food.

Hotel rooms are cheap in Vegas, encouraging people to come and spend as much as possible at the tables. Because of the lack of funds we have to go to the cheap end of the market and we end up in an hotel called Circus Circus.

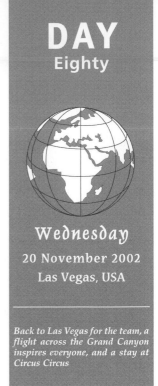

DAY
Eighty

Wednesday
20 November 2002
Las Vegas, USA

Back to Las Vegas for the team, a flight across the Grand Canyon inspires everyone, and a stay at Circus Circus

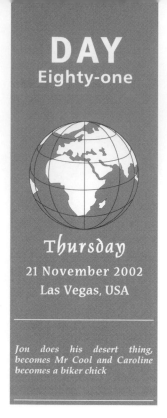

Tbursday

21 November 2002
Las Vegas, USA

Jon does his desert thing, becomes Mr Cool and Caroline becomes a biker chick

The adventurers must stay in Vegas to wait for Caroline's award ceremony which takes place on Saturday so Jon decides to give them the first day off.

He writes:

I took the day off today, a real day off from lifting, guiding, bottom examining for Mike, everything. Even when we have had days off in the past Miles and Mike needed some sort of assistance and there has always been something that needed doing. Now, after eighty days, I was on my own. The adventurers seemed to want to sleep in as late as possible but I headed off early to the Harley Davidson shop. A Harley for the day and a very big desert was my idea of a day that would be incredible: kicking up dust behind the bike, cruising in the warm wind and if I may say so, incredibly cool was just how I imagined it would be. Although I had a map I am not sure exactly where I ended up – I just sat, looking at the rocks and colours of the desert, feeling overawed by the space around me. I really don't understand why people flock to the tack of Vegas when there is so much peace and healing to be found in the desert just a few miles away. I could have stayed for ever.

Time raced away. I had promised Caroline a spin on the bike before I had to hand it back. Caroline had loved the biker chick experience on the Harleys in South Africa and had been nagging me for a ride so we met up and cruised through Vegas to the tip of the desert to catch the end of an amazing day.

Jon lives a dream on his day off – a ride on a Harley to the desert!

It is time to get back to the adventure. Stuart has sent out a message that they need to pack in more means of transport as some of the ones used have been very similar to others and may not be allowed.

John Hawthorne has arrived in Vegas from California and he has a couple of sand yachts in the boot of his car. Jon makes a beeline for him, explains what he and his team are up to, and asks if they can travel a sector by sand buggie.

'No, you can't do that today, there is no wind.'

Jon hunts around for an alternative and takes the adventurers along the famous Strip. He spots gondolas and asks if they can use them.

'Twelve dollars each' says the chap with the pole. No charity from him, he has his figures to meet.

Jon turns away. He is fast running out of money and feels the gondola ride is too expensive.

Stuart sends out a warning to the team. A lack of wind spoils a trip and the gondolas prove to be too expensive

He takes the team back to the hotel to consider what to do next. He decides that Las Vegas is not going to work and that as soon as Caroline's award is over, he must take the team off and head somewhere else in his bid to get them across the USA and back home by 3 December, the International Day for Disabled People.

DAY
Eighty-three

Saturday
23 November 2002

A flight in a hot-air balloon ends in a crash, but the same wind that caused it makes the sand yachts work

Peter Stoneberg had offered to take the adventurers hot-air ballooning in San Francisco but the fog had stopped the flight. It was very important to us that we went hot-air ballooning, for although Phileas Fogg never went up in one, everyone thinks he did because of the high prominence given to the film, where the producer included it to get some fantastic panorama shots.

To make up for our disappointment, Peter had donated funds to us instead, on the condition that the money had to be used in a hot-air balloon flight.

Jon tells the story:

Today the weather is perfect and we head out into the desert early in the morning. The mountains are glowing orange in the early morning sun and the team are busied in the process of filling a 140,000 cubic foot balloon. Mike is sitting in a kitchen chair which is tied inside the small basket, the rest of us cram into the small space and soon we are floating gently skyward. It is all so sedate as the slight breeze takes us south east.

We catch a thermal. We all laugh with excitement as the warm air causes us to ascend rapidly. Huw, the pilot, does not join in and suddenly I feel nervous. I realise that he is not happy, does not feel fully in control and he tries to get into the still air as quickly as possible.

The wind picks up. One side of the balloon bellows out, twisting the whole basket around. Huw decides it is time to land – fast. We head down chased by the ground crew.

I had heard that landing in a hot-air balloon is nothing more than a controlled crash and sure enough that is what happens. We thump into the ground, tip over on one side and then veer across rocks and dust before coming to a stop.

Mike is dangling by his waist strap inside the basket, Caroline is lying face down trying to support Mike, Miles is lying in and out of the basket, I am at the bottom trying to hold up Mike and Caroline. We all crawl out of the ruined basket, dust ourselves down, check for injuries and find none, and drink the traditional celebratory champagne.

It is time for our next means of transport, which is the Blokart sand yacht. We have a five mile strip of sand, absolutely flat, so we unzip the bags, erect the karts and climb on board. The wind is now our friend and

Caroline wonders which way is home, Mike heads off at fine speed and Miles and Jon admire the view

we zip across the dusty ground at an incredible speed. The buggies are instantly handleable by all of us and we spend an exciting time trying to see if we can get them up onto two wheels! There were no mishaps, but sheer joy – but I become increasingly aware of a pain in my chest.

Today, Caroline leaves to go to the MGM Grand where she will receive one of the 10 Outstanding Young People of the World Award, presented by the Junior Chamber Of Commerce International.

The MGM Grand is the largest hotel in the world, with five and a half thousand rooms along with theatres, shopping malls, six and a half acres of pools, and layer upon layer of casinos – a true playground for adults. Wearing her cowboy boots and now dusty jeans, carrying the elephant we had given to her, along with her by now battered and bedraggled luggage, and leaving a trail of dust behind her, she meets Joe Turner, one of the Irish Junior Chamber delegates. She is whisked away in a flurry of helpers, organisers and delegates, totally bemused by it all. Miles, Mike and Jon return to Circus Circus to eat, she enters the world of luxury, glamour, glitter and fame. It is heartrending, for the group have become so used to being a single unit, it seems as though a limb has been cut off.

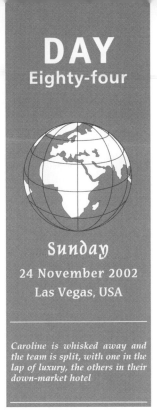
Caroline is whisked away and the team is split, with one in the lap of luxury, the others in their down-market hotel

Caroline picks up her Young People of the Year award

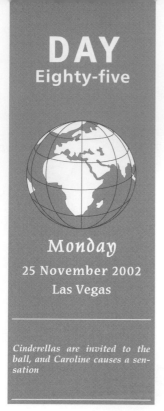

Cinderellas are invited to the ball, and Caroline causes a sensation

Miles, Mike and Jon are miserable. Caroline has been taken away to prepare for the awards tonight, the rest are mooching about in the Circus Circus hotel, wondering how to fill in the time. Caroline works a miracle and the news comes through that the whole group are invited to attend. At once morale soars sky high. There is going to be a party and everyone is going to be there after all.

It is a swish affair but like Cinderella the team, with the exception of Caroline, have nothing to wear but their duds. No good fairy turns up to dress them and there is no pumpkin to turn into a coach. Miles, Mike and Jon arrive by bus in cowboy boots, cargo shirts and jeans and are made welcome.

Caroline still has little idea what is going on, but banks on the fact that she is the second on the bill and will just take her lead from what the first person says. That plan is scuppered by the fact that he is Spanish and makes his speech in his native tongue.

Caroline has never written a speech in her life, she does not even know what she is going to say when she gets up, it is all spontaneous, a reaction to the audience, an adrenalin shot from the atmosphere, a potpourri of emotion, passion, power, and when she is on form she explodes enthusiasm and showers everyone around her with it.

She does it tonight – and creates a sensation. Caroline on form is sublime, infectious, irresistible and unavoidable and the whole audience rises to her passion. She finishes and the room is alive with excitement. Being a part of her show, the gang are instantly recognised and become award winners by proxy and suddenly the badges of office in their dusty and worn Around the World uniforms become a badge of pride.

'Did you ever think what would happen to the adventurers when they return home?' asks Mary.

DAY
Eighty-six

Tuesday
26 November 2002
Las Vegas to
Indianapolis

The team leader reflects on what to do next

No, is the simple answer. Always I had thought that the task was to get two people who are registered blind, and one who is paralysed and in a wheelchair, around the world using eighty different means of transport. What happens next to them has nothing to do with me.

But now I realise that for over eighty days, they have been together, shared excitement, some danger, been treated as celebrities, been wined and dined, experienced some severe discomfort and have bonded into a totally tight unit, dedicated to each other. Miles, Mike, Caroline and their manager Jon, are one person now, a combination of their different personalities, of course, but at the same time, the adventure has glued them together.

I start to think about the afterlife.

Miles has fought his own battle. Normally, he is the focus of attention when he undertakes his adventures, but Around the World is a team effort, and he has had to work with Mike and Caroline as a unit. He has found this hard at times, particularly when Mike needed help and Jon and Caroline, who could see a bit, would focus on his very special needs, often leaving Miles on the sidelines until the problem had been solved. Miles always said that when he looked at Mike's disablement, he felt that his difficulties were nothing compared to the challenges that Mike faces and he never begrudged the time that was spent in handling Mike's needs. Nevertheless he sometimes cuts a lonely figure as he sits on his own waiting for the others to join him.

Miles is also handling a different relationship to the one he normally enjoys with Jon. The two have been together through many adventures, working as a team. In all of his speeches, Miles pays tribute to Jon, saying that it is due to his enabling skills that he is able to live a full life. He also credits Jon with saving his life on at least two occasions. But the nature of Around the World means that Jon is team manager to three people and not just to Miles and that instead of devoting his full attention to Miles, he is often having to concentrate on Mike's particular requirements. Miles is a deep thinker, it is often hard to work out what is really going on in his mind. But most of all, at times I marvel at his enthusiasm and drive. He was the first of us to scuba dive, he had no fears of driving a super-fast Lotus car, and he wanted to try everything, at one time begging the Hong Kong Jockey Club to let him race a horse around their track.

When he left to go Around the World, Miles was working with the Royal National Institute of the Blind as their Motivational Development Manager. One of his tasks was to undertake a large amount of public speaking about his adventures, to show that blindness is simply a challenge to be overcome.

He liked to quote a Danish proverb.

Life does not consist in holding a good hand of cards, but in playing a poor hand well.

As a motivational speaker he is supreme. Now, after Around the World, he will have an even more amazing story to tell.

Mike has a different set of problems to meet. Before he set off, he had booked himself into the National Spinal Injuries Hospital at Stoke Mandeville on his return for the comprehensive check-up his medical team thought would be necessary after the stresses and strains of Around the World in 80 Ways. Mike never knows what is going to happen to him when he goes into hospital for something 'small'. Sometimes it is six months before he gets out again. We later learn that on completing the check, Dr Allison Graham said he was better and fitter than when he left and promptly cancelled the bed they were holding for Mike.

Mike has been astonishing, taking part in all the means of transport, even as unlikely as riding an ostrich. He has played a full part in the public speaking programme, and has established a massive bond of affection between himself and Miles, Caroline and Jon. Almost every day he has faced up to the media, be they television, radio or newspapers, and every time they have made him the centre of attraction as he is the most visibly disabled member of the team. Almost every day, there has been something exciting for him to do, a new adventure to undertake, a new area of the world to explore.

But Mike is going back home to live on his own, and all the trumpets, fanfares and bells will have stopped. Most of all, every day of the adventure Mike has felt love from Jon, Caroline and Miles and they would be gone, moved on to other adventures.

I think of two things for Mike. Clearly there is the speaking circuit, as he has an incredible story to tell; his life before injury, his battle back into life after it, and then his incredible achievement of getting around the world in 80 different ways.

But another job opportunity is apparent. Despite many hotels claiming that they have excellent facilities for disabled people, Mike has found that often some simple things elude them. Doors to toilets open inwards, leaving no room for anyone in a wheelchair, showers cannot be operated by someone in a wheelchair because the controls are out of reach or there is not enough space and so on. Mary has discovered that many business centres in hotels could not provide good access for wheelchairs. I believe that with his Around the World experience, Mike could carve out a new career for himself as a consultant with practical experience of how to cater for people with disabilities.

Caroline is a puzzle. At times she can be totally confident, at times she can be a piece of jelly. She needs someone who is very strong and understanding and with enormous patience to direct and control her enormous enthusiasms and passions. She is stubborn, determined and at times difficult, at times demanding her own way with frightening dedication. I know that on her return, she will throw herself with passion into her Aisling Foundation, the trust she set up when she returned from her Indian adventure on her elephant and which focuses on educating people on disablement and particularly in relation to employment. She also wants to set up a reservation park for elephants.

On completing Around the World Caroline will simply change gear and push Aisling, using contacts and experiences from Around the World.

Jon will miss Miles, Mike and Caroline. He is not doing the job of team manager as I thought it would be done. Over the days, Jon has evolved the role into being one of the adventurers himself. Certainly he has done a most magnificent job as an enabler, and indeed without him, it is hard to see how it would all have worked out. But the effect of the way it has worked out is that there are now two different factions, one being Jon, Miles, Mike and Caroline, and myself, Stuart and Mary as the other. Instead of being the pivotal person acting as the link between the adventurers and myself, Jon is now one of them and there is no middle link.

I realise that this was inevitable. Jon has been with Miles, Mike and Caroline every day of the entire adventure, he cares for them, he is the one to sort out on the ground problems, he takes the photographs and keeps control of the money. It was probably fanciful of me to believe that anyone could be with them all the time and not become one of them.

Jon will go back to his career on Rolls-Royce. Throughout the entire adventure, he has completed a daily interlink for Rolls-Royce and they have been able to feel a part of the whole adventure. Rolls-Royce support on the ground has been magnificent and I feel that the job Jon has done with us will be recognised by them in considering his future as a leader and developer of people.

Having thought about what lies ahead for Mike, Miles, Caroline and Jon, I decide it is none of my business. If they reach home safe and sound on 3 December then my job is over and they will look out for themselves. It is patronising of me to think otherwise. They are astonishing characters and they can work it all out for themselves.

I drag my mind go back to the present. The group are now well into their adventure sector and are flying to Indianapolis, where Jon has spoken to John Anfield, Career Development Manager for Rolls-Royce North America, based at Indianapolis. They have a mission to accomplish.

In conversations with Stuart Nussey, he has indicated some concerns about some of the means of transport that have been used. Some are similar, though not identical, to others and might be disqualified. Some were not completed by all the adventurers and some were so short in distance or duration that once again they may not be allowed. His urgent message to me, which I pass on to Jon, is to pack as many new means of transport in as we can whilst the team is in Indianapolis.

John Anfield has taken our mission to heart. He gives a briefing and it is clear that an astonishing action-packed day lies ahead, all in the determination to get in as many means of transport as possible. Only a drunken stoat would have tried to make the journey through Indianapolis that is to be used by the adventurers but it is all in a good cause.

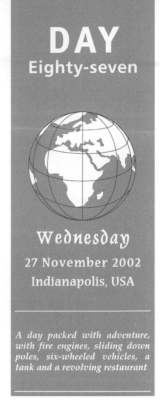

A day packed with adventure, with fire engines, sliding down poles, six-wheeled vehicles, a tank and a revolving restaurant

Jon has a problem. When he was in the sand buggies, he had felt a pain in his chest. Over the days, the pain had got worse and in the end he had to stop trying to hide it. We think back to the hot-air balloon crash and how Jon had tried to cushion the landing for Mike. He had ended up with Mike and Caroline on top of him and had clearly suffered a more serious injury than we had at first thought. Cracked ribs were now suspected.

At once I remember how a motoring hero of mine in Northern Ireland, John Baird, had suffered what seemed to be a minor injury of a broken rib whilst motor racing. Tragically the rib pierced his lung and he died.

Jon is reluctantly bundled off to the doctor for an examination whilst the rest of the adventurers set about scoring more means of transport.

The first is a fire engine provided by the Lawrence fire station on the outskirts of Indianapolis. Jon tries to forget about the fire engine we had used in Galway, because this one is brand-new and has a magnificent 105ft extending ladder. Of course it is different, we argued, even if we did not believe it.

All aboard and the team snort along on their journey, siren screaming, Miles shouting out his war cry TIGER, the parade being completed by a state of the arts fire service ambulance and the Fire Chief's car with enough high-tec communications systems to control a world war.

The team arrive at the fire station and spot one of those fire poles, so often spoken about but never seen – the one firemen and women slide down when rushing out to a fire.

Mischievous grins break out all round and Caroline and Miles are soon hurtling down the pole. Mike poses a problem for the whole key is to wrap your legs around the pole and control your drop with your hands. With no legs, Mike is at somewhat of a disadvantage. But if he can ride an ostrich, he can certainly ride a pole. Mike attaches himself to the pole, and lets fly.

Above: Mike uses a fork-lift truck to board
Below: Jon takes a look at the firepower before the off

With his developed upper body strength, his is the most controlled descent of all. There is satisfaction all round, for whilst Stuart may decide we have already done a fire engine, there is no way we have used a fire pole before as a means of transport.

But there is a surprise in store. A yellow school bus is outside the fire station. We have not used one of these before, so the adventurers clamber on board and head off. The destination is an extraordinary collection of tanks, guns and aircraft, sheer heaven for the adventurers who are trying to pack in as many means of transport as they can.

Astonishingly the adventurers find a massive self-propelled 105mm Howitzer gun. Mike is loaded on board by fork-lift truck, and the adventurers are soon roaring about on board. Shouts of TIGER mingle with Bang Bang as another means of transport is recorded. Take that Stuart, there is no way the adventurers have ridden a mobile howitzer gun before!

Still in the heaven of the weird collection of vehicles, the team move on to a six-wheel multi-terrain tracked vehicle and score one more means of transport. The famous Indianapolis Indy 500 track is nearby so a stop is made to take in go-karts. At first the owner is reluctant to let two blind people drive them, particularly when a race between them is mentioned, but a shot of the two of them on the Malaysian Grand Prix Circuit doing

Mike enjoys a bit of close support on board a six wheeler

Miles takes his go-kart round the circuit at Indianapolis and wonders if he is on the right track and in the right car

more than 150 kph soon makes the 40 mph go-karts seem tame and they are allowed to drive.

It has been a packed day and a celebration meal is called for. John Anfield takes the team to a revolving restaurant. This provides Miles and Caroline with a very special problem for the toilets were never in the place where they last used them! It has been a fantastic day, with the team confident that Stuart will accept the fire pole, yellow school bus, mobile howitzer, tracked vehicle and the Indianapolis go-kart as new means of travel.

But there is one more to be added to a very exciting day. Everyone argues whether going around in a revolving restaurant can be counted as a means of travel. We submit it and will let Stuart decide.

It has been a brilliant day for means of travel and full marks are awarded to John Anfield and his Rolls-Royce team.

This is Thanksgiving Day and the team go to spend it with John Anfield, his wife Ann and two friends, Robbie and Teresa McGregor.

Dinner is served; turkey, every imaginable vegetable, deliciously crispy roast potatoes, John's own recipe for pudding, pumpkin pie, apple pie, pecan pie and all the trimmings. It is hardly surprising that whilst watching the ball game on TV after – the game takes four hours with all the advertising – everyone falls sound asleep like beached whales in front of the massive TV. It is a simple recipe – eat yourself silly, half watch the game, fall asleep, eat again and sit satisfied, stuffed and warm until bedtime.

'Just like Christmas at home' is Jon's opinion.

A traditional Thanksgiving Day is celebrated, thanks to John and Ann Anfield

DAY
Eighty-nine

Friday

29 November 2002
Chicago to New York

Problems at home as Robin and Mary battle to put the last links in place and an anonymous sponsor saves the day

---

Time for the team to head for home and that reunion with partners and friends. John Anfield has again come up with the goods, for the means of transport to the airport is a massive 35ft long mobile home – again a brand-new item for Stuart to put in his book. The flight from Chicago Airport to The Big Apple is one of sadness, for it is the last stopping point before closing the circumnavigation and heading for London.

Back home, Mary and I are going frantic trying to set up the return home. An approach to the Reform Club brings a wonderful response. I had been told that they were sticky and formal, but this is not the case. They congratulate us warmly and say they would be delighted if, when we complete our mission, we would call in for coffee.

But the celebration luncheon is causing big problems. Our first sponsor was to have been the Leonard Cheshire Homes, with funds raised going to that excellent charity. However, a combination of difficulties has meant that they could not proceed. At that point, Jon asked Rolls-Royce and for a time it looked as though this would provide the answer. Sadly this too fell through.

The event was saved by an anonymous sponsor who knew what we were doing, was close enough to know about the difficulty in getting costs covered for the return to London celebration luncheon, felt we deserved it and stepped in. Our warmest thanks to Mr Anonymous, you know who you are and without your help we would have gone out, not with a bang, but a whimper.

But another unexpected problem has arisen. The adventurers have compiled their list of guests they wish to be invited, but somehow this has got lost. Mary appeals to the team to do them again, with no response. So we go into the files, pull out the family names that were there at the start and send invites to them.

Today should have been the big day for the adventurers to see New York but it was not to be. Exhaustion and end of team fever has set in over the past few days and Jon realises that he and the rest of the adventurers have simply not found the energy to attend to the mass of routine but detailed paperwork that our adventure requires.

As Jon says:

I just felt all gived out. I had got behind, the press were after pictures and details, Robin and Mary needed information back home to prepare for the return, Stuart needed information on the means of transport so we could have a completed list on our return.

So I decide that all of us should spend the entire day catching up with the paperwork and getting it in a fit state to present to the public on our return.

We did venture out in the evening, into the cold dark night. We had vowed that we could get a picture of ourselves at the Statue of Liberty to mark our stay in New York and our departure from America. The taxi driver dropped us and drove off before we realised that we were miles from the Statue. We could just see it in the distance so we got another taxi. He too dropped us off some considerable distance from the Statue, so we just took the picture there and then and caught another taxi back to the centre of Manhattan.

We ate our final on the road meal in fine style at the traditional Smith and Wollensky Steak House. As ever, Caroline managed to convince the management to donate a bottle of champagne to help us celebrate.

Then the adventurers retire to pack their gear for at least the 100th and final time. They know they are running out of steam and it is time to go home.

DAY
Ninety

Saturday

30 November 2002
New York, USA

An exhausted team catch up with paperwork and fail to find the Statue of Liberty

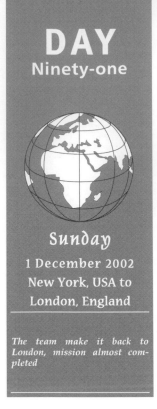

The team make it back to London, mission almost completed

Three months away is a long time and finishing a long trip is always an emotional time. When the trip involves the challenges posed by our adventure, it becomes even more emotional.

Everyone wants desperately to get back to families, friends, pets and normality but at the same time, ending the adventure means an end to the excitement of it, the challenges to be faced every day, and splitting up a team – Mary, Mike, Caroline, Miles, Jon, Stuart and myself – that has bonded into close friendship. In particular, Mike, Caroline, Miles and Jon have lived in each others pockets, sharing fun, difficulties and close comradeship.

Now the reunions are in two days time. Originally the team had wanted to return home on 2 December and go straight into the 3 December receptions but Mary had argued otherwise. Instinctively she felt that the team would have an emotional need to spend one last day together before facing the demands of the return and so she had booked everyone home on 1 December.

We are reunited at the airport. Mary and I have gone to Heathrow and are there at the time of their arrival. The sign shows that the plane from New York has landed but there is no sign of the team. Shades of Cairo!

Mary calls Jon on his mobile phone. He answers, and asks where we are. Then the truth dawns. Two planes have come in from New York at the same time, but to different terminals. Mary and I are at Terminal 4 whilst the adventurers are at Terminal 3!

It is just a small hitch and some fifteen minutes later we are in each others arms, tears steaming down our cheeks. It is an intensely private moment between the six of us and the people standing beside do not understand the emotion. In the mêleé, I hear Mike whisper to himself, 'I have done it.'

It is the afternoon before everyone is together again. Mary and I have planned a quiet celebration in a nearby Lebanese restaurant that Claire-Louise, Mary's daughter, has found for us. Claire-Louise has played a significant behind the scenes role throughout, and it was her research that led to the approach to the Hong Kong Jockey Club. Throughout she had been one of our most trusted advisors and workers, often unthanked and unrecognised, and it is right that she should be there at the end.

Home, a day of quiet reflection and a night of celebration in a Lebanese restaurant

We are joined by others who have played a massive part in our adventure. Mike Thomson has had the impossible role of trying to keep account of our finances. Not only did we operate in many different currencies, but often the accountant's love of receipts were totally defeated by circumstances – when you are slipping someone a big backhander to find luggage that has mysteriously disappeared, it is not always appropriate to ask for a receipt. Somehow Mike has turned bits of paper, perplexed expressions as to where the money has gone, scribbled notes, unidentifiable receipts and so on, into a properly ordered set of accounts.

Jimmy Spankie is also there. He had been the MC at our show at Cramond Kirk right at the start of the adventure and had remained a good friend to us throughout.

Aoife is there. Now fully recovered from her illness, there is an emotional reunion between her and the adventurers.

And so we dine and drink champagne, which we deserve. So many people had told us Mike would get ill, injured or even die on the trip, yet he is returning home fitter than he left. The wound on his bottom, which had been there right from the start, was in better - condition than it was at the start of the journey, due entirely to the nursing he had received from Jon and Caroline – we were later to learn that after a medical examination, the people at the hospital cancelled the booking he had made before leaving, saying that recovery treatment was completely unnecessary.

So many people told us what we were attempting to do was impossible. Yet Miles, Mike, Caroline, Jon, Mary, Stuart and I – magnificently supported by Mike Thompson, Carbonara and Aoife – had all ventured out and returned fit and well.

It is a wonderfully warm and informal occasion and everyone laughs a lot, cries a bit and tells stories of daring-do that have taken place over the past three months.

Towards the end, during coffee, Mary and I slip out, go to a bar across the road, and have a quiet toast to ourselves and what we have done. Then we return to the party and celebrate the night away. It is the last time that we and the team will be together, tomorrow it is back to our families, relatives and friends and the spotlight that has never left us since we departed and will shine upon us once more in the morning.

The final day of a two and a half year dream – and London is smiling on us. I wake up at 6:30 a.m., gulp down a cup of coffee and put on the Phileas Fogg outfit for the last time-the top hat, now battered and smelling of all sorts of concoctions that have visited it during the three months, the black frock-coat, seams now undone, white shirt well-stained, cravat, black trousers, socks with holes in them and shoes that would never again be good enough for church.

I go out of the hotel and look round the corner and there it is. The space shuttle which is to take us back to the Reform Club gleams in the morning sun, surrounded by puzzled pedestrians. Made by the people from Smurfit Europe, who had also made the cardboard boat on the Liffey in Ireland, it is magnificent.

Back in the hotel, the team is waiting for me – the adventurers Mike, Miles and Caroline, Project Director Mary Donaldson, team manger Jon Cook looking more and more like Indiana Jones each day, Aoife our journalist, Mike

Tuesday

3 December 2002
Reform Club, London

Mission complete and all back home safe and well

McNamara our cameraman and Claire Donaldson, our 'angel'. Mary sets off for the Reform Club to mastermind the return ceremony, Miles, Caroline, Mike Jon and I board the shuttle, with a police motorcycle escort to see us safely through the streets of London. We have planned that it will take a one hour to get from the hotel to the Reform Club allowing for Christmas traffic. But there is no Christmas traffic and it takes only fifteen minutes!

As we approach Piccadilly, I thump on the top of the lorry pulling us, and ask the driver to stop. We have three-quarters of an hour to fill in, so Caroline and Jon rush to a nearby café, and bring back refreshments. We exchange happy banter with the passers-by, who have no idea who we are and it is too hard to tell them. Then Mary calls. Standing at the Reform Club, surrounded by media, by friends, by Ian McCartney, Minister for Pensions and Works, by Stan Todd of Rolls-Royce, Doris Ho from the Hong Kong Jockey Club, Sir Jimmy Savile and Sir Tom Farmer, she picks up her mobile phone. 'Mission control, mission control, you are clear to land.' We board our space shuttle and then slowly and regally we pull up in front of the Reform Club and the waiting crowd. Sir Jimmy Savile greets us and the crowd applaud.

'Follow me' I shout for the last time and we all get down from the shuttle. Then Mary, Mike, Caroline, Miles, Jon and I hold hands in front of a ribbon that has been placed in front of us.

Safely back at the Reform Club

I read out the proclamation heralding the success of the mission, cut the ribbon and we all walk through to complete our journey, accompanied by enormous cheers from the crowd. We find our own way to the Clifton Ford Hotel where the celebratory lunch is to take place, starting with a champagne reception provided by Rolls-Royce. My son and daughter, Ashley and Elizabeth are there and it is wonderful to see them again. Doris Ho speaks on behalf of the charities we have helped, is overcome with emotion and has to stop. Tim Haddock whom we met in his wheelchair in Northern Ireland, has flown over to sing his own composition *Around the World* and is rewarded with a standing ovation. Jimmy Spankie from Scotland interviews the adventurers and Sir Tom Farmer concludes by reminding the team of the astonishing adventurers they have accomplished and pointing out that they will become legends. Then it happens. It is too much for us. Caroline starts crying and suddenly Mary, Caroline, Miles, Mike, Jon and I are in floods of tears, hanging on to each other. The dam has burst and the emotion pours out. It was always going to happen at some time, it is happening now, right in front of everyone.

Fifteen countries, over eighty means of transport, just under ninety speeches, a lot of money – estimated at £500,000.00 collected and all given away to charities around the world – many lives impacted, countless television, radio and newspaper interviews completed and the team home safe, sound and with the challenge accomplished.

The Around the World in 80 Ways project was all about being positive and refusing to take 'no' for an answer. Many people told us what we were trying to do was impossible. Miles, as always, has a quote that sums it all up. 'Those who think something is impossible should not interrupt those who are doing it.'

Where are they now?

Miles Hilton-Barber soon settled back into his old ways and in no time was planning a microlight flight to Australia with his companion Storm Smith. He left the RNIB and set up as a freelance motivational speaker, a career in which he now enjoys major success. He is still looking for more adventure, and is one of the UK's top motivational speakers.

Caroline Casey went back to the Aisling Foundation, but the travel bug has bitten in a big way. She returned to India for a reunion with her elephant Bhadra and travelled to Boston to pick up another award. She lobbies in Ireland for a better understanding of the challenges faced by disablement and undertakes an extensive public speaking role.

Mike Mackenzie was recalled to hospital some months after the conclusion of the adventure. An infection had set in and he went for a small operation. It ended up with the removal of part of his tail bone and an eight-month stay. Since then, he has been back to Sarajevo, the scene of his injuries, to raise funds for a day-school built to commemorate an aid worker who was killed by a sniper. He is also helping Darren Brooks and Jim Corbally to set up their charity to teach disabled people to scuba dive and has done some consultancy work with hotels on their provision of facilities for disabled.

Jon Cook returned to Rolls-Royce where he was quickly assigned to promote training, personal development and careers within the UK Aerospace sector. Most of his work is in conjunction with Government departments so he is currently living and working in London. Jon's ribs and toes, hurt in the balloon landing, mended, his hernia was fixed and then, catching a ball, he broke a finger which was in a splint for six months!

Mike McNamara made such an impression in San Francisco that he now returns there as a visiting lecturer. He still works as a freelance cameraman. Despite paying £14,000 for the brand-new camera he took with him on the adventure and which was stolen, and having it fully insured, so far the insurance company have only paid him a fraction of the cost.

Aoife O'Connell completed her journalism course and now works in journalism as a commercial featured editor with a media group in Dublin.

Stuart Nussey and his wife Alex retired and went to live in France. Stuart continues to serve the Scottish Business Achievement Awards as their Chief Executive.

Robin lost the use of his left eye shortly after returning home, the loss being related to his illness at the Red Sea. **Mary** returned to her work as Group Health and Safety Manager at one of the UK's leading housebuilders.

Robin and **Mary** got married on 18 October 2003, in Cramond Kirk, with Rev'd Dr Russell Barr performing the ceremony at which **Mike** represented the Around the World team and the choir sang the Irish Blessing

> May the road rise up to meet you
> May the wind be always at your back
> The sun shine warm upon your face
> The rain fall soft upon your fields
> And until we meet again may God
> Hold you in the hollow of his hand.